PROGRESS, STABILITY, *and the* STRUGGLE *for* EQUALITY

A Ramble Through The Early Years of Maine Law

1820–1920

PROGRESS, STABILITY, *and the*
STRUGGLE *for* EQUALITY

A Ramble Through The Early Years of Maine Law

1820–1920

BY HUGH G. E. MacMAHON

Drummond Woodsum & MacMahon, Publisher
2009

ISBN10: 0-9664015-4-9

ISBN13: 978-0-9664015-4-7

Drummond Woodsum & MacMahon, Publisher, with offices in
Portland, Maine and Portsmouth, New Hampshire.

Book design and production: Grace Peirce

The paper used in this publication meets the minimum requirements of
American National Standard for Information Sciences – Permanence of
Paper for Printed Library Materials

Additional copies of this book may be ordered at:

www.dwmlaw.com

ACKNOWLEDGMENTS

I would like to take this opportunity to express my thanks to many people who helped me in a variety of ways in completing this project.

I would first like to thank Frank M. Coffin, Retired Chief Judge, United States Court of Appeals for the First Circuit, and Vincent L. McKusick, Retired Chief Justice, Supreme Judicial Court of Maine, for their interest in this project and for their support of this effort as the project was coming along. Judge Coffin and Justice McKusick have been wonderful mentors for generations of lawyers, and their support was a great encouragement for me.

I would also like to express my gratitude to Herbert T. Silsby II, Retired Justice, Maine Superior Court, for generously sharing his knowledge of Maine legal history with me whenever I sought his counsel. Justice Silsby is widely regarded as the dean of Maine legal history, and I have found his enthusiasm for the topic contagious.

I deeply appreciate the support of my colleagues at our law firm, who made this project possible by providing the means to accomplish it, including office facilities, library, and research resources. I especially want to thank Harry Pringle, our firm's Managing Director, for his support of this effort from the beginning. I also owe special thanks to Harry, Melissa Hewey, Dick Spencer, and Ann Chapman for their helpful comments on various drafts of the manuscript and for encouraging me to see this project through to completion. I am also extremely grateful to Ruth Wentzel, who miraculously managed to make the time, on top of her numerous professional responsibilities, to help with formatting and navigating the book through the complexities of the publication process. I would like to express my appreciation to Louise Jensen, for help in locating books I needed to make this project possible, and Janet Tobkin, for assistance in organizing my notes of judicial decisions in the early stages of research. Everyone at our firm has been most helpful, and I greatly appreciate the support of all.

Several members of the faculty of the University of Maine School of Law have helped immeasurably by reading drafts of some of the chapters and graciously getting back to me with constructive comments. Many thanks to Orlando E. Delogu, Emeritus Professor of Law; Jennifer B. Wriggins, Sumner T. Bernstein Professor of Law; Deirdre M. Smith, Associate Professor of Law and Director, Cumberland Legal Aid Clinic; and Nancy Wanderer, Director, Legal Research and Writing Program.

Among others who have helped with their support, encouragement, and ideas, I would specifically like to acknowledge Joseph A. Conforti, Professor of American and New England Studies, University of Southern Maine, for his encouragement with this project when I first began thinking about it; John F. Woolverton, personal friend, author and historian of note, and formerly Professor of Church History, Virginia Theological Seminary, for his thoughtful commentaries on a draft of the manuscript; and Richard D'Abate, Executive Director, Maine Historical Society, for helping me see how legal history relates to the broader panorama of history as a whole.

I also owe special thanks to Nancy Rabasca, Librarian, The Nathan and Henry B. Cleaves Law Library, for help in locating law books and pictures of Maine jurists from the past; Arthur Dostie, Researcher at the Maine State Archives, for assistance in locating court records from Maine's early years; the librarians at the Donald L. Garbrecht Law Library, University of Maine School of Law, for assistance with legal research; and Adam Harvey, while a student at Colby College, for assistance with historical research concerning Civil War matters as this project was getting underway. I would also like to acknowledge several personal friends, Lee and Chuck Norris, Patrick McTeague, Raymond Kuhl, Dauna Binder, and Coleman Rogers, to all of whom I feel especially indebted for their encouragement and helpful insights.

I owe a large debt of gratitude to Sean Ociepka, a member of the Maine Bar and 2006 graduate of the University of Maine School of Law, where he was an Articles Editor of the *Maine Law Review*, for his editorial assistance in completing this project. Sean has been a great help with every part of that process, from cite checking, proof-reading, and coordinating tables with text, to suggesting improvements in the manuscript, and I feel very fortunate to have had the benefit of his writing and computer skills as well as his editorial judgment. This work has been significantly improved by Sean's contributions and could not have been completed without his assistance.

Finally, I owe special thanks above all to my wife, Barbara, whose well-known good humor I am sure I stretched to the maximum at numerous times over the years I have been working on this project. Throughout the time it took to pull this history together, she has been a constant source of support, assuring me that this effort was worthwhile and that it deserved to be completed and brought to publication. Her suggestions regarding the composition and content of this work have been extraordinarily helpful, and I know that I could not possibly have undertaken or completed this project without her help and inspiration. Words cannot express the depth of my appreciation.

Hugh G. E. MacMahon
Portland, Maine
August, 2008

CONTENTS

PREFACE

After practicing law for almost forty years, I became "of counsel" to our firm, Drummond Woodsum & MacMahon, of Portland, Maine. The term "of counsel" is a traditional designation in the legal world for a member of a law firm who serves as a senior consultant in semi-retirement status. This new role allowed me some time to pursue some interests I had been putting off over the years. With my less-demanding schedule at the office, I found myself thinking about the historical development of Maine law. Although from time to time I had researched the history of various legal principles, I had never taken a broader view of the development of law in Maine, from the time that Maine left Massachusetts and became a state in its own right in 1820.

It seemed to me that until I had researched this history, my understanding of Maine law would be incomplete. I felt I would remain somehow ungrounded in my understanding of Maine law until I had gone back and examined the roots of Maine law and how the law as we know it today came to be. So one day, I decided that I would read all the reported decisions of the Supreme Judicial Court of Maine beginning with the first term of that court in 1820.[1] It did not take me long to realize that I was biting off more than I wanted to

---

[1] The Supreme Judicial Court is Maine's highest court. It is variously referred to here as "the Maine Court" or "our Court," or by the name of its Chief Justice at a particular time, for example, "the Appleton Court." I have used similar shorthand in referring to the highest courts of other states. In its role as an appellate court, the Maine Court is commonly known as "the Law Court." The number of justices on the Court is determined by legislation. Over the years, the number of justices on the Court has ranged from as few as three to as many as eight. As originally established in 1820, the Court had three members, a Chief Justice and two Associate Justices. It currently has seven members, a Chief Justice and six Associate Justices.

chew. Accordingly, somewhere along the way I decided to restrict the scope of this project to the first hundred years of Maine law, 1820-1920.

After some time, I managed to complete my review of the decisions of our Court during those years. I cannot say that I read all of those decisions, but I did at least skim almost all of them and made notes on what seemed to be the most important cases. I then sat back and tried to figure out what to do with all of this. I had notes on hundreds of cases—my mind was full of nineteenth century law— and it seemed that I had rounded out my knowledge of Maine law as I had intended to do. Yet there also seemed to be something calling me to do something with all of this. The feeling persisted that there was some unfinished business for me in this review of early Maine case law.

As time went on, I found myself increasingly bothered by the idea that if I didn't do something with this project now, at some point down the road, I would regret not having done so. And thus it was that one day I decided to write and see where that might lead. Maybe, I thought, if I just start writing, I might begin to see the outline of a project that could be of some interest to others besides myself. Maybe someone starting out in the practice of law in Maine would find something here that, by providing historical context, would make their practice more interesting than it otherwise would be. Maybe something here would encourage someone to delve more deeply into the history of a legal concept and gain a new and helpful insight as a result. Maybe someone would encounter an idea here by which to test that person's own thoughts about the soundness of a rule of law. I am sure that I would have benefited if, when I began to practice law in Portland, I had made it a point to study the history of Maine law. In undertaking this project, I therefore feel a special obligation to lawyers who are today just entering the profession here in Maine.

The title of this volume, *Progress, Stability, and the Struggle for Equality*, refers to the three themes—the importance of economic progress, the importance of maintaining a safe and stable society, and the struggle for equal rights under the law—that, for me, stand out most prominently in looking back over the entire sweep of the first hundred years of the development of Maine law. Those themes are the topic of the final chapter, "Concluding Thoughts."

I call these reflections on the development of Maine law a "ramble" through the early years of Maine law because the topics discussed follow no particular sequence or order. This ramble is nothing more than a brief, and sometimes opinionated, discussion of selected topics of Maine law during the first hundred years of Maine's statehood. This effort makes no pretense at being a comprehensive history of Maine law. I have simply included here a collection of some of the topics in the early development of Maine law that I have found most interesting. At the same time, however, those subjects seem sufficiently diverse and broad enough in scope to provide at least a starting-point for beginning to understand the mind of our Court as it went about its business of deciding cases in its early years.

I realize that the interjection of personal opinion runs the risk of violating one of the canons of good writing as prescribed by the eminent Strunk and White in *The Elements of Style*, their classic work on the art of writing ("Unless there is a good reason for its being there, do not inject opinion into a piece of writing."). But mere commentary without the addition of personal opinion seems inadequate here. Any opinions offered in this discussion of the law in Maine's early years are presented less to persuade than to generate fresh thinking, to prompt the reader to think anew about some of the issues discussed, to respond, to react, to agree or to disagree. All of those opinions are, of course, made with the benefit of hindsight. Had I been in the shoes of jurists who decided cases in years gone by, living in a culture markedly different from the culture we live in today, I have no reason to think that my judgment concerning the legal issues presented would have been any different or "better" than theirs.

That being said, however, it is important to remember that history has much to teach us, in terms both of errors to avoid and examples to emulate. Thus, while it is true that the historian considers the past with the advantage of hindsight—and often from the perspective of a different culture—it does not follow that the historian should on that account refrain from expressing personal opinions about circumstances that existed in the past. Indeed, because the historian's personal opinions might help to illuminate errors to avoid and examples to emulate, the historian would seem to be duty-bound to offer those opinions up for consideration by the reader.

In addition to my personal opinions about this and that, I have also included many quotations from judicial decisions instead of simply paraphrasing them, thereby violating another rule I once read regarding the writing of nonfiction. I believe, however, that the quotations are important here because the style of judicial writing, the turns of phrases, and the particular manner of expression provide valuable insight into the mind of a court that paraphrasing simply cannot capture.

One observation I would like to make at the outset is that throughout my reading of judicial opinions, I was struck by how hard our Court worked. The work of judges is difficult and demanding. Seldom do they get recognition for the diligence and care with which they perform their demanding judicial duties. During a time when they lacked the most basic labor-saving tools of the modern law office, and when they had to travel over the breadth of the state, with horse and carriage—over roads that were often nothing more than muddy or snow-covered trails—the members of our Court managed to generate a substantial corpus of well-written decisions that thoughtfully addressed the issues at hand. Indeed, many of those decisions have not lost any of their luster and remain authoritative to the present day.

WHY LEGAL HISTORY MATTERS

In setting out on this ramble through the early years of Maine law, I feel obliged to try to explain why I believe this exercise is worthwhile or, otherwise stated, why legal history matters. Such an explanation is particularly necessary now because most lawyers today seem to have little, if any, time to pursue an interest in the historical development of the law. They generally consider the citation and research of old court decisions to be a waste of time if more recent decisions are at hand. The idea that sometimes the weight and authority of a precedent improves with age is likely to be ignored or overlooked in haste to find more recent cases to cite. The prevailing sentiment seems to be that modern lawyers need modern law and that no one can afford to rummage around in search of "old" court decisions, meaning decisions older than twenty years or so.

Carrying the weight of responsibilities to their clients in an increasingly competitive and hurried professional environment, lawyers, as a whole, are now often too busy to be concerned with how the law originated and how it came to be what it is today. The demands of keeping abreast of client needs and emergencies necessarily take priority and leave little time for contemplating the history of the law. In any event, time spent on such activity is apt to be considered nonproductive because it adds nothing to the financial statement's bottom line.

Yet, I would suggest that the more hurried the times are, the more important it is for lawyers to have some understanding of the history of the law. For in times of rush-and-hurry, such as the present, it is all too easy for lawyers to become caught up in a treadmill-like round of work, which prevents their seeing their place in the historical development of the law and the legal profession.

This brings us to the first reason for understanding the history of the law, which is that it provides a foundation that is essential for anyone who would truly be a member of the legal profession. Here I am not referring to particular, practical uses to which an understanding of the history of the law can be put, to the advantage of the practitioner; rather, I am speaking here of the broader benefit of a lawyer's having a grounding in the historical development of the law. Without some understanding of how the law we live with today came to be, a lawyer resembles an adventurer who embarks on a journey through the winter wilderness without a map, compass, or any other kind of positioning device. On becoming lost in a snowstorm, our adventurer will find that he has no idea of the direction from which he came or the direction in which he was headed. And if, by a stroke of good fortune, he were to discover a landmark in the drifting snow, he would not know what to make of it. It would tell him nothing of any use to him and would point him in no particular direction.

Like our unfortunate adventurer, a lawyer who ignores legal history soon finds himself severely hampered in his ability to understand his legal surroundings. If he encounters a landmark judicial ruling or other pivotal development in the history of the law, he is unable to appreciate its historical importance, what it means for the present, what it portends for the future, and what it might mean for the development of the law in other fields beyond that to which it immediately pertains. Viewing each judicial decision and rule of law in isolation, and overlooking the ways in which those decisions and rules relate to each other over time, the lawyer who disregards legal history is likely to misconceive the direction in which the law is currently tending and the historical forces involved in that movement, and thus in any given case is unsure whether he is going with or against the grain. In that state, the lawyer's judgment will lack an essential element of soundness, and his advocacy will not be as persuasive as it might be. Something very basic, something important, is missing. Most notably, lacking grounding in the history of the law, the lawyer is unable to assess the merits of legal developments generally, or the merits of the case at hand, against the evaluative judgment of history.

The sense of being grounded in our past, in history, is a fundamental, existential aspect of our nature as human beings. It is, however, such a fundamental aspect, so inseparable from our being, that we scarcely take note of it. Its significance therefore is not generally appreciated. This sense of being grounded in history is intangible. It is not something that is easy to express. Occasionally, though, we come across writers who have captured the sense of enlarged vision that comes from a growing awareness of our relationship with the past. This is the grounding I am trying to get at here.

In his book, *Drawn with the Sword,* the eminent Civil War historian James M. McPherson quotes from a letter he received from a reader who was deeply affected by *Battle Cry of Freedom*, McPherson's great history of the Civil War: "You have," the reader said, "grounded my existence, my present, into a past."[2] That simple statement really says it all.

The sense of connection with the past, and the significance of that connection, has perhaps never been better expressed than by James Howard Kunstler in his book, *Home from Nowhere*, a perceptive commentary on the phenomenon of suburban sprawl and the current state of urban architecture and design. Kunstler there describes the value of what he calls "chronological connectivity":

> Chronological connectivity lends meaning and dignity to our little lives. It charges the present with a more vividly conscious validation of our own aliveness. It puts us in touch with the ages and with the eternities, suggesting that we are part of a larger and more significant organism. It even suggests that the larger organism we are part of *cares* about us, and that, in turn, we should respect ourselves, our fellow creatures, and all those who will follow us in time, as those preceding us respected us who followed them. In short,

[2] James M. McPherson, *Drawn with the Sword: Reflections on the American Civil War* (New York: Oxford University Press, 1996), 252.

chronological connectivity puts us in touch with the holy. It is at once humbling and exhilarating. I say this as someone who has never followed any formal religious practice. Connection with the past and the future is a pathway that literally charms us in the direction of sanity and grace.[3]

If that moving description seems remote from the study of the history of the law, we might, to bring this somewhat closer to home, consider the similar sentiments expressed by Justice Oliver Wendell Holmes, who in 1897 penned these words:

> And happiness, I am sure from having known many successful men, cannot be won simply by being counsel for great corporations and having an income of fifty thousand dollars. An intellect great enough to win the prize needs other food beside success. The remoter and more general aspects of the law are those which give it universal interest. It is through them that you not only become a great master in your calling, but connect your subject with the universe and catch an echo of the infinite, a glimpse of its unfathomable process, a hint of the universal law.[4]

As Holmes so clearly saw, the chief advantage for a lawyer in studying the history of the law—the law's "remoter and more general aspects"—is that such a study takes the lawyer back to the origins of the law, to its ultimate foundation in principles of morality and justice, and gives the lawyer a "hint of the universal law." In that way, such a study expands the lawyer's vision and ultimately gives the lawyer a new and deeper appreciation—some might even say, "reverence"—for the law and for the craft. The lawyer who has acquired that sort of reverence for the law will inevitably feel a

---

[3] James Howard Kunstler, *Home from Nowhere: Remaking Our Everyday World for the Twenty-First Century* (New York: Simon & Schuster, 1996), 89.

[4] Oliver Wendell Holmes, Jr., "The Path of the Law," 10 *Harvard Law Review* 457, 478 (1897).

heightened sense of responsibility for the law and become a more effective counselor and advocate as a result.

Closely related to the foregoing, but on a less cosmic scale, another benefit for the lawyer in studying the history of the law is simply the pleasure that comes from becoming more intimately acquainted with the law and historical figures in the law. Just as our lives are enriched by becoming better acquainted with friends over time—discovering where they grew up, their likes and dislikes, how they live, in a word, their history—our enjoyment of the law is deepened by the study of its history. A similar sentiment about the pleasure of the study of history was long ago articulated by the Greek biographer, Plutarch, in his "life of Timoleon." Explaining that he used his study of historical characters to expand his circle of friends and improve his own character, Plutarch said:

> Using history as a mirror I try by whatever means I can to improve my own life and to model it by the standard of all that is best in those whose lives I write. As a result I feel as though I were conversing and indeed living with them; by means of history I receive each one of them in turn, welcome and entertain them as guests and consider their stature and their qualities and select from their actions the most authoritative and the best with a view to getting to know them. What greater pleasure could one enjoy than this or what more efficacious in improving one's own character?[5]

From my reading of old Maine cases, I have derived similar pleasure in becoming better acquainted with the judges who decided those cases. The personalities of those jurists have a way of shining through their written words. And the testimonials in their honor at their decease give the reader added appreciation of their values and character. For example, at memorial proceedings in 1891, Chief Justice John A. Peters included these observations in a tribute to his predecessor, Chief Justice John Appleton:

---

[5] *See* Roger Kimball, *Lives of the Mind: The Use and Abuse of Intelligence from Hegel to Wodehouse* (Chicago: Ivan R. Dee, 2002), 18 (quoting Plutarch).

Another dominant element in Judge Appleton's character—both an intellectual and moral power—was temperament.
This is a product of all the elements of character blended
together,—a balance-wheel that guides them all,—an indicator
of the general character. He was a person of even and unruffled
temper, courteous and kindly in all places and conditions. He
was utterly unconscious of prejudice or resentment against any
one. He was more likely to see the good side of men than their
faults. He was tolerant of the views of those who did not agree
with his own. During the almost half-century that I knew him I
never heard an angry word from his lips. Charity, sympathy,
liberality, courtesy, forbearance, lenity, and kindred qualities
were elements in his disposition. Not that he did not have
firmness. Gentleness is the sure sign of firmness. He possessed
good-natured firmness and perseverance in an uncommon
degree.[6]

Concerning those testimonials, it is interesting to note that the
qualities of the deceased's character most admired by the person pre-
senting a testimonial were sometimes the same qualities of character
by which the presenter would himself like to be remembered down
through the ages. Those who offered tributes in honor of the
deceased sometimes seem unconsciously to have provided a partial
sketch of their own eventual obituaries.[7]

In addition to the enlightenment derived from becoming
acquainted with the judicial temperament and character of individual

---

[6] Remarks of Chief Justice John A. Peters at memorial proceedings of the
Penobscot Bar for Chief Justice John Appleton in Bangor, June 20, 1891, 83 Me.
587, 606-07 (1891).

[7] *See, e.g.*, Remarks of Hon. John F. Lynch, of Machias, Maine, at memorial
proceedings for Chief Justice John A. Peters in Bangor, June 14, 1904, 99 Me. 541,
555 (1905) (remarking that Peters' memorial for another judge expressed Peters'
own views of life (quoting from Horace Walpole): "To act with common sense,
according to the moment, is the best wisdom I know; and the best philosophy, to
do one's duties, take the world as it comes, submit respectfully to one's lot, bless
the goodness which has given us so much happiness with it whatever it is, and
despise affectation.").

lawyers and jurists from the past, the student of legal history can also benefit from learning something about the litigants, whose difficulties and controversies, reported for posterity in court decisions, are the raw materials of legal history. In reading old Maine cases, I have found myself feeling sympathy for these litigants and their relatives on a very close and personal level, particularly in those cases that involved grim circumstances such as poverty, suffering, disabling injuries, and the death of loved ones. The litigants in those cases are themselves now long since dead. They went to their graves never thinking that their lives would be memorialized in the annals of the court, and certainly never thinking that their circumstances might, years later, be cited as illustrations of the consequences of injustice. Yet their stories are there after all these years for the reader to peruse and to reflect upon. The student of legal history who reads cases with an empathetic feeling for the people involved, like the reader of an historical novel or biography, will inevitably gain a deeper understanding of human nature and a refined sense of justice.

Another important reason for a lawyer to be concerned with the history of law is that the soundness of any common law rule cannot be assessed without understanding the reason why the rule was adopted by the courts in the first place. If the advocate is suggesting that the rule should be changed, one of the best arguments for that position is that the original reasons for the rule no longer exist.[8] Conversely, if the advocate is contending that the rule should not be changed, the advocate would argue that the rationale that supported the rule when it was originally adopted is still viable today. Whatever side of the issue is taken, an understanding of the historical development of the rule is essential.

One of many Maine Court decisions involving this aspect of legal history is a case decided by the Maine Court in 1889 that concerned the question of whether a will executed by a woman when she was single was revoked by her marriage. The name of the case, as

---

[8] That argument is summed up by the Latin maxim, *cessante ratione legis, cessat ipsa lex* (the reason of the law ceasing, the law itself ceases).

reported, is simply, *George A. Emery, Appellant.*[9] Under the old common law (court-made) rule, the will would be deemed to have been revoked upon that woman's marriage. The reason for that rule was that under another old common law rule a married woman was deemed, as a matter of law, to be incapable of writing a will. That being the case, unless a will executed by a woman before her marriage was deemed to have been revoked by her marriage, that will, upon her death years later, might be wholly inappropriate in light of personal and family circumstances that occurred since her marriage. To prevent that result, the courts developed the old common law rule that a will written by a woman before her marriage was deemed to have been revoked upon her marriage. In *Emery*, the Court decided that that common law rule should no longer be applied because the reason for it—the incapacity of a married woman to execute a will—had ceased to exist. More specifically, by 1889, when *Emery* was decided, the Maine Legislature had enacted legislation allowing a married woman to make, alter, or revoke a pre-existing will as fully as if she were not married. Under these circumstances, the Court asked, "Why, then, should her marriage revoke a pre-existing will? We think it should not." The Court went on to explain:

> *Cessante ratione legis, cessat ipsa lex.* Reason is the soul of the law, and when the reason of any particular law ceases, so does the law itself.... In this state, a *feme covert* [married woman] can [now] make or revoke a will as freely as a *feme sole* [single woman]; and the reason no longer exists for holding that the will of a *feme sole* will be revoked by her marriage. It will not be.[10]

---

[9] 81 Me. 275, 17 A. 68 (1889).

[10] *Id.* at 277-78, 17 A. at 69. In an earlier case, the Court had expressed considerable skepticism about a jurisprudence that would change whenever the reasons underlying it no longer applied, at least as regards legal principles involving the matter of real estate: "Where the common law has been adopted in this country, we are not at liberty to disregard it, because the reasons, in which it originated, no longer exist. Much of the law in relation to real estate, as at present administered, can be explained only by reference to institutions, and to a

A more recent illustration of the important role played by legal history in the judicial process is the U.S. Supreme Court's 2003 decision in *Lawrence v. Texas*.[11] The Supreme Court there held that a Texas statute that made it a crime for two persons of the same sex to engage in certain intimate conduct was unconstitutional. In so ruling, the Court overruled its 1986 decision in the case of *Bowers v. Hardwick*,[12] in which the Court had upheld the constitutionality of a similar Georgia statute. In upholding that statute, the Court in *Bowers* had stated that laws prohibiting the conduct at issue had "ancient roots." In the more recent *Lawrence* case, however, the Court noted that the historical premises underlying its decision in *Bowers* were more complex than the Court had indicated in that case and that in fact "there is no longstanding history in this country of laws directed at homosexual conduct as a distinct matter."

Having demonstrated the shortcomings of the historical premises on which its decision in *Bowers* was based, the Court noted that in any event, more recent legal developments "show an emerging awareness that liberty gives substantial protection to adult persons in deciding how to conduct their private lives in matters pertaining to sex." As the Court's extensive discussion of legal history in *Lawrence* indicates, an accurate appraisal of relevant legal history was central to the Court's ultimate conclusion striking down the Texas criminal statute involved in that case. Indeed, legal history played such a critical part in the *Lawrence* case that a lawyer whose focus was limited to the present state of the law would be wholly at sea in evaluating the legal merits of the issues in that case.[13]

---

state of society, very different from ours; but until changed by the legislative power, it must be regarded as the law of the land." *Crowell v. Merrick*, 19 Me. 392, 393 (1841).

[11] 539 U.S. 558 (2003).

[12] 478 U.S. 186 (1986).

[13] The significance of the history of the law in the outcome of that case is further illustrated by the Supreme Court's reliance on many scholarly amicus briefs submitted to assist the Court in evaluating the historical premises of the *Bowers* decision, including, as the Court expressly noted, a brief submitted by a number of history professors.

Yet another value of delving into legal history is that the student will inevitably come across cases out of the past that discuss a legal topic in an historical context that the reader has not previously considered. Considering a legal issue in that light, from an entirely new perspective, may well make such a compelling impression that the reader is moved to reconsider the soundness of his or her current judgment concerning the matter. A good illustration of reconsideration such as that, from the early years of Maine law, is the Maine Court's decision in *Portland v. Bangor* (1876),[14] where the Court, reconsidering its previous jurisprudence, overruled two of its own decisions (from 1834 and 1856), which had upheld the legality of the practice of towns summarily committing paupers to workhouses without providing them the rudiments of a fair hearing. Against the background of the Civil War, and the ratification of the Fourteenth Amendment in 1868, the Maine Court in 1876 saw that issue in an entirely new light, noting the similarity between the summary confinement of paupers and the evil of slavery.

For the practicing lawyer, an understanding of legal history is also useful in cases that turn on the meaning of statutes. For example, just as in any given case the lawyer must be familiar with relevant judicial precedents, the lawyer must also understand the historical development of any statutes that might bear on the case. A significant body of law exists regarding the history of statutory law, or as it is customarily called, "legislative history." That body of law primarily concerns the circumstances in which votes, debates, and other actions of legislative bodies may be used to elucidate the meaning of words contained in statutes.[15] For example, a lawyer urging a court to narrowly interpret the ambiguous scope of a particular statute might find it helpful to discover that the legislature had

---

[14] 65 Me. 120 (1876). This case is discussed further in the chapter entitled "Paupers."

[15] One of the most reliable keys for understanding the meaning of an ambiguous statute is to determine the purpose of the statute, that is, the object that the legislative body was trying to accomplish by enacting the statute. That purpose may itself be clarified by the legislative history of the enactment.

previously rejected a bill that had proposed a broadening of the statute. Against that background, that legislative history, the lawyer on the other side of the case would have a difficult row to hoe in persuading the court to adopt a similarly broad construction of the statute.

Perhaps the greatest value of studying legal history is that it sharpens our awareness of present-day injustices and, in doing so, forces us to consider our responsibility for correcting those injustices. In looking back on the history of the law, generally, we come across rules of law that, from the distance of many years and with the advantage that comes from hindsight, seem plainly unjust today. Some of these in the early years of Maine law—such as the early Maine Court's jurisprudence concerning contributory negligence, assumption of risk by employees in the workplace, the "fellow servant rule," the legal rights and status of married women, and the exclusively male character of the judiciary—are discussed in the chapters that follow. Yet when the Maine Court and courts in other states were developing and applying those rules, they probably sincerely believed that they were doing the right thing. Indeed, the Maine Court's assessment of its own work product in its first hundred years was unreservedly positive.[16]

---

[16] *See* Address of Chief Justice Leslie C. Cornish, "A Century of the Supreme Judicial Court of Maine," 22 *Report of the Maine State Bar Association* 109, 143 (1921):

"This Association has done well to turn aside from its customary program and to devote this day to remembrance; to call back from the receding past those men who laid the foundations of our jurisprudence broad and deep and firm; and also to remember those who in later years have built upon the foundations so laid, and have extended them to meet the ever expanding necessities of the times, moulding the common law in a spirit of conservative progressiveness, meting out justice between man and man with all the exactness of which the finite mind is capable, tempering the severities of the law with the mercy of equity, jealously safeguarding the rights of the individual, while faithfully protecting the public weal, and thereby in all ways helping to guide the ship of State in a safe and sane and prosperous course.

"It is an honorable record. The present generation may study it with pride and with reverence. The body of law which has been built up by

No doubt a hundred years from now, students of legal history will similarly look back on the present time and be struck by the fact that we, the lawyers of today, seem to have been blind to many injustices that stare us in the face every day. Just as certain wrongs seem to have been invisible to the Maine Court in its early years, injustices exist today that are generally "below the radar" of lawyers and courts. In sharpening one's sense of justice, it is useful to consider how we, the legal establishment of today, will fare in the judgment of history. What issues that today do not rise to the level of litigable issues will be seen in the future as issues of justice that seem to have been largely overlooked by lawyers in the past? Will it be the plight of employees who have been displaced by the outsourcing of their jobs? Will it be the misfortune of the most vulnerable among us, for whom the basics of adequate housing and medical care are increasingly out of reach? Will it be the working conditions of workers in Third World countries to which American corporations have transferred work in order to increase profits and add to the wealth of their officers and shareholders? Will it be other issues of international justice that will continue to emerge with increasing frequency, and become more difficult to ignore, with the advancing interconnectedness of the cultures of the world and the globalization of the world economy?

Just thinking about issues such as these, and the roles that lawyers and courts might play in addressing them, is sufficiently jarring to cause most lawyers to retreat to the relative comfort of a billable-hour practice. But seeing how the judgment of history illuminates injustices that existed in the past, we clearly risk the judgment of history if we close our minds to the injustices of the present day.

---

the one hundred and eighteen Maine Reports represents the finest purpose, the best thought, the soundest judgment and the highest devotion to public duty on the part of these men of the first century."

FINDING AND MAKING THE COMMON LAW

When, on March 15, 1820, the District of Maine separated from the Commonwealth of Massachusetts and became a separate state in its own right, it became the responsibility of the Maine Supreme Judicial Court to develop the common law of the new State of Maine. The term, "common law," as used here, refers to law developed by courts, as distinguished from statutes enacted by legislatures. In its early years, the Maine Court frequently relied on decisions ("precedents") of English courts and the Massachusetts Court in determining the rules and principles of the common law that would apply in Maine. In doing so, the Maine Court was continuing the practice with which judges and lawyers in the District of Maine had become accustomed over the years before Maine became a separate state. After the separation, Maine lawyers and judges relied on judicial precedents in the same way they had done when Maine was part of Massachusetts. The process of developing a body of common law in the new State of Maine, therefore, proceeded quite smoothly and without interruption.

That orderly approach to the early development of the common law in Maine is similar to the approach taken by Maine and Massachusetts in providing for the development of statutory law in Maine following Maine's separation from Massachusetts. In anticipation of the separation, the Massachusetts legislature, in 1819, enacted a statute, commonly known as the "Act of Separation," which contained a number of provisions relating to the separation.[17] One of those provisions was designed to prevent any inadvertent break in continuity of legislation as a result of the separation process. Section 6 of the Act of Separation addressed that concern by providing that "all the laws" in force in the District of Maine, as of March 15, 1820, would remain in force in Maine until "altered or repealed" by the government of Maine. The only laws excepted from that "carry-over provision" were those laws that "may be inconsistent with the situation and condition of said new State, or repugnant to the Constitution thereof." That provision stated:

> That all the laws which shall be in force within said District of Maine, upon the said fifteenth day of March [1820], shall still remain, and be in force, within the said proposed State, until altered or repealed by the government thereof, such parts only excepted as may be inconsistent with the situation and condition of said new State, or repugnant to the Constitution thereof.

The carry-over provision in the Act of Separation thus established a framework for the orderly transition of statutory law at the time of the separation.[18] In 1824, Maine's first Chief Justice, Prentiss Mellen, explained the purpose of that provision as follows:

> It was evidently designed to prevent the confusion consequent upon a suspension of law, and the injury which would thereby result to the community and individuals. It was for the purpose of giving time to the legislature of this State to re-enact, modify, or repeal those laws as, on consideration, they

---

[17] The full text of the Act of Separation is set forth at 1821 Me. Laws 817-28 and 1822 Me. Laws 16-25.

[18] Maine's counterpart to the carry-over provision of the Act of Separation is Article X, Section 3 of the Maine Constitution. As originally enacted and as it still reads today, that section provides: "All laws now in force in this State, and not repugnant to this Constitution, shall remain, and be in force, until altered or repealed by the Legislature, or shall expire by their own limitation."

should determine most for the interest and best adapted to the situation of the State.[19]

In its early years, the Maine Court frequently looked to decisions of the Massachusetts Court and English courts for guidance in cases that concerned the common law. Although as we shall see, the Maine Court did not feel that it was invariably required to follow English precedents, Maine's jurisprudence from the beginning was not affected by "Anglophobia," a condition characterized by the rejection of all things English. That condition, which resulted from the trauma of the Revolutionary War, was for a time prevalent in some parts of the country. For example, that state of mind led the State of New Jersey to enact a statute in 1799, not repealed until 1819, which forbade the citation in court proceedings of any English case decided later than July 4, 1776.[20] The fact that Anglophobia did not affect Maine's early jurisprudence, however, does not mean that the common law tradition was warmly received by the citizenry at large in Maine. The complexities of the substantive and procedural rules of the common law that pertained in Maine's early years, as well as the cost of "going to law," were significant irritants in that regard.

As the years passed, the Maine Court became increasingly willing to look to the decisions of the courts of other states for guidance in determining the rules of the common law for Maine. For example, in 1842 we find our Court praising the jurisprudence of the Supreme Court of New York:

> And without intending to make any invidious comparisons between the decisions of the Courts of Pennsylvania and New York, in this particular, we are free to confess, that we entertain great respect for the decisions of the Supreme Court of the latter State.... The fountains of the venerated common

---

[19] *Towle v. Marrett,* 3 Me. 22, 25-26 (1824).

[20] *See* Grant Gilmore, *The Ages of American Law* (New Haven: Yale University Press, 1977), 22.

law are nowhere in *America* more copiously drawn upon for the correct rule of decision than in that State.[21]

In addition to relying for precedents on the decisions of English courts, the Massachusetts Court, and courts in other states, the early Maine Court sometimes rested its decisions on certain English statutes that the Massachusetts Court considered to be part of the common law, broadly construed. For example, in *State v. Temple* (1835),[22] the Maine Court considered whether the Latin phrase, *vi et armis* (with force and arms), was necessary in indictments for offenses concerning an actual disturbance of the peace. In holding that those words were not essential in that setting, the Court relied on an English statute that provided that the absence of those words in an indictment was immaterial. In so ruling, the Court cited for authority the opinion of Chief Justice Theophilus Parsons of the Massachusetts Supreme Judicial Court in *Commonwealth v. Knowlton* (1807).[23] Chief Justice Parsons there stated:

> Our ancestors, when they came into this new world, claimed the common law as their birthright, and brought it with them, except such parts as were adjudged inapplicable to their new state and condition. The common law, thus claimed, was the common law of their native country, as it was amended or altered by English statutes in force at the time of their emigration. Those statutes were never reenacted in this country, but were considered as incorporated into the common law.[24]

In its search for authorities on which it could support its decisions, the Maine Court, like other state courts, also relied heavily on treatises written by legal scholars who collected and explained judicial decisions concerning the rules of the common law. In the

---

[21] *Frontier Bank v. Morse*, 22 Me. 88 (1842).

[22] *State v. Temple*, 12 Me. 214 (1835).

[23] 2 Mass. (1 Tyng) 530 (1807).

[24] *Id.* at 534.

early years of Maine law, one of the most authoritative of those treatise writers was William Blackstone, an eighteenth-century English scholar, whose *Commentaries on the Laws of England,* published in 1765-69, were for many years widely read and used by lawyers and judges throughout the United States. Other extremely significant authors of legal treatises on whom the Maine Court relied extensively in its early years were Chancellor James Kent of New York and U.S. Supreme Court Justice Joseph Story of Massachusetts. In a new nation, lacking its own established jurisprudence, the influence of these treatise writers was immense.

In developing the common law, our Court also relied on the "customs and usages" of the people. Under this approach to finding or making law, customary behaviors that have created settled expectations in the ways people relate to one another may be regarded as if they were a reflection of unwritten laws. One rather graphic illustration of the Maine Court's reliance on customs and usages in determining the rules of the common law is the Court's decision in 1910 in the case of *Conant v. Jordan.*[25] In that case, the plaintiffs claimed to be the owners of a tract of land that contained a pond measuring "about 175 acres," situated in the town of Cape Elizabeth and known as the Great Pond property. The plaintiffs sought a ruling that they were the exclusive owners of that land and pond, and asked that the defendants be enjoined from entering thereon and from fishing and hunting there.

Under Maine law at that time, a pond larger than ten acres was deemed a "great pond," meaning that such a pond was a public pond upon which the public had the right of free fishing and fowling. The plaintiffs maintained that those rules were not applicable to their property because their chain of title to the real estate in question dated back in private ownership to 1631, several years prior to the enactment of the Massachusetts Colonial Ordinance of 1641-47, which granted public access to great ponds for fishing and fowling. The Court had "considerable doubt" as to whether the plaintiffs' title

---

[25] 107 Me. 227, 77 A. 938 (1910).

to their land originated in private ownership before 1641, as they claimed, but the Court assumed, *arguendo*, that this was the case. Even so, the Court decided that the plaintiffs were not entitled to the relief they sought.

In ruling against the plaintiffs, the Court concluded that as a matter of practice and usage, the principle that great ponds were open to the public for fishing and fowling was in force in Maine as long ago as 1631, the assumed year of the origin of their title, even though that principle had not been codified at that time. As the Court stated:

> The same conditions which led the people of Massachusetts to declare "free fowling and fishing" as one of their "liberties" [in the Massachusetts Colonial Ordinance of 1641-47] existed here. There was the same necessity for a resort to fishing and fowling for sustenance. In both cases, the colonists were in a comparatively uninhabited and not very fertile country. It was a wilderness. They gained only a scanty subsistence from the soil. Husbandry was attended with failure of crops and depredations from savage foes. The common law of England, which restricted the use of ponds and streams to private owners was not suited to their conditions and necessities.... The picture of these struggling colonists, so familiar to every reader of history, clearly shows how very inapplicable to their conditions was that principle of the [English] common law which gave the exclusive right of fishery in a pond to the owners of the soil underneath. Such undoubtedly was the origin of the "liberty" which was declared in Massachusetts in 1641.[26]

Based on the conditions, customs and usages of the colonists that existed in the area now known as Maine, from the earliest times, the Court decided that as a matter of the common law of Maine, the plaintiffs' property interests in the Cape Elizabeth land and pond in question were, from the beginning of their chain of title, subject to the

---

[26] *Id*. at 234-35, 77 A. at 940-41.

public right of free fishing and fowling and that the old English common law rule that restricted the use of great ponds to private owners had never been applicable in Maine. The Court also took the occasion to reaffirm that, as the result of custom and usage, the Massachusetts Colonial Ordinance of 1641-47 had itself become part of the common law of Maine. As the Court explained, that ordinance had not been extended to Maine by any legislative act; rather, it had become law in Maine because the Court found that it had been "so acted upon and acquiesced in as to have become a settled, universal right."

When judicial precedents and statutes were not available, and when established customs and common usages could not be discerned, the Court developed the common law on the basis of its judgment regarding the result that would best promote the public interest. This approach to judicial law-making is illustrated by an 1829 case, *Lassell v. Reed*,[27] which concerned the right of a tenant of a farm to remove manure from the farm at the end of the lease—a matter of more than minor significance in the agricultural economy that prevailed at that time. The lease contained no provisions concerning the subject of manure. Some of the cattle kept on the farm belonged to the owner of the farm, and some belonged to the tenant. The Court was not aware of any established custom or court decision regarding the legal issue presented. Under these circumstances, the Court explained that it would decide the issue on what it called "the principles of policy and the public good."

Distinguishing the case at hand from cases in which courts upheld the right of a tenant to remove fixtures he built on leased premises for carrying on his trade, the Court decided that to protect the "interests of agriculture," the tenant should not be permitted to remove manure from the farm when the lease was over:

> It is our duty to regard and protect the interests of agriculture
> as well as trade. It is obviously true, as a general observation,
> that manure is essential on a farm; and that such manure is

---

[27] 6 Me. 222 (1829).

the product of the stock kept on such farm and relied upon as annually to be appropriated to enrich the farm and render it productive. If at the end of the year, or of the term where the lease is for more than a year, the tenant may lawfully remove the manure which has been accumulated, the consequence will be the impoverishment of the farm for the ensuing year; or such a consequence must be prevented at an unexpected expense, occasioned by the conduct of the [tenant]; or else the farm, destitute of manure, must necessarily be leased at a reduced rent or unprofitably occupied by the owner. Either alternative is an unreasonable one; and all the above mentioned consequences may be avoided by denying to the [tenant] what is contended for in this action. His claim has no foundation in justice or reason, and such a claim the laws of the land cannot sanction.[28]

The Court noted that the rule that allows a tenant, at the end of his lease, to remove fixtures erected at his own expense for the purpose of carrying on his trade encourages "enterprise and industry" and thus "best advances the public interest and accords with good policy." But to protect the interests of agriculture, a contrary rule was called for where the removal of manure from a farm was concerned, in order to prevent the "impoverishment of the farm for the ensuing year." In both situations, the Court explained, the ultimate consideration, in the absence of controlling judicial precedent, was what rule would best serve the public good.

The common law in Maine thus developed from several sources—judicial precedents from England, Massachusetts and other states; a few English statutes that were considered part of the early common law of Massachusetts; scholarly legal treatises; customs and usages of the people; and considerations of justice and public policy. From these several strands, the Maine Court over time wove together a richly textured fabric that constitutes the common law of our state. We should note here, however, that the process of developing the

---

[28] *Id.* at 224-25.

common law is an ongoing judicial process that continues, case by case, from one generation to another and is never "completed" once and for all. The continuous and creative nature of that process has been well described by Learned Hand, one of our nation's most distinguished jurists:

> Our common law is the stock instance of a combination of custom and its successive adaptations. The judges receive it and profess to treat it as authoritative, while they gently mould it the better to fit changed ideas. Indeed, the whole of it has been fabricated in this way like a coral reef, of the symmetry of whose eventual structure the artificers have no intimation as they labor.[29]

Before we consider some of the ways in which the Maine Court "gently moulded the common law to fit changed ideas," two observations seem appropriate here. First, the natural, evolutionary way in which Maine inherited the common law tradition from England via Massachusetts allowed the new and independent State of Maine to become established at the outset with a minimum of disruption. Maine, it could almost be said, was born into a system of law that was ready-made to receive it. Because that process occurred so naturally, we are apt to overlook the advantage that process bestowed on the State of Maine in its earliest years, in terms of the continuity of the law and the consequent stability of the body politic. The significance of that advantage can perhaps be better appreciated by comparing Maine's common law heritage with the confusing legal situation that existed in the early years of California's statehood:

> It is safe to say that, even in the experience of new countries hastily settled by heterogeneous crowds of strangers from all countries, no such example of legal or judicial difficulties was

---

[29] Learned Hand, "Is There A Common Will?" in *The Spirit of Liberty*, ed. Irving Dillard (New York: Alfred A. Knopf, 1952), 52-53. Learned Hand served with great distinction as a judge on the U.S. District Court for the Southern District of New York from 1909 to 1924 and as a judge on the U.S. Court of Appeals for the Second Circuit from 1924 until his death in 1961.

ever before presented as has been illustrated in the history of California. There was no general or common source of jurisprudence. Law was to be administered almost without a standard. There was the civil law, as adulterated or modified by Mexican provincialisms, usages, and habitudes, for a great part of the litigation; and there was the common law for another part, but *what that was* was to be decided from the conflicting decisions of any number of courts in America and England, and the various and diverse considerations of policy arising from local and other facts. And then, contracts made elsewhere, and some of them in semi-civilized countries, had to be interpreted here. Besides all which may be added that large and important interests peculiar to this State existed—mines, ditches, etc.—for which the courts were compelled to frame the law, and make a system out of what was little better than chaos.[30]

The second point that should be noted here is that as the result of the explosive growth of statutory law in the twentieth century, the relative importance of the common law in the ordering of society and the adjustment of disputes has declined from what it was in the nineteenth century. During the nineteenth century, judicial decisions based on common law precedents and principles constituted a much larger part of the legal landscape than they do today. Nevertheless, despite the increased significance of statutory law, the common law continues to play a crucial role in the administration of justice because statutes, regardless of how many or how detailed they may be, cannot cover the entire canvas of human life. To the present day, many areas of law, including such far-reaching topics as the law of contracts and torts, which directly concern the lives of every citizen, continue to be shaped and applied by courts through the traditional

---

[30] Joseph G. Baldwin, "Judge Field," in *Some Account of the Work of Stephen J. Field*, ed. Chauncey F. Black & Samuel B. Smith (1881; reprint, Littleton, Colo.: Fred B. Rothman & Co., 1986), 18. The quoted passage describes the legal landscape of California in 1857, when Stephen J. Field was elected to the Supreme Court of California. Field later served as a Justice of the U.S. Supreme Court.

processes of the common law. And our complex, technological society continues to generate novel legal issues at an increasingly rapid rate, as if defying courts and legislative bodies to keep pace.

CHARTING NEW COURSES

Although during the nineteenth century the Maine Court frequently relied on the common law of England when applicable English precedents could be found, the Court made it clear from the outset that it would not slavishly follow the rulings of English courts if those rulings were not suited to the needs and ways of life in Maine. The Maine Court was not alone in its willingness to depart from English common law precedents in such circumstances. The U.S. Supreme Court encouraged that cautious approach to the adoption of English common law precedents, and courts in other states followed suit when they believed that local circumstances warranted a different rule.[31] The Maine Court's concern for the particular needs of Maine is demonstrated by its decisions in several early cases.

One such case, *Cottrill v. Myrick* (1835),[32] concerned the constitutionality of a Maine statute that had been enacted to preserve and regulate the fishery in the Damariscotta River. That statute, enacted by the Maine Legislature in 1821, made it the duty of certain local officials "to open, and cause to be kept open, a sluice or passageway for Alewives and other fish to pass up Damariscotta river, on what is now called New River streams to the great pond at the head thereof, called Damariscotta Pond...."[33] That statute also provided that

---

[31] As U.S. Supreme Court Justice Joseph Story explained, "The common law of England is not to be taken in all respects to be that of America. Our ancestors brought with them its general principles, and claimed it as their birthright; but they brought with them and adopted only that portion which was applicable to their situation." *Van Ness v. Pacard*, 27 U.S. 137, 144 (1829).

[32] 12 Me. 222 (1835).

[33] An Act to regulate the Fishery in Damariscotta River, Me. P. & S.L. 1821, ch. 50, §1.

24

those officials could go through any land as necessary in the performance of their duties, without being considered trespassers. When one of those officials opened a portion of a dam on that stream in order to allow fish to ascend the stream, the landowners whose land bordered the stream at that location sued the official for trespass and for destroying that dam. Relying on the rights of riparian owners (owners of land abutting a waterway) under the common law in England, the landowners contended that the statute pursuant to which the defendant had acted was unconstitutional because it violated their property rights. The Maine Court, however, rejected that claim and upheld the constitutionality of the statute.

As the Court explained, the English common law rule regarding the rights of riparian owners, on which the plaintiffs relied, had never taken root in Massachusetts. Under that English rule, the Court noted, "fisheries in streams not navigable, belong to the riparian proprietor." In contrast, however, in Massachusetts, "from its earliest settlement," a different rule applied on account of the paramount public interest in preserving the salmon, shad and alewife fisheries. Under the Massachusetts rule, which the Court described as being based on "common consent, manifested by legislative acts, and by general acquiescence," the rights of riparian owners had always been considered to be subject to the superior right of government to regulate fisheries in the public interest. Explaining the rationale behind the Massachusetts rule, the Maine Court stressed the importance of the public interest in fisheries in the New World:

> By the common law in England, fisheries in streams not navigable, belong to the riparian proprietor. In Massachusetts, from its earliest settlement, this principle has been modified. It was deemed most conducive to the public good, to subject the salmon, shad and alewive fisheries to public control, whenever the legislature thought proper to interpose. They were much relied upon, as among the means of subsistence, afforded by the common bounty of Providence, and some regulation became necessary for their preservation.... In Massachusetts, then, by common consent, manifested by legislative acts, and by general acquiescence, the common law

rights of the riparian proprietor, yielded to the paramount claims of the public. It was implied in all grants of land, made by them, and in all conveyances by individuals, upon streams through which these fish passed, to cast their spawn. The right of the public to regulate the interior fisheries, is proved both by legislative acts ... and by judicial construction.[34]

Following the lead of Massachusetts, the Maine Court declined to adopt the rule of the English common law on which the landowners relied. Consistent with the Massachusetts rule that recognized the paramount interests of the public, the Court rejected the landowners' claim. The Court explained that because the property rights of the landowners and their predecessors in title had always been inherently subject to the superior right of the public to regulate fisheries, the statute in question—which had been enacted by the Maine Legislature in furtherance of that superior right—could not be deemed a violation of the landowners' property rights.

Similarly, in *Woodman v. Pitman* (1887),[35] the Maine Court pointed out that, contrary to the English common law rule, American courts had generally held that rivers may be considered navigable, and therefore available for public use, even though they are not affected by a flow of tides from the sea. This was an especially important principle of law in Maine, given the lumbering and paper-making economy of the state. For many years, those essential industries depended completely on rivers and streams for transporting logs from forests to sawmills and paper mills. As the Court explained, "public necessity" and the needs of the public in Maine justified the Court's not following the old common law of England in this respect:

> The court of no state has probably ventured so far as this court has, in maintaining that small streams have floatable

---

[34] *Cottrill*, 12 Me. at 229-30. Our Court's reminder that our ancestors looked upon our fisheries as "the common bounty of Providence" is a refreshing counterpoint to the current view that looks upon our natural resources (including even our drinking water) as material for private acquisition and economic gain.

[35] 79 Me. 456, 10 A. 321 (1887).

properties belonging to the public use. Our climate and forests, together with the interests and wants of the community, make the doctrine here reasonable—a reasonable interpretation of the law. While in some of the states, where less necessity for the doctrine exists, it is considered by their courts to be untenable as subversive of private rights.[36]

In *Owen v. Boyle* (1842),[37] our Court indicated its willingness to construe English common law liberally in order to promote commerce and to support mercantile interests. That case involved some 600 bushels of salt that had been stored by a shipper in a warehouse located on a wharf in New Brunswick, Canada. The warehouse was operated by the tenant of the owner of the warehouse. The tenant was behind in his rent. At issue was whether the owner of the warehouse could enforce his claim for unpaid rent by seizing the bushels of salt that were stored in the warehouse. The Court first decided that the matter should be resolved in accordance with the common law of England, which was then the basis of the common law of New Brunswick.

The Court found that under the common law of England, as a general rule, to collect unpaid rent, the owner of leased premises could claim a lien on any personal property located on the leased premises, even if that property belonged to a third party who had no connection with the lease. One established exception to that general rule concerned goods that were only temporarily in the possession of the tenant for the purpose of being worked on by the tenant—for example, a horse left at a blacksmith's shop for the purpose of being shod, cloth left at a tailor's shop to be made into garments, or corn sent to a mill for processing. The law was unclear, however, regarding the scope of this exception. To resolve this issue, the Court considered the purpose of this exception to the general rule, and found that the purpose was "to favor trade and commercial dealing in general." Based on that broadly stated purpose of the exception to

---

[36] *Id.* at 460, 10 A. at 323.

[37] 22 Me. 47 (1842).

the general rule, the Court concluded that the salt in question could not be subject to a lien asserted by the owner of the warehouse as a way of securing his claim for unpaid rent. Explaining its decision to broadly protect goods in commerce from being seized by owners of warehouses for nonpayment of rent by tenants who operated those warehouses, the Maine Court showed what a high value it placed on mercantile operations, generally:

> What species of goods could be more a proper subject of protection in a country like England, whose pride, whose wealth, whose strength and whose fame have arisen and are continued by the liberality and far-sightedness of their mercantile regulations, than that which is brought into their ports, entered at their custom houses, the duties for the support of the government being paid, and deposited in a warehouse, like the one used by the defendant, for security, till a satisfactory sale can be made?[38]

In a dissenting opinion, Chief Justice Ezekiel Whitman criticized the majority of the Court for having construed the exception to the general rule so broadly that the exception was allowed to swallow up the general rule itself. In his judgment, the Court's broad application of the exception to the general rule could not be squared with English case law.[39]

Five years later, in *Pierre v. Fernald* (1847),[40] the Maine Court decided that the old English common law doctrine of "ancient lights" was not suited to Maine. Under that English common law doctrine, the owner of a dwelling, who for twenty years had enjoyed access to light and air through its windows, could prevent a neighbor from

---

[38] *Id*. at 66.

[39] As an illustration of the potentially far-reaching and lasting persuasive power of a judicial decision, it is interesting to note that in 1967, 125 years after *Owen* was decided, a federal court in Maryland cited *Owen* with approval and remarked that the Maine Court's 1842 decision in that case contains a "full discussion of the development of the law" on the issue decided. *United States v. Nat'l Capital Storage & Moving Co.*, 265 F. Supp. 50, 55 (D. Md. 1967).

[40] 26 Me. 436 (1847).

erecting a structure that would block such access to light and air. The Court rejected that doctrine, noting that it had been "very justly remarked" by the Supreme Court of New York, in a case decided in 1838, that the doctrine of ancient lights "cannot be applied to the growing cities and villages of this country without working the most mischievous consequences." Consistent with the Maine Court's approach to English precedents, the New York Court in that case said, "[T]hose portions of the common law of England which are hostile to the spirit of our institutions, or which are not adapted to the existing state of things in this country, form no part of our law."[41]

In *Rangely v. Spring* (1848),[42] our Court decided that under the common law of Maine, a person who has induced another to convey real estate to a third party may under certain circumstances be precluded from subsequently claiming title to the property. Although at that time, that rule had not yet been adopted as a rule of the common law in England, our Court, appealing to fundamental principles of justice and fairness, adopted that rule here. In doing so, the Court pointed out that other state courts had similarly adopted principles of common law that "were not to be found in the common law of the mother country":

> What are the objects of legal rules? Surely the promotion of justice. The common law aims at that object; and especially at the promotion of fair dealing among men, and the prevention, in an especial manner, of whatever would be in effect a fraud. Whatever rule would be conducive to this end it would ordinarily adopt.... The common law is characterized, as being founded upon reason, and as being "the perfection of reason, acquired by long study, observation and experience, and refined by learned men in all ages." Its principles accumulate with the experience of ages, adapting themselves to the progress of society in knowledge and civilization. Accordingly, no one of the elder States in the union is without its common law principles, not to be found in the common

---

[41] *Parker v. Foote*, 19 Wend. 309, 318 (N.Y. Sup. Ct. 1838).

[42] 28 Me. 127 (1848).

law of the mother country, adapted to its own peculiar situation and wants.[43]

Our Court's willingness to modify old rules of English common law in order to fit circumstances existing in Maine is also demonstrated by its decision in *Whitney v. Slayton* (1855).[44] That case involved the validity of the defendant's agreement not to compete with the plaintiff in the iron-casting business for a period of ten years following the plaintiff's purchase of the defendant's iron-casting business in Calais, Maine. Under the terms of that agreement, the defendant had agreed not to engage in the business of iron casting for that period of time within sixty miles of Calais, Maine. When the plaintiff (purchaser) sued the defendant (seller) for having broken that agreement, the defendant contended that under the common law, his "non-compete agreement" was void and unenforceable because it amounted to a "restraint of trade." Sustaining a jury verdict in favor of the purchaser, however, our Court decided that as a matter of the common law of Maine the agreement was valid and enforceable.

Our Court first noted that under English common law, non-compete agreements were generally considered to be in restraint of trade and therefore void, subject to certain limited "exceptions" for cases in which the agreed-upon restrictions on competition were narrowly tailored in duration and geographic scope. Next, however, the Court noted the ease with which entrepreneurs could start up businesses in the rough-and-tumble, free-enterprise economy of mid-nineteenth century America. Against that background, the Court reasoned that agreements not to compete served the beneficial purpose in this country, at that time, of protecting the purchaser of a business from possibly ruinous post-purchase competition by the party from whom he had purchased the business. Under those

---

[43] *Id.* at 143-44. Our Court's reminder that the common law aims to promote justice and fair dealing, and to prevent whatever would be in effect a fraud, jolts us sharply back to first principles that are apt to get lost in the welter of statutes and regulations that exist today.

[44] 40 Me. 224 (1855).

circumstances, the Court indicated that in its view such agreements should receive a more favorable reception in American courts than they would have received under ancient rules of English common law. As the Court put it,

> In this country, particularly, such is the facility with which persons are enabled, without capital, to embark in various enterprises, and such the desire to try experiments therein, that it often turns out, when these experiments have been successful, in some of these undertakings, others will enter into them in such numbers that ruin to most of them so engaged is the consequence. Hence those who retire, and for a proper consideration contract with others not to engage in any particular business for a limited time, and in a particular place, have often, if not generally, been the successful party. This, then, is not the country, or the time, when it is expedient to enforce rigorously the ancient common law rule, and restrict the exceptions to narrow limits, but rather to give the latter a liberal construction.[45]

In *Drown v. Smith* (1862),[46] the Court rejected another English common law rule on the ground that it was ill-suited to the needs and circumstances of the citizens of Maine. There, the Court held that the trial judge had not erred in instructing the jury that cutting and selling trees by one occupying land under an agreement with the owner to manage that land in a "prudent and husband-like manner" did not necessarily constitute "waste," even though such activities might be considered "waste" under English common law. In this context, the term "waste" means harm to real estate that would allow a claim for damages. The Court explained that the English common law rule, which looked with disfavor on the removal of trees, was ill-suited to a new country that was developing from a wilderness. Under these conditions, the Court stated that "[t]o clear wild land, so as to fit it for cultivation, is not necessarily waste."

---

[45] *Id.* at 231.

[46] 52 Me. 141 (1862).

Although these several cases show that the Court was willing to reject or modify English common law rules in order to meet the particular needs of the State of Maine, it would be a mistake to conclude that the Maine Court during its first hundred years was an "activist" court. Far from it. For the most part, the Court seems to have been comfortable with the maxim that "the law is subject to slow and gradual growth"[47] and based its decisions on judicial precedents, in accordance with the principle of *stare decisis*.[48] That conservative approach to the development of the common law was eloquently described by Oliver Wendell Holmes, Jr., in an opinion he wrote in 1900 while serving as Chief Justice of the Massachusetts Supreme Judicial Court:

> We do not forget the continuous process of developing the law that goes on through the courts, in the form of deduction, or deny that in a clear case it might be possible even to break away from a line of decisions in favor of some rule generally admitted to be based upon a deeper insight into the present wants of society. But the improvements made by the courts are made, almost invariably, by very slow degrees and by very short steps. Their general duty is not to change but to work out the principles already sanctioned by the practice of the past. No one supposes that a judge is at liberty to decide with sole reference even to his strongest convictions of policy and right. His duty in general is to develop the principles which he finds, with such consistency as he may be able to attain.[49]

---

[47] *Woodman v. Pitman*, 79 Me. 456, 460, 10 A. 321, 323 (1887).

[48] The Latin phrase, *stare decisis*, means "to stand by decided cases."

[49] *Stack v. New York, New Haven, & Hartford R.R. Co.*, 177 Mass. 155, 158, 58 N.E. 686, 687 (1900). Holmes, however, also cautioned against a jurisprudence so conservative that it would allow the common law to become a collection of outmoded doctrines of no relevance to present times. As he stated in an essay published in 1897, "It is revolting to have no better reason for a rule of law than that so it was laid down in the time of Henry IV. It is still more revolting if the grounds upon which it was laid down have vanished long since, and the rule simply persists from blind imitation of the past." Oliver Wendell Holmes, Jr., "The Path of the Law," 10 *Harvard Law Review* 457, 469 (1897).

As we saw in the preceding chapter, our Court's reliance in its early years on judicial precedents from England and Massachusetts provided continuity in the development of Maine's common law in much the same way that the carry-over provision of the Act of Separation provided continuity in the early development of Maine's statutory law. Similarly, the Court's willingness in those early years to reject or modify English common law principles that it believed were ill-suited to local conditions in Maine paralleled the approach taken by the Act of Separation, which excepted from its carry-over provision those Massachusetts statutes that "may be inconsistent with the situation and condition of said new State [of Maine]." In declining to follow certain English common law precedents that it considered ill-suited to the situation and conditions in Maine, the Maine Court no doubt felt supported by the general sense of that exception, which recognized that what worked in Massachusetts might not work so well in Maine.

FOUNDATIONAL CONSTITUTIONAL PRINCIPLES

Shortly after Maine became a separate state, two cases arose that allowed our Court the opportunity to establish significant foundational principles of constitutional law. These cases were *Proprietors of the Kennebec Purchase v. Laboree* (1823)[50] and *Lewis v. Webb* (1825).[51] The *Laboree* case concerned the power of the Court to declare acts of the Legislature unconstitutional. *Lewis* concerned the doctrine of the separation of judicial and legislative powers under the Maine Constitution. The Court's rulings in these cases established rules of central and lasting importance to the governance of Maine. Chief Justice Prentiss Mellen, who authored the opinions for the Court in both cases, fully understood the importance of the constitutional issues involved. His opinions in these cases are masterly and magisterial expositions of the law that rank among the most important decisions in the history of Maine law.[52]

The third case, which rounds out this trilogy of early foundational constitutional cases in Maine, is *Allen v. McKean* (1833),[53] which

---

[50] 2 Me. 275 (1823).

[51] 3 Me. 326 (1825).

[52] In an address delivered in 1921, Chief Justice Leslie C. Cornish left us this nice description of Mellen's personality and dedication to the law: "Fond of people, and therefore people fond of him, cheery and optimistic, full of wit and anecdote, and yet deeply learned in the law and strictly conscientious in the discharge of his official duties, he was a remarkable combination of jurist, scholar and companion." *See* Address of Chief Justice Cornish, "A Century of the Supreme Judicial Court of Maine," 22 *Report of the Maine State Bar Association* 109, 118 (1921). For an insightful biography, see Ellyn C. Ballou, "Prentiss Mellen, Maine's First Chief Justice: A Legal Biography," 28 *Maine Law Review* 315 (1977).

[53] 1 F. Cas. 489 (C.C.D. Me. 1833) (No. 229).

was decided by U.S. Supreme Court Justice Joseph Story. That case involved the question of the constitutionality of a Maine statute, enacted in 1831, that was intended to remove the President of Bowdoin College from that post.

Proprietors of the Kennebec Purchase v. Laboree

At issue in *Laboree* was the constitutionality of a Maine statute, enacted in 1821, that made it easier for settlers to obtain title to real estate based on their "adverse possession" and "occupancy" of land for a period of years prescribed by law.[54] The statute helped settlers by changing the rules of "occupancy."

As the Court explained, under rules of Massachusetts law that applied before the 1821 statute was enacted, a settler claiming title to a tract of land on the basis of adverse possession, without a recorded deed of any kind, had to prove that he had occupied the tract for thirty years in such an "open and visible" way that the lawful title holder "may at once be presumed to know" that the settler's claim extended to the whole tract. In contrast, under the new statute, as interpreted by the Court, a settler making the same claim might be able to obtain title to the whole tract even though he had "openly and visibly" occupied only part of the tract, for example, the acreage that contained his dwelling, outbuildings, cleared fields, cultivated land, etc.

The *Laboree* case, which concerned a tract of land in the town of Whitefield, presented the latter situation. The settlers there had openly and visibly occupied only part, the west half, of the 175-acre tract they claimed by adverse possession. The east half had never been fenced or cleared. Based on principles of adverse possession, the settlers had a good claim to the west half, regardless of whether the old rules or the new statute applied. As to that half, the Court concluded that the settlers had established a good and valid title. But the settlers' claim to the east half was less certain because it

---

[54] Me. P.L. 1821, ch. 62, § 6.

depended on applying the new statute to circumstances that occurred over a period of years before it had been enacted.

The Court was troubled by the consequences of applying the new statute retroactively. As the Court remarked, if this new statute were given retrospective effect, it would "punish the rightful owner of lands, by barring him of his right to recover the possession of them, when, by the existing laws, he was not barred...." The Court noted there was no provision in Maine's Constitution, as there was in New Hampshire's Constitution, that expressly prohibited the Legislature from enacting "retrospective" laws.[55] Nevertheless, the Court found that such a prohibition was implicit in Maine's Constitution, Article I, Section 1, which, "among other things, secured to each citizen the right of *'acquiring, possessing,* and *protecting* property, and pursuing and obtaining safety and happiness.'"[56] Otherwise, the Court stated, that section would seem to secure "no other right to the citizen, than that of being governed and protected in his person and property by the laws of the land, for the time being."

The Court also found a prohibition against the enactment of retrospective laws implicit in Maine's Constitution, Article I, Section 21, which prevented private property from being taken for public uses without just compensation. This provision was relevant because it presupposed that the private property of one person cannot be taken for the private purposes of another in any event. As Chief Justice Mellen explained:

> But the *private* property of one man cannot be taken for the *private uses* of *another* in any case. It cannot by a *mere act of the legislature* be taken from *one man,* and vested in *another directly;* nor can it, by the *retrospective operation* of laws be indirectly transferred from one to another; or subjected to the

---

[55] Maine's Constitution, Art. I, § 11, prohibits the enactment of "ex post facto" laws, but at an early date, the U.S. Supreme Court determined that the same phrase in the U.S. Constitution concerns crimes and their punishment as distinguished from civil matters. *Calder v. Bull,* 3 U.S. (3 Dall.) 386 (1798).

[56] *Laboree,* 2 Me. at 290.

government of principles in a Court of Justice, which must necessarily have that effect.[57]

Based on that analysis, the Court declared that the 1821 statute was unconstitutional insofar as it operated retrospectively because such operation would "impair and destroy *vested rights*, and deprive the owners of real estate of their titles thereto, by changing the principles and the nature of those facts, by means of which those titles had existed and been preserved to them in safety." Simply put, the Court was not going to allow the Legislature to change the rules retroactively in the middle of the game. With that ruling, the settlers' claim to the undeveloped east half of the tract in question was remanded to the lower court where its prospects at that point would seem to have been less than dim.

Aware of the gravity of its decision to declare an act of the Legislature unconstitutional, the Court relied on a then-recent Supreme Court decision that made it clear that the judiciary cannot avoid its responsibility as the ultimate authority of the meaning and application of the Constitution. As Mellen stated:

> It is always an unpleasant task for a judicial tribunal to pronounce an act of the legislature in part or in whole unconstitutional. We agree with the Supreme Court of the United States, in the case of *Fletcher v. Peck*, that "the question whether a law be void for its repugnance to the constitution is, at all times, a question of much delicacy, which ought seldom, if ever, to be decided in the affirmative, in a doubtful case. But the Court, when impelled by duty to render such a judgment, would be unworthy of its station, could it be unmindful of the obligation which that station imposes."[58]

Mellen then concluded with a balanced description of the Court's duties under the Constitution:

---

[57] *Id.* at 290-91.

[58] *Id.* at 297 (quoting *Fletcher v. Peck*, 10 U.S. 87, 128 (1810)).

> [T]he oath of office, under which we conscientiously
> endeavour to perform our duties, imposes upon us as solemn
> an obligation to declare an act of our legislature *unconsti-*
> *tutional,* when, upon mature deliberation, we believe it to be
> so; as it does to give prompt and full effect to all *constitutional*
> laws, in the administration of justice.[59]

The *Laboree* case, which established the power of the Maine
Court to declare Maine statutes unconstitutional, could be said to be
Maine's *Marbury v. Madison,*[60] the U.S. Supreme Court's 1803 decision
that established the similar authority of the Supreme Court to declare
acts of Congress unconstitutional. By 1823, when *Laboree* was
decided, the principle that courts were the ultimate arbiter of the
meaning of constitutions was generally accepted in view of *Marbury*
and other Supreme Court decisions. Accordingly, our Court's brief
reference in *Laboree* to the Supreme Court's decision in *Fletcher v. Peck*
sufficed to explain and justify the power of our Court in that regard.
Laboree remains a most significant landmark in the history of Maine
law, not only because it established the authority of the Court to
declare legislation unconstitutional, but also because it established
the important principle that vested property rights cannot be taken
away by the retrospective operation of a law.[61]

Lewis v. Webb

Two years after it decided *Laboree*, the Court took up the case of
Lewis v. Webb. In that case, the Court established the important
constitutional point that there is a judicially enforceable line that

---

[59] *Id.* at 297-98.

[60] 5 U.S. 137 (1803).

[61] Several years later, in a case it decided in 1852, the U.S. Supreme Court
commended Mellen's opinion in *Laboree,* observing that it "contains an elaborate
and searching analysis of the subject, and it is evident, that learned court
considered it with all the care demanded by a question of so much delicacy and
importance, and brought to its adjudication sound principles of constitutional
jurisprudence." *Webster v. Cooper,* 55 U.S. 488, 503 (1852).

separates the business of the legislature from the business of the courts. The case involved a probate court order that held the administrator of an estate personally liable for certain debts related to the estate. After the time established by statute for appealing that order had passed, sureties on the administrator's bond, who found themselves ultimately liable for the administrator's liability, obtained a resolve from the Maine Legislature granting them the right to appeal the probate court order to the Maine Supreme Judicial Court. In *Lewis*, the Maine Court decided that this action by the Legislature constituted impermissible legislative intermeddling with the authority of the judiciary and was therefore of no legal force or effect.

Chief Justice Mellen first articulated the significance of the issue before the Court:

> This cause assumes an importance from the very nature of the question before the Court; because it has immediate respect to the boundary lines of those powers which are given by the constitution of this State to the legislative and judicial departments. These lines are not drawn in the constitution with distinctness, but by the use of certain general expressions, which will be presently considered. It seems at the present day to be an established principle in our country, as well as in many other parts of the world, that the three great powers of government, the legislative, the executive, and the judicial, should be preserved as distinct from, and independent of each other, as the nature of society, human imperfections, and peculiar circumstances will admit. And the more this independence of each department, within its constitutional limits, can be preserved, the nearer the system will approach the perfection of civil government, and the security of civil liberty. Thus the wisdom and virtue of society are called upon to give strength and support to this vital principle; thereby guarding the system against those disorders and diseases which are too apt to endanger its stability and derange its operations.[62]

---

[62] *Lewis v. Webb*, 3 Me. 326, 328-29 (1825). Some years before, in 1788, James Madison left no doubt about his view of the importance of the constitutional

Having described the importance of the question at hand, Mellen explained that the principle of the separation of the powers of government—legislative, executive, and judicial—is expressly recognized and mandated by Maine's Constitution.[63] It therefore followed, as Mellen put it, that "if the legislature undertake to exercise judicial power, they invade the province of the judiciary." The Court then decided that by allowing an appeal that was statutorily barred by the passage of time, the Maine Legislature had in effect set aside a judgment of a court of law. In doing so, the Court concluded, the Legislature had exercised a power that was "purely judicial" in nature and had thereby exceeded the limits of its constitutional authority.

As if that were not enough to dispose of this ill-fated legislative resolve, the Court went on to point out that, in addition, the resolve was unconstitutional for two further reasons: first, because it had the effect of retroactively disturbing vested rights; and second, because it had the effect of suspending the operation of existing statutes for the benefit of certain favored individuals (the sureties involved in the case) while leaving those statutes in effect as to all others. In the latter respect, Mellen concluded that the resolve violated what he called "the great principle of constitutional equality."

Lewis v. Webb surely ranks as one of the Maine Court's most important decisions because from the outset of Maine's statehood, that decision gave teeth to the fundamental constitutional principle of the separation of governmental powers. It is one of the key

---

principle of the separation of powers: "The accumulation of all powers, legislative, executive, and judiciary, in the same hands, whether of one, a few, or many, and whether hereditary, self-appointed, or elective, may justly be pronounced the very definition of tyranny." *The Federalist No. 47*.

[63] Me. Const. Art. III, §1 ("The powers of this government shall be divided into three distinct departments, the legislative, executive and judicial."). The separate nature of these three branches of government is further underscored by the second section of that article, which provides: "No person or persons, belonging to one of these departments, shall exercise any of the powers properly belonging to either of the others, except in cases herein expressly directed or permitted."

building blocks by which the independence of the Maine judiciary is secured. *Lewis's* lasting significance is further assured because, as the following quotations from Mellen's opinion in that case illustrate, that opinion is a virtual anthology of maxims of constitutional law:[64]

> [I]f the legislature undertake to exercise judicial power, they invade the province of the judiciary; because the constitution and the laws have placed all the judicial power in other hands.
>
> ....
>
> ...It is one of the striking and peculiar features of judicial power that it is displayed in the decision of controversies between contending parties.... It is the province of the legislature to make and establish laws; and it is the province and duty of Judges to expound and apply them.
>
> ...The genius of our government and the nature of our civil institutions are such as to render it most proper that all questions between litigating parties should be discussed and decided in a judicial Court; there is the place to settle questions of law....
>
> ....
>
> ...[A] law retrospective in its operations, acting on past transactions, and in its operation disturbing, impairing, defeating or destroying vested rights, is void, and cannot and must not receive judicial sanction....
>
> ...On principle then it can never be within the bounds of legitimate legislation, to enact a special law, or pass a resolve dispensing with the general law, in a particular case, and granting a privilege and indulgence to one man, by way of exemption from the operation and effect of such general law, leaving all other persons under its operation. Such a law is neither just or reasonable in its consequences. It is our boast that we live under a government of laws and not of men. But this can hardly be deemed a blessing unless those laws have

---

[64] In a case decided in 1968, our Court relied on, and quoted extensively from, Mellen's opinion in *Webb*, remarking that after 143 years Mellen's opinion remained "fresh and clear." *See Maine Pharm. Ass'n v. Bd. of Comm'rs of the Profession of Pharmacy*, 245 A.2d 271, 273 (Me. 1968).

for their immoveable basis the great principle of constitutional equality.[65]

Although only five years of age in 1825, our Court, by its decisions in *Laboree* and *Lewis*, had already firmly established foundational principles of constitutional law concerning the extent and limits of the powers of the Legislature and the judiciary. The principles established in *Laboree* and *Lewis*—that the judiciary is the ultimate judge of the constitutionality of legislation, and that the powers of the judiciary are separate from those of the Legislature, and are not to be exercised by the Legislature—are lasting contributions to Maine's constitutional jurisprudence that remain authoritative and compelling to the present day.

Allen v. McKean

This case, which was decided by U.S. Supreme Court Justice Joseph Story in 1833, concerned the constitutionality of a Maine statute that resulted in the removal of William Allen from his office as President of Bowdoin College in Brunswick, Maine.[66] The statute in question, which was passed by the Maine Legislature in 1831, purported to terminate the tenure of any person holding the office of president of any college in Maine as of the date of the next college commencement, unless the incumbent were to be re-elected by a two-thirds vote of the boards of trustees and overseers of the college. That statute further provided that any person elected or re-elected to the office of president of a college in Maine, after the statute was passed, would thereafter hold that office at the pleasure of college trustees and overseers.

Although written in language of general applicability, this statute was really aimed at Bowdoin's President Allen. There were only two colleges in Maine at that time, Bowdoin College and Waterville College, later re-named Colby College. As Charles C.

---

[65] *Lewis*, 3 Me. at 331-36.

[66] *See* An Act Respecting Colleges, Me. P.L. 1831, ch. 517.

Calhoun explains in his comprehensive history of Bowdoin College, "Since no one at Waterville objected to [its President], who would easily be re-elected, it was clear on whom the axe was descending."[67] After Allen failed to be re-elected, he sued Bowdoin's treasurer in federal court for his salary and other perquisites of office, contending that the Maine statute that led to his removal violated his contractual rights.

The case was argued in Portland, Maine in 1833 before Justice Story, in his capacity as Circuit Justice for the First Circuit, which then included Maine, New Hampshire, Massachusetts, and Rhode Island. At that time, Supreme Court justices were required to hear federal court cases within their circuits in addition to their Supreme Court responsibilities.[68] The U.S. District Judge for Maine, Ashur Ware, would ordinarily have sat with Story as a circuit court panel of two, but being a Bowdoin trustee, Ware was unable to sit in judgment of the case.[69] In a characteristically scholarly decision that addressed every facet of the legal issues presented, Story concluded that the Maine Legislature's attempted ouster of President Allen was entirely unconstitutional:

> In every view, therefore, in which I have been able to contemplate this subject, it seems to me, that the [Maine Legislature's] act of 1831 is unconstitutional and void, so far as it seeks to remove President Allen from office. The legislature could not constitutionally deprive him of his office,

---

[67] Charles C. Calhoun, *A Small College in Maine: Two Hundred Years of Bowdoin* (Brunswick, Maine: Bowdoin College, 1993), 85-86. I am indebted to Calhoun's superb history for much of the background information contained in this discussion.

[68] Circuit court duty became such a burdensome, additional responsibility of Supreme Court justices that in 1891 Congress established intermediate circuit courts of appeal, resulting in the demise of the old circuit courts as a practical matter. In 1911, Congress took the final step of officially abolishing the old circuit courts. *See* Russell R. Wheeler & Cynthia Harrison, *Creating the Federal Judicial System* (Federal Judicial Center, 1994), 18.

[69] *See* Calhoun, *A Small College in Maine*, 98 n. 62.

or of his right to the salary and the perquisites annexed thereto.[70]

In reaching that conclusion, Story first observed that for purposes of constitutional analysis, Bowdoin was a private, not a public, corporation. "It answers," said Story, "the very description of a private college, as laid down by Mr. Chief Justice Marshall in *Dartmouth College v. Woodward....*" In the *Dartmouth College* case, decided in 1819, the Supreme Court held that a private corporation's charter was a contract that was protected from impairment by state legislation by virtue of the Contracts Clause of the U.S. Constitution.[71] Consistent with that ruling, Story decided that the Maine Legislature's attempt to legislate Allen out of office was a nullity because the power to take such action was exclusively conferred on college authorities by Bowdoin's original charter. Moreover, Story concluded, Allen's tenure in office was itself protected by his contract with the College. The obligations of his contract, Story stated, "could not, consistently with the constitution of the United States, be impaired by the state legislature."

The characters that played key roles in *Allen v. McKean* were a most interesting group. The defendant, Joseph McKeen (whose name was misspelled, McKean, in the official report of the case), was the treasurer of Bowdoin College. His interests were represented by Stephen Longfellow, a prominent member of the Portland Bar, father

---

[70] *Allen v. McKean,* 1 F. Cas. 489, 503 (C.C.D. Me. 1833) (No. 229).

[71] *Trustees of Dartmouth Coll. v. Woodward,* 17 U.S. (4 Wheat.) 518 (1819). The Contracts Clause, in Article I, Section 10 of the U.S. Constitution, forbids states from enacting laws impairing the obligation of contracts. Some commentators have suggested that "[h]istorians have probably exaggerated the impact of the early contracts clause decisions [like *Dartmouth*] on American economic and legal developments." Kathleen M. Sullivan & Gerald Gunther, *Constitutional Law*, 14th ed. (New York: Foundation Press, 2001), 498. They note that Justice Story himself, in his concurrence in *Dartmouth*, "pointed out what state political leaders already knew well: 'If the legislature mean to claim such an authority [to alter or amend corporate charters], it must be reserved in the grant.'" *Id.* In the wake of *Dartmouth*, most states, including Maine, did reserve that authority with regard to charters thereafter granted.

of the poet, Henry Wadsworth Longfellow, and Harvard College classmate of Justice Story. President Allen was represented by equally able counsel, Simon Greenleaf of Portland, Maine. Greenleaf was soon to join Story as a colleague on the faculty of Harvard Law School where he, like Story, had a distinguished academic career for many years. Among Greenleaf's many impressive accomplishments was his successful representation of the prevailing parties in the famous "Charles River Bridge case" decided by the U.S. Supreme Court in 1837.[72] Greenleaf's treatise on the law of evidence was for many years the leading authority in that branch of the law.

The plaintiff, William Allen, was well-acquainted with the legal issues involved in his struggle to maintain his position at Bowdoin. Before being called to become President of Bowdoin, Allen had served as President of the short-lived Dartmouth University in New Hampshire. Dartmouth University was short-lived because it was disestablished as the result of the Supreme Court's 1819 decision in the *Dartmouth College* case mentioned above. In that decision, the Supreme Court determined that the New Hampshire legislature violated the Contracts Clause of the U.S. Constitution by enacting legislation (in 1816) that in effect converted Dartmouth College, a private corporation, into a state institution named Dartmouth University. Ironically, the Supreme Court's decision in the *Dartmouth College* case, which resulted in Allen's losing his university post (and university) in New Hampshire, turned out to be the basis for Story's decision in *Allen v. McKean*, which led to Allen's regaining his position at Bowdoin.[73]

The influence of Justice Story in the development of our nation's law in its early years cannot be overstated. Story served for nearly thirty-four years on the U.S. Supreme Court, having been appointed

---

[72] *Proprietors of the Charles River Bridge v. Proprietors of the Warren Bridge*, 36 U.S. (11 Pet.) 420 (1837). In that case, a majority of the U.S. Supreme Court decided that the Massachusetts legislature had not unconstitutionally impaired the charter of a toll-bridge corporation by chartering a competing free-bridge corporation because the terms of the charter of the toll-bridge corporation did not expressly or impliedly restrict the powers of the legislature in that respect.

[73] *See* Calhoun, *A Small College in Maine*, 85.

to the Court in 1811 at the youthful age of thirty-two. He was Chief Justice John Marshall's close personal friend and colleague throughout the many years they served together on the Supreme Court. In the entire history of the Court, he was probably the most learned jurist to have served on that bench. Story's capacity for work was prodigious. His breadth of knowledge of the law, both here and abroad, was unsurpassed. Story authored numerous significant decisions while on circuit court duty, wrote several authoritative treatises on a wide variety of legal topics, all of which went into multiple editions, and served as a professor of law at Harvard Law School for many years while performing, in addition, his weighty responsibilities as an Associate Justice of the Supreme Court of the United States.

Story also found time generously to help other judges who frequently sought his advice on questions of law. He was highly respected and well-liked by lawyers who found him to be not only an oracle of the law, but a congenial and amiable companion as well. A letter written in 1846 by a leading member of the Maine Bar paints a vivid picture of Story and the impact of his arrival in Maine for his circuit court duties:

> I hardly know how you will understand me when I say, that his annual or biennial coming among us, seemed like something between an avatar and an avalanche; for, it seemed, at first, a coming down upon us with a weight from his judicial power and genius and knowledge, and the prestige that attended them, that would have been felt more heavily, if it had not been so soon relieved, I might say, at once, by the cordiality and warmth with which he greeted his brethren, as he always made them feel, of the Bar; and the animating kindness, with which he invited them to their tasks.[74]

---

[74] Charles S. Daveis, Esq., of Portland, to William W. Story, September 15, 1846, *Life and Letters of Joseph Story*, vol. 2, ed. William W. Story (Freeport, N.Y.: Books for Libraries Press, 1851), 587-595. For informative biographical sketches of Daveis and other important lawyers and jurists in Maine's early years, see William Willis, *A History of the Law, the Courts, and the Lawyers of Maine: From its*

Looking back at this trilogy of foundational constitutional cases that arose in the infancy of Maine's statehood, it seems both remarkable and extremely fortunate that jurists of the quality of Prentiss Mellen and Joseph Story were on hand and willing to undertake the formidable responsibility of building a solid structure of constitutional law, sufficient to last through the ages. It seems, moreover, equally remarkable and fortunate that in those early years, the Maine Bar included lawyers as able as Stephen Longfellow and Simon Greenleaf, who represented the parties in *Allen v. McKean*. As Story remarked in that case, referring to those distinguished advocates, "This cause has been argued with a degree of learning and ability proportionate to its importance."

First Colonization to the Early Part of the Present Century (Portland, Me.: Bailey & Noyes, 1863). For more on notable lawyers and judges in Maine's early years, including numerous anecdotes along with a wealth of biographical and historical information, see Herbert T. Silsby II, *Memorable Justices and Lawyers of Maine: A Historical Perspective* (Ellsworth, Me.: Dilligaf Publishing, 2006).

PAUPERS

T hroughout the first hundred years of Maine's history as a separate state, municipalities were responsible for the support of the poor and indigent members of their communities, who, on receiving public support, were known in the law as "paupers." Municipal authority regarding paupers was administered by municipal "overseers of the poor" who were chosen at annual town meetings. By statute, any two overseers could commit paupers to confinement in municipal workhouses so that they could be gainfully employed and be less of a burden on the taxpayers. By statute, any two overseers could also commit to workhouses all persons "able of body to work," who "live a dissolute, vagrant life, and exercise no ordinary calling or lawful business, sufficient to gain an honest livelihood."[75] The commitment to Portland's workhouse of persons allegedly within that "dissolute-vagrant" category gave rise to litigation in three cases that reached the Maine Supreme Judicial Court in the nineteenth century.

The Court's decisions in this trilogy of cases provide some insight into the way the early Maine Court regarded the poor, the less fortunate, and the most vulnerable citizens of Maine. These cases are also particularly interesting from an historical point of view because they show how it was that, over time, the Court came to

---

[75] The full text of that category was "all persons able of body to work and not having estate or means otherwise to maintain themselves who refuse or neglect to do so; live a dissolute, vagrant life, and exercise no ordinary calling or lawful business, sufficient to gain an honest livelihood." *See* An Act for erecting Work Houses for the reception and employment of the Idle and Indigent, Me. P.L. 1821, ch. 124. This statute derived from a Massachusetts statute bearing the same name, enacted January 10, 1789. *See* Laws and Resolves of Massachusetts, 1788-9, ch. 30, at 42.

accept the idea that some form of hearing was required before municipal officials could deprive anyone of their "liberty" by committing that person to a workhouse.

Adeline G. Nott's Case

The first of these cases was an 1834 case, reported simply as *Adeline G. Nott's case.*[76] Adeline Nott was committed to Portland's workhouse on the basis of a written statement signed by two of Portland's overseers of the poor, who alleged that she lived a dissolute, vagrant life and exercised no lawful business. Thereafter, her attorney moved for her discharge, contending that the statute under which she had been committed was unconstitutional in several respects: that it violated the natural rights of every citizen of the state by authorizing the commitment of a citizen to a "dungeon" or workhouse without a trial or hearing; that it violated the spirit and genius of the Constitution and laws of the land, especially the provision in Maine's Constitution, Article I, Section 1, that declared that "[a]ll men are born equally free and independent, and have certain natural, inherent and unalienable rights, among which are those of enjoying and defending life and liberty"; and that it violated constitutional provisions securing rights incident to a criminal prosecution.

"How," Nott's attorney asked, "can it be said that the citizen of this State can enjoy liberty, if at any time he may be committed by two others, to a dungeon, without a hearing, without a trial—without even a complaint on oath, and the imprisonment being, as by the law it may be, for life?"

From the vantage point of the present day, one would think that Nott's attorney, with this rhetorical question, made an overwhelmingly compelling case. But in Maine, in 1834, that advocacy proved insufficient. First, the Court noted that this was not a criminal prosecution and that therefore the constitutional rights of the accused in criminal cases were not involved. Turning to the

---

[76] 11 Me. 208 (1834).

claimed constitutional right to a hearing of some kind—some measure of due process—*prior to* committal to a workhouse, the Court concluded that it sufficed that the lawfulness of a committal could be challenged after the fact by a claim for damages or by a petition for habeas corpus.

In upholding the constitutionality of the workhouse committal statute, as it applied to paupers generally, the Court began by noting that it was "not unreasonable" that those receiving public assistance "should be made to contribute to their own support, by some suitable employment." The Court then offered this justification for municipal officials to commit paupers to workhouses:

> The indigent have no claim to be supported in idleness; and it is but just that they should remunerate those, charged with their maintenance, by their own industry. Their poverty generally grows out of an unwillingness to labor, or is occasioned by reckless and improvident habits. Thus circumstanced, and while receiving alms from the town, they have no just right to complain, if they are sent to, employed and governed in a work-house, provided for the purpose of making their support less burthensome. It would probably not be contended that their rights would be thereby infringed; unless the restraint should be continued beyond the necessity which occasioned it.[77]

At this juncture, it seems worth pausing to note that, as that passage shows, the Court's observation that "poverty generally grows out of an unwillingness to labor, or is occasioned by reckless and improvident habits" was at the basis of its conclusion that committal to a workhouse, the form of "workfare" involved in that case, was "not unreasonable." In contrast with that judgment, which blamed the poor for their lot in life, the U.S. Supreme Court has more recently observed, "We have come to recognize that forces not within

---

[77] *Id.* at 210.

the control of the poor contribute to their poverty."[78] These differing perceptions of the roots of poverty will no doubt continue to affect the deliberations of courts and legislatures as they wrestle with the challenging issue of how best to care for the poor and indigent within the constitutional framework in the years that lie ahead.

In upholding the constitutionality of the workhouse-committal statute, as it applied to Adeline Nott (who had neither claimed nor received public assistance from Portland), the Court explained that in its view, Nott was "but one degree removed" from becoming a public charge. By her "dissolute habits," she was "prostrating" her health and strength, and "unless her course can be arrested, she may become entirely unable to do anything towards her own support." From that perspective, Nott's committal was a cautionary measure "to enable the town, with less expense, to provide for her support, which is about to be thrown upon them." Moreover, the Court added, her committal was intended "to save instead of punishing [her]." Based on that speculative and paternalistic line of reasoning, the Court concluded that Nott's committal was properly within the jurisdiction of the overseers of the poor.

In addition, the Court explained, Nott's committal to the workhouse could be justified as "a police regulation, to preserve the community from contamination." From that perspective, a person living "a dissolute, vagrant life" had no greater rights to due process than the "victim of contagious sickness," who, the Court said, "may at the discretion of the selectmen, be taken from his own house, from the aid and solace of his family, and assigned to such place, and subjected to such care, as they may adjudge necessary." Clearly, the Court felt that the citizenry was well served by Nott's summary removal from the streets of Portland.

Adeline Nott lost her case before the Maine Court, but as noted below, arguments that had been made by her attorney would eventually prevail in later years.

---

[78] *Goldberg v. Kelly*, 397 U.S. 254, 265 (1970) (holding that the Due Process Clause of the Fourteenth Amendment requires that a state provide an evidentiary hearing before terminating a recipient's welfare benefits).

Portland v. Bangor (1856)

In *Portland v. Bangor* (1856),[79] the Maine Court again addressed the question of the legality of the procedure for committing paupers to municipal workhouses. In this case, one Betsey Brown and her daughter, Almedia, had been committed to Portland's workhouse on the basis of a warrant signed by two overseers of the poor, who alleged that it appeared to them that Mrs. Brown and her daughter lived a dissolute, vagrant life and exercised no ordinary calling or lawful business sufficient to gain an honest livelihood. In proceedings before the Court, Portland sought reimbursement from the city of Bangor for the cost of pauper supplies that Portland had provided Mrs. Brown and her daughter while they were in Portland's custody. Bangor would ordinarily have been responsible for those costs because it was the place where the Browns had their "legal settlement," or residency as defined by Maine's pauper laws. But in this case, Bangor contested Portland's reimbursement claim. Bangor took the position that Portland had unlawfully committed the Browns to Portland's workhouse because, as Bangor saw it, they were able to support themselves and were not in need of immediate relief. The Maine Court disagreed. Upholding the legality of Portland's actions, the Court said that the evidence "tends to confirm, rather than confute" the overseers' statement that the Browns were living "a dissolute, vagrant life" and exercising "no ordinary calling or lawful business, sufficient to gain an honest livelihood."

The Court's decision, however, was not unanimous. One member of the Court, Justice Richard D. Rice, filed a dissenting opinion. Rice was of the view that, although the evidence might have been sufficient to justify the filing of a criminal complaint against the Browns for keeping a house of ill-fame, the Browns should not have been sent to the workhouse without there first having been some kind of proceeding to determine the validity of the overseers' allegations against them. As Rice saw it, the evidence supported none of those allegations. Rice also agreed with Bangor's position that

---

[79] 42 Me. 403 (1856).

Portland's reimbursement claim was not justified because there was no evidence that the Browns, at the time of their committal, were in need of immediate relief.

Justice Rice's dissenting opinion in this case is an important landmark in the history of Maine constitutional law because with prescience it articulated the now well-established constitutional principle that a state may not deprive a person of liberty without due process of law. Rice first clarified the importance of the "liberty interest" at stake:

> Pauperism works most important changes in the condition of the citizen. Through its influence, he is deprived of the elective franchise, and of the control of his own person. The pauper may be transported from town to town, and place to place, against his will; he loses the control of his family, his children may be taken from him without his consent; he may himself be sent to the work-house, or made the subject of a five years contract, without being personally consulted. In short, the adjudged pauper is subordinated to the will of others, and reduced to a condition but little removed from that of chattel slavery, and until recently...like the slave, was liable to be sold upon the block of the auctioneer, for service or support.[80]

Rice then proclaimed, in words that presaged the Fourteenth Amendment's protection of the constitutional right of liberty:

---

[80] *Id.* at 411. One year earlier, Justice John Appleton had described the plight of the pauper under Maine law in similar terms: "The pauper, who receives aid from the town, while that condition of things exists, is deprived of the rights and privileges of citizenship. He cannot serve on the jury. He is not permitted to vote. He is eligible to no office. His control over his children ceases. They may be taken from him and bound to service. Where he shall reside is no longer a matter dependent upon his own will, but is determined for him by the action of the town or its constituted authorities. It may be in the poor house, if one there be. It may be where the person who has contracted to take charge of the poor may reside. The place where he may live is not one selected by himself, nor is his continuance there the result of his own volition." *Starks v. New Sharon*, 39 Me. 368, 380 (1855) (Appleton, J., dissenting).

A condition in life so undesirable, not to say revolting, to all that is manly and ennobling in human character, should not be *established* unnecessarily, nor by doubtful nor precipitate action.[81]

Pointing out the injustice of a system that allowed paupers and persons considered "likely to become paupers" to be committed to workhouses, without a hearing or due process of any kind, Rice stated:

Thus, while rogues, vagabonds and beggars; night-walkers, brawlers, pilferers, common drunkards, fortune-tellers, common pipers, fiddlers and the like, may not be sent to the house of correction, except upon trial before a magistrate and on complaint on oath with a right of appeal, or before the Supreme Judicial Court, and then restrained only for a limited period of time; [paupers and other categories of persons described in the workhouse-committal statute] may be sent to the work-house, by the overseers thereof, for an indefinite period, without any complaint, trial, or right of appeal. And this unrestrained power is exercised over a class of persons not paupers, nor even *quasi* paupers, but who, it is supposed, are likely to become such.[82]

Sometimes dissenting opinions have no lasting consequence, but Rice's powerful dissenting opinion in *Portland v. Bangor* (1856) was not of that kind. Twenty years later, in another case having the same name, the Court unanimously acknowledged the validity of the concerns that Rice had so forcefully stated in that dissenting opinion.

Portland v. Bangor (1876)[83]

Like the 1856 case discussed above, this 1876 case involved a claim by Portland for reimbursement from Bangor, the place of a

---

[81] *Portland*, 42 Me. at 411 (Rice, J., dissenting).

[82] *Id.* at 412.

[83] 65 Me. 120 (1876).

pauper's legal settlement, for the cost of supplies Portland had furnished that pauper while she was in Portland's workhouse. The pauper had been committed there on the basis of a warrant signed by two overseers of the poor, who alleged that she was "a dissolute vagrant, exercising no lawful business and liable to become chargeable to the city." In this case, however, in contrast with the 1856 case, the Court rejected Portland's claim for reimbursement on the ground that the proceedings that resulted in the pauper's committal to Portland's workhouse were illegal. In reaching that conclusion, the Court in effect overruled both its 1834 decision in *Adeline G. Nott's case* and its 1856 decision in *Portland v. Bangor*. As the Court stated, "If the decisions in [those cases] were correct when made, the power therein sanctioned can be exercised no longer." The Court's decision, negating those earlier decisions, was based on the Fourteenth Amendment to the U.S. Constitution, which had been ratified in 1868.

Noting that the Fourteenth Amendment "declares that no state shall deprive any person of life, *liberty*, or property, without due process of law," the Court concluded that the commitment of a person to a workhouse, based simply on the say-so of two overseers of the poor, was an "arbitrary exercise of power" that "very clearly violates the fourteenth amendment of the federal constitution." Echoing the principle of "equal protection of the laws," embodied in that Amendment, the Court also remarked that "[i]f white men and women may be thus summarily disposed of at the north, of course black ones may be disposed of in the same way at the south; and thus the very evil which it was particularly the object of the fourteenth amendment to eradicate will still exist."[84]

It is interesting to note that until the aftermath of the Civil War, including the ratification of the Fourteenth Amendment, the Court as a whole seems to have been unable to appreciate that the deprivation

---

[84] In the same year that the Court issued that ruling, based on the Fourteenth Amendment, the Maine Legislature enacted a due process statute to the same effect, specifying that henceforth a person could be committed to a workhouse "only upon conviction of the offenses, acts, or conditions for which such commitments are by law authorized, before some municipal or police court, or trial justice." Me. P.L. 1876, ch. 147.

of liberty resulting from the committal of paupers to workhouses bore some resemblance to the shackles of slavery. Once that connection was made, the Court seems to have readily accepted the argument that some form of due process, prior to committal, was required. At the same time, however, the Court was careful to note the limitations of due process (today commonly known as "procedural due process") in this context:

> The objection to [a workhouse-committal] proceeding does not lie in the fact that the persons named may be restrained of their liberty, but in allowing it to be done without first having a judicial investigation to ascertain whether the charges made against them are true. Not in committing them to the workhouse, but in doing it without first giving them an opportunity to be heard.[85]

Maine's old laws concerning paupers are noteworthy today in at least three other respects. First, during Maine's first hundred years, those laws spawned a vast amount of litigation regarding the issue of which of two or more towns was ultimately responsible for the cost of supporting a pauper. Those disputes produced an elaborate fact-specific jurisprudence for determining that issue and consumed an enormous amount of judicial time and resources. Given that state of affairs, it seems surprising that some form of alternative dispute resolution process, such as an administrative fact-finding procedure, was not put in place at an early date to deal with those repetitive and time-consuming factual inquiries.

Second, looking back on the long chapter of history during which Maine courts routinely adjudicated controversies regarding the support of paupers, and reading those cases through the lens of the present day, one cannot help but be struck by the amount of personal information that was included in the public record, not only in cases in which the right of a pauper to support was at issue, but also in cases where the only issue in dispute was which of two towns was

---

[85] *Portland*, 65 Me. at 121.

responsible for a pauper's support—support that all agreed was warranted. For example, in a case decided in 1882, in which the only real issue was which of two towns, Strong or Farmington, was responsible for the pauper's support at "the insane hospital," the Court, referring to the pauper by name, described him as "a person of weak mind, of filthy and disgusting habits, careless of his personal appearance, able to labor, but requiring for successful labor, supervision."[86]

With the benefit of hindsight, it seems surprising that neither the Court nor the Legislature took steps to protect the confidentiality of personal information such as that. Yet in the early years of Maine law, the public may generally have been of the view that by seeking public support, a pauper in effect waived any right of privacy, and that in any event, personal information related to the expenditure of municipal funds would inevitably become public knowledge, regardless of any protective shield of confidentiality that might be erected by the law for the benefit of the pauper.

Third, if the Court's moralistic feelings about paupers, as expressed in its 1834 decision in *Adeline G. Nott's case*, were any indication of public opinion generally, there must have been a particularly painful stigma attached to anyone's need for public assistance at that time. The likelihood that a request for public assistance would result in the details of a pauper's personal history becoming a matter of public record must have made that stigma all the more painful. It is distressing also to contemplate that the fear of public humiliation must have deterred many deserving citizens of our state from seeking public assistance for themselves and their families in times of real need.

---

[86] *Strong v. Farmington*, 74 Me. 46, 47 (1882).

MAINE LAW'S DEBT TO ANIMALS

D uring Maine's early years, domestic animals were present in abundance in every Maine community. Horses, hogs, chickens, oxen, cows, sheep, cats, and dogs were then as much a part of the fabric of everyday life as the automobile is today. And just as the automobile today is a frequent subject of litigation, animals, because of their ubiquitous presence in Maine's early years, were then frequently at the center of litigated cases and other controversies. Many of those cases ultimately reached the level of the Maine Supreme Judicial Court, where they resulted in decisions of significance in the history of Maine law.

Looking back over the entire first century of Maine law, the considerable debt that the development of Maine law owes to animals becomes very clear. For example, the common law rules of liability in Maine for negligent acts and omissions originally developed in large measure from early cases in which horses and their owners were injured as the result of defects in roadways, which towns were required by statute to keep in good repair. Horses, sadly, also figured prominently in the development of Maine's jurisprudence concerning the rights and duties of parties in cases involving railroad-crossing accidents. Some other branches of the law in which animals made significant contributions in the early years of Maine law are illustrated by the cases discussed below.

Before turning to those cases, however, it seems worth noting here that there is something about our connection with animals—probably our sense of empathy for them—that makes these cases and the legal principles for which they stand distinctly memorable as contrasted, for example, with cases that involve inanimate items of personal property such as pieces of equipment, machinery, and the like. When we read about animals, we relate to them, we feel for them, and we remember them. For these reasons, I have found that cases in which animals played leading roles can be extremely helpful in understanding legal rules and principles that, in a different setting, might seem abstract and of fleeting interest at best.

A Stallion Named "Sir William" and Caveat Emptor: Let the Buyer Beware

At the center of the case of *Briggs v. Hunton* (1895)[87] was a stallion by the name of "Sir William." The plaintiff, the owner of Sir William, brought this case to recover damages in the amount of $50 from the defendant, that sum being the agreed-upon price for the services of Sir William in breeding the defendant's mare. Sir William duly rendered those services, but the resulting colt was born weak, sick, and diseased, and lived only four days. The defendant refused to pay the plaintiff, claiming that Sir William was afflicted with a disease at the time his services were provided and that the agreement to provide those services was subject to an implied warranty that the stallion was not diseased at that time. The Maine Court, however, rejected the defendant's contentions and decided the case in favor of the plaintiff, Sir William's owner.

The Court first noted that the plaintiff was not guilty of fraud because there was no evidence that he knew his stallion was diseased. As the Court saw it, the buyer was in as good a position as the seller to determine the state of the stallion's health. Next, the Court noted that the seller had not expressly warranted that his stallion was fit to beget offspring. As the Court interpreted the transaction, the plaintiff had not sold the services of a stallion fit to beget offspring, but only the services of a stallion fit to impregnate the defendant's mare. Under those circumstances, the Court concluded that the parties' agreement was not subject to an implied warranty that the stallion was free from disease that might be transmitted to offspring. Having found that the defendant's implied warranty theory did not hold water, the Court dismissed the

---

[87] 87 Me. 145, 32 A. 794 (1895).

defendant's appeal on the basis of the old common law rule of *caveat emptor* (let the buyer beware).

If the Court's decision in this case was a disappointing outcome for the buyer of Sir William's services, whose sickly colt died just days after it was born, that result was no more severe than the outcome of a Massachusetts precedent, *Giroux v. Stedman* (1888),[88] on which the Maine Court relied. The defendant in that Massachusetts case was a farmer who sold butchered hogs, knowing that the purchasers intended to use them as food. The hogs had been infected by disease, and the purchasers became seriously ill when they ate the pork. The Massachusetts Court nevertheless held that the sale was not subject to an implied warranty that the hogs were fit for food. The Massachusetts Court explained the basis for its ruling as follows:

> In making casual sales from a farm of its products, to hold the owner to the duty of ascertaining at his peril the condition of articles sold, and of impliedly warranting, if sold with the knowledge that they are to be used for food, that they are fit for the purpose, imposes a larger liability than should be placed upon one who may often have no better means of knowledge than the purchaser.[89]

Like the Maine Court, which, in Sir William's case, indicated that the purchaser of the stallion's services was in as good a position as the seller to determine the state of the stallion's health, the Massachusetts Court justified its decision by suggesting that the seller of a farm product may often have no better means of knowing the condition of the product than the purchaser. As a practical matter, however, it is difficult to see why that would be so. Would not an animal's owner, who has had the care and custody of the animal, ordinarily be in a much better position than the purchaser to know the state of the animal's health and physical condition? Plainly, as these cases indicate, these nineteenth-century courts were disinclined to impose upon

---

[88] 145 Mass. 439, 14 N.E. 538 (1888).

[89] *Id.* at 442-43, 14 N.E. at 540.

sellers implied liabilities that went beyond terms to which they had expressly agreed. These courts simply did not feel it was right to impose their version of fairness and justice on transactions that had been freely entered into by consenting parties.

The rule of *caveat emptor*, on which these decisions were based, was deeply embedded in the common law. Courts justified the rule on the ground that it served the public interest. As the Maine Court in *Bean v. Herrick* (1835) put it, "The rule of *caveat emptor* is useful in the community. It leads to vigilance and circumspection; and serves to check litigation."[90] By shielding sellers from litigation and liability for selling defective products, the rule of *caveat emptor* has no doubt been a significant boost for economic progress and development. But what the Court left unsaid, in saying that *caveat emptor* is a rule that is "useful in the community," is that *caveat emptor*—a rule that always favors sellers at the expense of consumers—could hardly be described as a model of justice.

Over the years, courts and legislatures have made some significant inroads on the common law rule of *caveat emptor* in order to protect the interests of consumers.[91] In the meantime, purchasers of defective products and services, such as the purchaser of Sir William's services, were generally out of luck in the absence of warranties expressly set forth in written agreements—not the most comfortable situation for farmers and others who could not afford to retain lawyers and who were apt to be skeptical about the value of lawyer-drafted agreements in any event.

---

[90] 12 Me. 262, 269 (1835).

[91] For example, the Uniform Sales Act, enacted by the Maine Legislature in 1923, spelled out a number of circumstances that would give rise to an implied warranty of quality or fitness in the sale of goods. That statute was superseded in 1964 by the Maine Legislature's adoption of the Uniform Commercial Code, which expanded the scope of implied warranties in the sale of goods. Since then, Congress and the Maine Legislature have both enacted many consumer protection statutes.

A Horse Named "Prince" and the Law of Bailments[92]

A horse by the name of "Prince" played a tragic yet central part in *Sanford v. Kimball* (1910),[93] a case that concerned the issue of a bailee's liability to a bailor for damage to property that was the subject of the bailment. In the summer of 1908, the plaintiff and the defendant, being two farmers in the town of Kennebunk, agreed "to exchange work in haying, with teams and men." Under that agreement, the plaintiff let the defendant have the plaintiff's horse, Prince. About two weeks thereafter, the plaintiff went to pick up his horse, but as the defendant was not yet done haying, it was agreed that the defendant could keep the horse for another day and return him on the day following. The defendant used the horse that day, fed him for the evening, and left him for the night unhitched in a sixteen-foot square stall on the defendant's farm.

The following morning, the defendant found the horse in that stall with what would prove to be a mortal wound. As described by the Court, the wound was "a clean cut three or three and one-half inches long and from one to one and a half inches deep, across the upper part of the off forward leg." The wound was not bleeding. There were no traces of blood on the floor of the barn or in the stall. According to the record in the case, there were marks of blood on a pail, as if someone had washed the wound. Prince's wound was treated, but the horse died about ten days later. Thereafter, Prince's owner sued the defendant for negligence in his use and care of Prince. The defendant testified that he had no idea of how the injury was inflicted. The jury returned a verdict in favor of the defendant, and the plaintiff appealed. On appeal, the Maine Court affirmed the verdict.

The plaintiff (bailor) contended that he was entitled to damages because the defendant had not satisfactorily explained how Prince

---

[92] A bailment is an arrangement whereby personal property is delivered by one person (bailor) to another (bailee), to be kept by the bailee and returned by the bailee to the bailor at the conclusion of the bailment.

[93] 106 Me. 355, 76 A. 890 (1910).

had been injured. The Court, however, rejected that argument, stating that "[t]he law does not require so much [of a bailee], amounting in this case to an impossibility, because the cause or source of this injury is admitted to be a mystery." The Court then stated that to impose liability on the bailee under these circumstances would amount to treating the bailee as an insurer. That, the Court would not do. The bailee in a case such as this, the Court said, need only give the reason why the horse was not returned, and in this case "this was done." Evidently, the Court believed the bailee had satisfied his burden of proof simply by explaining that the horse had not been returned to the bailor because it had died after having been injured by causes unknown. Accordingly, Prince's owner had no legal recourse despite the fact that the injury suffered by Prince occurred while Prince was in the defendant's custody and control, and despite the fact that the arrangement was for the defendant's benefit in the haying of his farm.

Under these circumstances, it seems unfair that the defendant could avoid liability simply by saying he had no idea how the injury happened to Prince. As between the plaintiff-bailor and the defendant-bailee, wasn't the latter in a much better position to know how Prince was injured? Shouldn't it have been the business of the defendant to know how that injury could have occurred? After all, Prince's injury occurred on the defendant's premises and on the defendant's watch, so to speak. One leaves this sad tale of the fate of Prince with the sense that an injustice was done. Yet here again, as was the situation in Sir William's case, it is certainly understandable that a court would hesitate to impose liability on anyone without proof of actual fault.

The case involving the sorry fate of the horse, Prince, would prove not to be the final word on the rights and obligations of bailors and bailees in Maine. Just as the rule of *caveat emptor* has been modified by legislation over the years following the Maine Court's 1895 decision in "Sir William's case," the rules of the common law concerning the rights and obligations of bailors and bailees have been refined by the Maine Court over the years following its 1910 decision in "Prince's case." For example, in *Levasseur v. Field* (1975),[94] a case that involved a boat that was damaged while it was in winter storage, the Maine Court explained that once a bailor has shown that his property was damaged while in a bailee's possession, the bailee will not necessarily be exonerated simply because he has presented *some* evidence that the damage occurred without his fault.

As these developments illustrate, the evolution of rules of law over time is a continuing process in which courts and legislatures both play important roles. The lively, almost fluid nature of that process stands in marked contrast with the commonly held, but inaccurate, perception that "the Law" is as firmly fixed and unchanging as granite blocks in courthouse walls.

The Invalidity of Agreements That Violate Public Policy

At the center of the case of *Sager v. Portsmouth, S. & P. & E. Rail Road Co.* (1850),[95] was a horse that suffered serious injury from exposure to the weather while being transported from Boston to Portland in an open car on the defendant's railroad on a cold November day in 1848. The horse's owner won his case against the railroad company for negligence in transporting his horse in an open car under those adverse weather conditions. On appeal to the Maine Supreme Judicial Court, the railroad company argued that the plaintiff's verdict should be set aside because, prior to the shipment of this horse, the plaintiff had signed a waiver agreement prepared by the railroad company, which exonerated it from "all damages that may happen to any horses" sent over the railroad. The Maine Court was not persuaded by that argument.

First, the Court interpreted the language exonerating the railroad company from damages that "may happen," as referring to accidental occurrences that might happen unexpectedly, as distinguished from losses caused by the company's own negligence. In addition, and most significantly, the Court also decided that, in any event, an

---

[94] 332 A.2d 765 (Me. 1975).

[95] 31 Me. 228 (1850).

agreement that would exonerate a railroad company from liability for its own negligence in transporting property would be invalid as a matter of law. The Court explained that its ruling to that effect was based on the importance of protecting the interest of the public in safe transportation by rail. Referring to railroad companies, the Court stated:

> The very great danger to be anticipated, by permitting them to enter into contracts to be exempt from losses occasioned by misconduct or negligence, can scarcely be over estimated. It would remove the principal safeguard for the preservation of life and property in such conveyances.[96]

In so ruling, the Court noted that railroad companies and other common carriers had a "public character" that differentiated them from mere bailees-for-hire, who, having no obligation to receive goods for shipment, are at liberty to prescribe the terms on which they will be shipped.

The implications of this decision were far-reaching. For if the Court had decided the case the other way, railroad corporations, as a practical matter, in view of their commanding economic power, would have been able, through the use of waiver agreements, to effectively immunize themselves from all liability to their customers for harm resulting from negligent conduct of the railroad corporations themselves.

The Maine Court's decision in the *Sager* case is an early example of judicial intervention to prevent one party—there, the railroad corporation—from taking undue advantage of parties with a weaker bargaining position. In *Sager*, we see our Court as an active agent of justice, invalidating an agreement in order to protect paramount interests of the public at large. By its decision in *Sager*, our Court in effect served notice that in some circumstances it was willing to tell contracting parties that significant public policy considerations will limit their ability to establish the terms of their own contracts.

---

[96] *Id.* at 238.

It is interesting to compare the Maine Court's decision in *Sager* with its decisions in the cases involving the stallion, Sir William, and the horse, Prince, discussed above. In the latter two cases, which were disputes between individuals that did not directly involve any significant public interests, the Court was not inclined to impose its sense of justice on the parties and burden them with obligations beyond those to which they had expressly agreed. In *Sager*, by contrast, the Court told the railroad corporation that even if the express terms of its waiver agreement could be construed as exonerating it from liability to its customers for its own negligence, the Maine courts would not enforce that agreement because it violated important principles of justice and public policy.

Ultimately, the question of the validity of such waiver agreements reached the U.S. Supreme Court in the case of *Railroad Co. v. Lockwood* (1873).[97] After noting that state court decisions concerning that question were sharply divided, with some courts allowing such waiver agreements, and others not, the Supreme Court in *Lockwood* sided with the position taken by the Maine Court in the *Sager* case some twenty-three years before and declared that such waiver agreements were void and invalid as a matter of law. The Supreme Court's decision to that effect was grounded on principles of morality, justice, and public policy. As the Supreme Court put it,

> [W]hen [common carriers] ask to go still further, and to be excused for negligence—an excuse so repugnant to the law of their foundation and to the public good—they have no longer any plea of justice or reason to support such a stipulation, but the contrary. And then, the inequality of the parties, the compulsion under which the customer is placed, and the obligations of the carrier to the public, operate with full force to divest the transaction of validity.[98]

---

[97] 84 U.S. 357 (1873).

[98] *Id*. at 381-82.

Judicial Notice

An unexpected benefit of reading early decisions of the Maine Court is that the reader inevitably learns a good deal about particular behaviors of horses. We have today become so accustomed to more modern means of transportation that, for the most part, we have no first-hand knowledge of those animal behaviors today. In the early years of Maine law, however, Maine people generally had an every-day familiarity with horses and their characteristics, a circumstance that played a significant role in our Court's development of the law of "judicial notice."

Certain facts that have become matters of general knowledge may be established in court proceedings by what is called "judicial notice," meaning that such facts may be taken as established without their having to be proved by evidence presented in those proceedings. At one time, characteristic behaviors of horses were so well known throughout Maine that our Court considered those behaviors to be proper subjects of judicial notice. As the Court stated in *State v. Maine Central Railroad Co.* (1894),[99] a case that arose from a fatal accident at a railroad crossing,

> But it seems to us that, at this day the fact that horses are liable to be frightened by locomotive engines and moving trains of cars, and that collisions at highway crossings are often caused thereby, are facts sufficiently notorious to be taken judicial notice of....[100]

Having concluded that those characteristics of horses were proper subjects of judicial notice, the Court explained that it therefore followed that there was no merit to the plaintiff's contention that the trial judge's instructions improperly allowed the jury to consider those characteristics in the absence of any evidence in the record to support them. The trial judge's instructions to the jury in this case included the following description of equine behaviors:

---

[99] 86 Me. 309, 29 A. 1086 (1894).

[100] *Id.* at 312, 29 A. at 1086.

In your common observation, it may be that you have
observed sometimes that when you are driving a horse
ordinarily kind and manageable, in the vicinity of a railroad,
while you hear no noise of an approaching train, the horse
does hear it, with its keen instinct, and springs into a faster
speed at once, and you may wonder why it is, until in a
moment you hear the sound also. And you may have
observed that a horse is anxious, approaching a railroad-
crossing, to spring into speed and get across as soon as
possible. If that is the case, and results from the character of
the horse, and is not caused by any means of fright resulting
from the wrongful act of the railroad company or its servants,
then it does not lay the foundation for [a lawsuit].[101]

Similarly, in *Bradbury v. Lawrence* (1898),[102] a case that concerned
the issue of whether the bailee of a horse that died while in the
bailee's custody was liable to the horse's owner for that loss, the
Maine Court approved jury instructions that stated:

And in your experience you probably have, all of you or the
most of you, if not all, have had experience with horses and
you may know that sometimes even a safe horse and a gentle
horse, if he hasn't been used for a few days or if he has been
hitched some time and becomes annoyed either by flies or by
anything else, will sometimes become restless and uneasy,
and for the time, a comparatively unsafe horse, that ordinarily
and usually is a perfectly reliable one. That is a matter that
might be within your knowledge and you have a right to
judge all matters according to your experience and dealing
with horses and your observation.[103]

Although certain facts concerning the behavior of horses may
have been proper subjects of judicial notice in the nineteenth century,
on account of their being matters of common knowledge at that time,

---

[101] *Id.* at 311, 29 A. at 1086.

[102] 91 Me. 457, 40 A. 332 (1898).

[103] *Id.* at 460, 40 A. at 333.

those same facts today would no longer qualify as such unless it could be said that they are still matters of common knowledge. Conversely, facts that at one time were not matters of common knowledge may, with the passage of time, become so commonly known that they would qualify as facts of which judicial notice may be taken. As our Court in *Maine Central Railroad*, the first judicial notice case mentioned above, explained:

> There are many facts in relation to electricity and its uses that to-day are known to almost every school boy, which, a few years ago, were known only to a few. To-day, they may be taken judicial notice of. Then, they could not.[104]

The evolving nature of the concept of judicial notice thus provides another illustration of the point that to one degree or another, the development of law over the years reflects changes that are continually occurring in the society of which the legal system is an integral part.

Competing Interests: Animals and Economic Development

When Maine became a separate state in 1820, horses were just about the only means of ground transportation. During the next hundred years, however, horses and their owners would have to compete and contend with railroads, electric street railways and ultimately, the automobile. Each of these emerging means of transportation created grave dangers to horses and to all who relied on them for travel. In addition, horses had to deal with all kinds of new and startling noises, such as whistles and loud hisses of steam emitted by locomotives and steam-powered machinery. Industrial development also brought with it novel objects of menacing size and unusual shapes and colors, the mere sight of which could cause otherwise gentle horses to panic, resulting in injury or death to persons and horses as well. The reports of old Maine cases contain many sad stories of horses that became skittish and panicked when

---

[104] *Me. Cent. R.R.*, 86 Me. at 312, 29 A. at 1086.

alarmed by sights and sounds to which they were not accustomed. The way in which the Maine Court resolved the competing interests of horse owners on the one hand and industrial development on the other, as shown by the following three cases, provides a good example of how the common law of Maine has evolved to meet the changing needs and values of the community.

The case of *Lynn v. Hooper* (1899)[105] involved a personal injury claim brought by the driver of a wagon who was thrown from the wagon when his horse became frightened and bolted at the sight of a white cloth "hay cap" that had been placed by the defendant over a pile of hay situated near the traveled part of the highway. The corners of the hay cap were fastened with ropes to four stakes driven in the ground, giving the cap the appearance of a white cloth tent that fluttered up and down when blown by the breezes. The plaintiff obtained a verdict in his favor, and on appeal that verdict was affirmed. In ruling for the plaintiff, the Court decided that the jury could have properly found that the hay cap, "because of its color, its fluttering, flapping movement when disturbed by the breezes, and its proximity to the traveled way, was an object naturally calculated to frighten horses of ordinary gentleness...."

Three years later, the Court addressed a similar claim in the case of *Witham v. Bangor & Aroostook Rail Road Co.* (1902).[106] This was an action to recover damages for injuries sustained by the plaintiff when she was thrown from her carriage in the town of Guilford, while traveling on the highway next to the defendant's railroad tracks. The accident was caused by the plaintiff's horse becoming suddenly frightened at seeing three large culvert pipes, each weighing more than three tons, which had been left by the defendant next to the roadway four days before the day on which the accident occurred. There was no question concerning the fact that the appearance of those culvert pipes would frighten horses of ordinary gentleness.

---

[105] 93 Me. 46, 44 A. 127 (1899).

[106] 96 Me. 326, 52 A. 764 (1902).

Citing the Court's decision just three years earlier in the "hay-cap" case, the plaintiff's attorney argued that the culvert pipes constituted an unlawful nuisance for which the defendant corporation was liable. In this case, however, the Court rejected that contention and entered judgment in favor of the defendant. In ruling for the defendant, the Court explained that in its view the defendant had not acted unreasonably in allowing the culvert pipes to remain near the roadway for four days. With specific reference to the vital importance of railroads, the Court stated:

> The public which creates these great channels of travel and commerce, and whose safety and convenience demand that they be maintained in repair, must submit to such inconveniences as are necessarily incident to their management and operation.
>
> ....
>
> ...Some latitude and discretion must be allowed to those intrusted with the construction and operation of great public works as to the manner in which, and the means by which, they will perform the duties imposed upon them. If they act in good faith, with a proper regard for the rights of others, and without carelessness or negligence, they are exempt from liability.[107]

If, after this case, there was any question as to where the Court stood on the need of the common law to keep pace with economic development, that doubt was dispelled by the Court's decision six years later in the case of *Simonds v. Maine Telephone & Telegraph Co.* (1908).[108] *Simonds* was an action for damages for personal injuries that were caused when the plaintiff's horse became frightened and ran away upon encountering a large reel of wire cable enclosed in "bright lead pipe" (flexible tubing) that had been left on the side of Main Street in the town of Madison by workers who were stringing telephone cable on poles at that location. Like the culvert pipes in

---

[107] *Id.* at 334-35, 52 A. at 765.

[108] 104 Me. 440, 72 A. 175 (1908).

Witham, here there was no dispute concerning the fact that the reel, with the lead pipe coiled around it, was the kind of object that might frighten a horse unaccustomed to seeing such a thing.

Relying on the Court's decision in the "hay-cap" case, the plaintiff's attorney contended that the reel and lead pipe, situated where they were, amounted to an unlawful nuisance for which the defendant should be found liable. The jury agreed with that assessment of the case and issued its verdict in the plaintiff's favor. On appeal, however, the Maine Court set that verdict aside on the ground that in the absence of negligence on the part of the telephone company, the plaintiff could not prevail:

> It is not the law that economic progress is to be arrested or even turned aside, whenever a well broken horse, carefully driven, is frightened or likely to be frightened thereby. To say that well broken horses, carefully driven, must not be frightened, is to say that no new appliance, however useful, shall be used on or near highways....
>
> In this age of economic progress it is the more reasonable and workable, and hence the legal rule, that owners and drivers of horses should recognize that the highways are not exclusively for their use; that other and new instrumentalities for transportation and transmission, and appliances for their construction and maintenance, are often legally allowed upon the highways; and that they should early accustom their horses to whatever new conditions thus arise and be on their guard against them. In this case it was as much incumbent on the plaintiff as on the defendant to foresee that his horse might be frightened by the reel or the lead pipe, and have taken measures to avoid or prevent the possible consequences. The reel and the lead pipe being otherwise lawfully where and when they were in the street, the mere fact that they were likely to frighten horses unaccustomed to them did not make their presence there unlawful.[109]

---

[109] *Id.* at 442-43, 72 A. at 176-77.

The Court could not have made it clearer that in "this age of economic progress" the interests of horse owners would often have to give way to the interests of economic development. The horse-and-buggy days would soon be passing into history, and the Court was making it emphatically clear that it would not stand in the way of economic progress. Indeed, as these cases show, the Court was shaping the common law to enable that development to occur without undue interference.

Domestic Animals and the Law

When I went to law school, the first-year curriculum included a course on Property Law. The first cases we studied in that course involved the ownership of animals, especially wild animals. We discussed questions such as who is the rightful owner of a whale that is harpooned by A but is thereafter found dead on a beach by B; and who is the owner of a deer found dead in the woods by B, the deer having been killed by an arrow shot by A. These cases involving wild animals and competing claims to their ownership were a good introduction to the subject of property law because they required students to think broadly about the meanings of property and ownership and why the ownership of property is protected by law.

I was recently reminded of those law school days when, in reading reports of old Maine cases, I came across two animal cases, one of which concerned a dog, *State v. Harriman* (1884),[110] the other, a cat, *Thurston v. Carter* (1914).[111] These cases called upon the Maine Court to decide whether dogs and cats were domestic animals or wild animals. The opinions authored by the justices in these cases are in their own way classics in the history of Maine judicial lore.

The first of these cases, *Harriman*, concerned the validity of a criminal indictment that charged the defendant, Mr. Harriman, with having maliciously killed a Newfoundland named "Rich" in violation of a Maine statute that made it a crime to maliciously kill or wound a

---

[110] 75 Me. 562 (1884).

[111] 112 Me. 361, 92 A. 295 (1914).

"domestic" animal. Harriman maintained that the indictment was defective because, he argued, a dog is not a domestic animal. All of the members of the Court, except for Chief Justice John Appleton,[112] agreed with the defendant that a dog is not a domestic animal, but instead belongs to that class of animals known in ancient law as *ferae naturae*, or wild animals.

Writing for the majority of the Maine Court, Justice Charles Danforth stated that a distinction between domestic and wild animals had been recognized in the law "from the origin of the common law, from the earliest date of authentic history, when the wealth of individuals was reckoned by the number of their flocks and herds." Danforth then launched into a description of the "wild characteristics" of dogs that would hardly endear him to dog lovers, especially owners of Newfoundlands:

> That by the common law the dog belongs to the wild class of animals is recognized by all the authorities, and in that state he was and is utterly worthless, his flesh even being unfit for food, so that legally he was said to have no intrinsic value....
> [A]s they still retain in a great measure their natural

---

[112] John Appleton served on the Maine Court for thirty-one years, first as a Justice (1852-1862) and then as Chief Justice (1862-1883). Among his many achievements was the reform of an old common law rule of evidence that generally prohibited the parties to a lawsuit and all others having a direct interest in the outcome of a lawsuit from testifying. *See Murray v. Joyce*, 44 Me. 342 (1857). As a result of Appleton's work, the Maine Legislature, in 1856, enacted a statute that effectively abolished that rule in civil cases. Me. P.L. 1856, ch. 266. Then, in 1864, the Maine Legislature enacted a law that allowed defendants in criminal cases to testify in their own defense if they chose to do so. Me. P.L. 1864, ch. 280. As the U.S. Supreme Court later recognized, that statute was "the first such statute in the English-speaking world," and was "largely the work of John Appleton of the Supreme Court of Maine." *Ferguson v. Georgia*, 365 U.S. 570, 577 (1961). For more on John Appleton, see David M. Gold, *The Shaping of Nineteenth-Century Law: John Appleton and Responsible Individualism* (New York: Greenwood Press, 1990); Charles Hamlin, "The Supreme Court of Maine (Part II)," 7 *The Green Bag* 504, 510 (1895); and Remarks of Chief Justice Vincent L. McKusick Before the Bangor Rotary Club, May 6, 1986, "Chief Justice John Appleton and His Bangor Judicial Colleagues" (catalogued at the Donald L. Garbrecht Law Library, University of Maine School of Law).

propensities, they may more properly be called domestic animals with vicious habits. They still keep their wild characteristics which ally them to the class of animals *ferae naturae*, so much so, that in their domestic state they furnish no support to the family, add nothing in a legal sense to the wealth of the community, are not inventoried as property of a debtor or dead man's estate, or as liable to taxation unless under a special provision of the statute; but when kept it is for pleasure, or if any usefulness is obtained from them it is founded upon this very ferocity natural to them by which they are made to serve as a watch or for hunting.[113]

Danforth's opinion for a majority of the Court carried the day and effectively disposed of the criminal indictment against Mr. Harriman for having killed the Newfoundland, Rich.

Chief Justice Appleton's dissenting opinion, however, will for all time stand as one of the great judicial testimonials to dogs—a tribute that will be treasured by dog lovers throughout the ages. Describing the domestic qualities of dogs, Appleton got immediately to the point:

He is a domestic animal. From the time of the pyramids to the present day, from the frozen pole to the torrid zone, wherever man has been there has been his dog. Cuvier has asserted that the dog was perhaps necessary for the establishment of civil society and that a little reflection will convince us that barbarous nations owe much of their civilization above the brute to the possession of the dog. He is the friend and companion of his master—accompanying him in his walks, his servant, aiding him in his hunting, the playmate of his children—an inmate of his house, protecting it against all assailants.

It may be said that he was *"ferae naturae"* but all animals, naturalists say, were originally *"ferae naturae"* but have been reclaimed by man as horses, sheep or cattle, but however

---

[113] *Harriman*, 75 Me. at 563-64.

tamed, they have never like the dog, become domesticated in the home under the roof and by the fireside of their master.

The dog was a part of the agricultural establishment of the Romans and is treated of as such. There were the *canes villatici* to guard the villa of the Roman senator, the *canes venatici* accompanying him in his hunting expeditions, and the *canes pastorales* by whom his flocks were guarded. Virgil in his Georgics, has given direction as to their management and education. Today, in many countries they are used for draught, as in France and Holland, and every where regarded as possessing value and as the subject matter of traffic.[114]

It would be difficult within the genre of judicial opinions to find a more learned and moving tribute to animals than Appleton's praise of dogs in *Harriman*, but Justice George E. Bird's tribute in honor of cats in *Thurston v. Carter* is a respectable runner-up. Mr. Thurston sued Mr. Carter for having shot and killed Thurston's fox-hound. Carter acknowledged killing the fox-hound, but maintained that he was justified in doing so because Thurston's fox-hound was chasing and worrying Carter's cat while it was on Carter's property. A Maine statute then provided that "Any person may lawfully kill a dog which… is found worrying, wounding, or killing any domestic animal when said dog is outside of the enclosure or immediate care of its owner or keeper."[115] The issue therefore came down to whether Carter's cat was a "domestic animal." The trial court found that the cat was a domestic animal and directed a verdict in Carter's favor. On appeal, the Maine Court, in an opinion authored by Justice Bird, affirmed that ruling, agreeing with the trial court that a cat is a domestic animal within the meaning of that term in the relevant statute.

Justice Bird might well have rested his opinion on the plain meaning and dictionary definition of "domestic animal," but he probably felt called upon to offer a few more words on behalf of cats,

---

[114] *Id.* at 566.

[115] An Act for the Licensing of Dogs, Me. P.L. 1909, ch. 222, § 17.

having in mind Chief Justice Appleton's glowing testimonial in honor of dogs some thirty years earlier in the *Harriman* case. Not to be outdone by Appleton's historical references, Bird took the domestication of the cat as far back as "the mists of the dawn of history":

> The time of its first domestication is lost in the mists of the dawn of history, but it is apparent that the cat was a domestic animal among the early Egyptians by whom it came to be regarded as sacred as evidenced by the device of Cambyses during his invasion of Egypt, B.C., 525 or 527 which could scarcely have been feasible if the animal was then wild. From that day to this it has been a dweller in the homes of men. In no other animal has affection for home been more strongly developed and in none, when absent from home, can the *animus revertendi* be more surely assumed to exist.[116]

Besides providing the Court an opportunity to expound upon the domestic virtues of cats, the *Thurston* case is also of interest from an historical point of view because the Court there noted an increasing and "admirable" tendency of society at that time (1914) to protect animals from cruelty and abuse. As the Court stated:

> The change of sentiment respecting animals and the light in which they are regarded at the present day is admirably shown in the provisions of law punishing cruelties inflicted upon them and their sweeping character is indicated in the provision that the word animal as employed in our statutes upon this subject "includes every living brute creature."[117]

In addition to being memorable parts of Maine's judicial lore, the decisions of Justices Appleton and Bird in these dog and cat cases are important landmarks in the long and continuing history of our state's recognition of the importance of domestic animals in our lives and the importance of protecting animals from cruelty and abuse. Maine's many animal-welfare statutes, enacted by the Legislature

---

[116] *Thurston*, 112 Me. at 363, 92 A. at 295.

[117] *Id.* at 364, 92 A. at 296.

over the years, are additional milestones in that long history that continues to the present day. For example, to mention but one of many recent statutes in that line, the Maine Legislature in 2006 enacted a law, the first of its kind in the nation, to protect pets in homes where there has been domestic abuse.[118] One particularly noteworthy landmark in the history of our state's recognition of the importance of animals in our lives is an 1891 amendment to the Maine statute requiring the teaching of moral values in schools. That amendment, which added the requirement that students be taught "the principles of kindness to birds and animals," was again amended in 1917 and restated in a 1984 amendment to require that students be taught "the great principles of humanity as illustrated by kindness to birds and animals...."[119] As is evident, the sympathies displayed by these legislative enactments are at one with the sentiments expressed by Justices Appleton and Bird in the opinions they wrote many years ago in the dog and cat cases discussed above.

---

[118] An Act Amending the Animal Welfare Laws, Me. P.L. 2005, ch. 510, § 12 (amending 19-A M.R.S.A. § 4007(1)(N)).

[119] *See* Me. P.L. 1891, ch. 29; Me. P.L. 1917, ch. 228; and "An Act Concerning the Teaching of Certain Subjects," Me. P.L. 1983, ch. 767, § 1 (amending 20 M.R.S.A. § 1221). The Maine statute that requires the teaching of moral values in schools, 20 M.R.S.A. § 1221, derived directly from a statute enacted by Massachusetts in 1789, entitled "An Act to provide for the instruction of youth and for the promotion of good education." Maine inherited the substance of that statute when Maine became a separate state in 1820. *See* "An act to provide for the Education of Youth," Me. P.L. 1821, ch. 117, § 2. As most recently amended, in 1984, this Maine statute, now entitled "Teaching of virtue and morality," provides as follows: "Instructors of youth in public or private institutions shall use their best endeavors to impress on the minds of the children and youth committed to their care and instruction the principles of morality and justice and a sacred regard for truth; love of country, humanity and a universal benevolence; the great principles of humanity as illustrated by kindness to birds and animals and regard for all factors which contribute to the well-being of man; industry and frugality; chastity, moderation and temperance; and all other virtues which ornament human society; and to lead those under their care, as their ages and capacities admit, into a particular understanding of the tendency of such virtues to preserve and perfect a republican constitution, secure the blessings of liberty and to promote their future happiness." 20 M.R.S.A. § 1221 (2008).

CONTRIBUTORY NEGLIGENCE AND RAILROAD CROSSING COLLISIONS

One of the most striking subjects of interest in the early development of Maine law is a series of cases, toward the end of the nineteenth century and into the early years of the twentieth, in which the Maine Court set aside jury verdicts against railroad companies in cases involving injury and death resulting from railroad crossing accidents. These cases are particularly worthy of our attention in several respects. First, they show how far the early Maine Court was willing to go in protecting railroad companies—by applying rules of law that favored defendants and by limiting the jury's role in deciding the ultimate question of liability. Second, these cases show that the integrity of the judicial process can be strained to the breaking point where the rules of law that juries are expected to apply fail to meet minimal standards of fairness. And finally, these cases are of continuing interest because they so clearly illustrate the point that the extent to which cases are decided by juries instead of by judges can be every bit as important, in terms of the outcome of cases, as the rules of law that apply.

Before turning to these cases, I would be remiss if I didn't note that most of them could just as well have been mentioned in the chapter entitled "Maine Law's Debt to Animals," because in the early years of Maine law horses were as frequently victims in railroad crossing accidents as those they transported by carriage, cart, wagon, or sleigh. Horses did not get along well with trains.

The Contributory Negligence Doctrine

The rapid growth of industry and rail transportation that took place in the nineteenth century brought with it many new hazards and risks of injury. Reflecting those developments, personal injury cases began to appear with increasing frequency on the Maine Court's docket during the last half of that century. At first, most of those cases involved workplace injury claims. By the last quarter of the century, however, claims involving injury and death in railroad crossing accidents also became a regular feature of the Court's docket. For the most part, these cases came to the Court on appeal by defendants, employers and railroad corporations, from jury verdicts in favor of plaintiffs, injured parties or their surviving family members. In these cases, the doctrine of "contributory negligence" proved to be an extremely useful tool for defendants and an extremely formidable obstacle for plaintiffs.[120]

Under the doctrine of contributory negligence, as developed and applied by the early Maine Court, the plaintiff's claim failed in its entirety if any amount of carelessness (contributory negligence) on his part contributed in the slightest degree to causing the injury for which he sought damages from the defendant—even though the negligence of the defendant might have been much greater than that of the

---

[120] The doctrine of contributory negligence originated in Maine with our Court's decision in *Crumpton v. Inhabitants of Solon*, 11 Me. 335 (1834). That case involved a claim against the town of Solon for damages for injuries to the plaintiffs' cattle, which occurred when a bridge maintained by the town, over which the cattle were passing, collapsed. The claim was based on an early Maine statute that allowed suits against towns for damages resulting from a town's failure to make necessary repairs to a bridge within its bounds, provided the town was aware of the defect. Although the plaintiffs received a jury verdict in their favor, the Maine Court, on appeal by the town, remanded the case for a new trial on the ground that the trial court should have instructed the jury that it was for them to decide whether the plaintiffs exercised "ordinary care" in deciding to drive some twenty to forty cattle, of a combined weight of from six to nine tons, over the bridge, all at once, particularly where it appeared that a defect in the bridge might have been visible to the plaintiffs. From that humble and pastoral beginning, the doctrine of contributory negligence would eventually become an important factor in litigation involving financial stakes of considerable magnitude.

plaintiff.[121] And the plaintiff had a double burden of proof. He not only had to prove that the defendant's negligence caused his injury; in addition, he had to prove a negative—that his injury was not attributable to any carelessness on his part. Making things even more difficult for the plaintiff, the Court also required that the plaintiff prove the absence of contributory negligence on the part of the injured person— even in those cases in which the injured person on whose account the suit was brought had died as the result of the accident in question.[122]

These rules, which the Maine Court applied rigorously over a period of many years, provided the means by which it overturned numerous jury verdicts in favor of injured plaintiffs or their surviving family members in cases when death ensued.[123] In retrospect, and with the benefit of hindsight, it seems fair to say that the doctrine of contributory negligence, as developed and applied by our Court during the early years of Maine law, fell short of the ideal of evenhanded justice. Indeed, in recent years, our Court has itself acknowledged that the doctrine of contributory negligence "resulted

---

[121] See, for example, *Ward v. Me. Cent. R.R. Co.*, 96 Me. 136, 144-45, 51 A. 947, 950 (1902), where our Court stated: "It is too well settled in this State to permit of discussion, that whenever a plaintiff's want of ordinary care contributes as a proximate cause to the injury for which he brings suit, he cannot recover. In such case the degree of his negligence, or the extent of its effect, as one of the causes for the injury is of no consequence. More than this, the burden is upon him to show affirmatively that no want of ordinary care upon his part contributed in the slightest degree to the injury of which he complained."

[122] *See State v. Me. Cent. R.R. Co.*, 76 Me. 357 (1884).

[123] It should be noted that the Maine Court was not the only court that adopted the doctrine of contributory negligence. During the nineteenth century, that doctrine was also adopted by the federal courts and by virtually every other state court throughout the county. But the doctrine, as developed by the Maine Court, was especially harsh on plaintiffs. For example, the Maine Court was one of a minority of state courts that required the *plaintiff* to prove the *absence* of contributory negligence on his part. In contrast, the federal courts and a substantial majority of state courts required that the *defendant* bear the burden of proving the plaintiff's contributory negligence if the defendant claimed that the plaintiff's contributory negligence was a factor in causing the injury. *See* Thomas G. Shearman & Amasa A. Redfield, *A Treatise on the Law of Negligence*, vol. 1, 6th ed. (New York: Baker, Voorhis & Co., 1913), §§ 106-109.

in an unfair hardship having to be borne by one party alone under circumstances where ordinary fairness and justice should make possible a division of this loss according to equitable principles."[124]

A review of some of the Court's early railroad crossing decisions shows how the doctrine of contributory negligence directly benefited railroad corporations at the expense of those who sought recompense for injuries or deaths in railroad crossing accidents.[125] A good vantage point from which to begin that review is the Maine Court's decision in *State v. Maine Central Railroad Co.* (1884),[126] otherwise referred to here as "Dr. Pickard's case." Dr. Pickard's case is a pivotal case in the history of Maine law because it marks the point at which our Court began systematically to limit the scope of the authority of juries to have the final say on questions of contributory negligence in railroad crossing cases.

Dr. Pickard's Case

At about half past six in the evening on December 26, 1882, Dr. Pickard of the town of Carmel was struck and instantly killed by a passing train in that town. At the time of the collision, Dr. Pickard, traveling in his horse-drawn sleigh, was en route to pick up one of his children who had been visiting with a friend on that day after Christmas. At that time, a Maine statute provided that the State, for the benefit of the widow and children, could bring a legal proceeding against a railroad company for having negligently caused someone's death. That statute did not provide for damages, as such, but did allow a jury to assess a fine or "forfeiture" for the benefit of surviving family members.[127] In accordance with that statute, this case was brought by the State, representing the interests of Dr. Pickard's widow and children.

---

[124] *Crocker v. Coombs*, 328 A.2d 389, 391 (Me. 1974).

[125] In the chapter entitled "Employee Injuries," we will see how this doctrine also benefited employers in cases involving workplace injury claims.

[126] 76 Me. 357 (1884).

[127] The early development of Maine law concerning claims for damages in cases involving death caused by negligence is discussed in the chapter entitled "Wrongful Death Claims." It was not until 1891 that the Maine Legislature

As advocates for Dr. Pickard's widow and children, the State's attorneys contended that the defendant railroad company had negligently caused Dr. Pickard's death. The jury agreed and entered a verdict against the defendant. But on the defendant's appeal, the Maine Court vacated that verdict on the ground that the Court thought that Dr. Pickard himself was negligent in not having ascertained that a train was approaching the crossing, or, in the alternative, that he had knowingly attempted to cross the tracks in front of the train.

The State presented a strong argument that if the defendant tried to avoid liability by suggesting that Dr. Pickard's carelessness was a contributing factor in the accident, the defendant should bear the burden of proving that point. In that regard, the State noted that a rule that requires a plaintiff to prove that his negligence was *not* a contributing factor in a collision amounted to an arbitrary presumption that the plaintiff was always negligent unless the plaintiff could prove otherwise. A rule of law that automatically presumes at the outset that one of two parties in a collision was negligent certainly seems less than fair on its face. And why, in any event, given the human instinct for self-preservation, would it make any sense for the law to presume that a person who suffered injury or death had carelessly exposed himself to the risk of those consequences? Wouldn't it be more even-handed and fair for the law to presume that neither of two parties involved in a collision was negligent until one of them has established that the other was negligent? The State also noted that several other state courts—and the U.S. Supreme Court itself— had adopted the rule that the defendant bears the burden of proving contributory negligence on the part of the plaintiff.[128]

---

passed a general "Wrongful Death" statute, allowing damages to be recovered when a person was killed as the result of the negligence of a person or corporation. In England, a similar statute, known as "Lord Campbell's Act," was enacted in 1846. In 1848, the Maine Legislature enacted a wrongful death statute, enforceable by the State, which was limited to deaths caused by wrongful acts of railroads and steamboats. That statute, as later amended, was the basis of the State's claim on behalf of Dr. Pickard's widow and children in Dr. Pickard's case.

[128] In the U.S. Supreme Court decision relied on by the State, the Supreme Court had stated: "While it is true that the absence of reasonable care and caution, on

Moreover, as the State noted, when a collision results in death, it seems particularly unfair as well as unrealistic to impose on the plaintiff the burden of proving that contributory negligence on the part of the person killed did not contribute to produce the accident in any way. After all, as the State noted, Dr. Pickard, having been killed in the collision, was hardly in a position to be of any help in proving that he had not been negligent. In any event, the State suggested, the jury should be allowed to have inferred the absence of negligence on the part of Dr. Pickard from the surrounding circumstances, without direct proof: "With a wife and four children whom he had just left, and going to get a fifth child to carry home with him, it is incredible that he should knowingly risk or be careless of his own life."

The Maine Court, however, in an opinion written by Justice Charles W. Walton, summarily rejected all of these arguments out of hand, without discussing the merits of those arguments or the Court's reasons for rejecting them. Citing two of its earlier decisions, the Court simply stated that it is "settled law in this state" that the plaintiff has the burden of showing "that the person injured or killed, did not by his own want of ordinary care contribute to produce the accident." In Dr. Pickard's case, the Court concluded that there was "a total want of such evidence," despite the jury's verdict in favor of the plaintiff.

The Court, moreover, vacated the plaintiff's jury verdict in Dr. Pickard's case even though there seems to have been at least some evidence that, as claimed by the State, the train had failed to sound a whistle or ring a bell at the crossing. As the Court decided the case, however, any negligence of the defendant in that respect was immaterial because in its view, Dr. Pickard could have seen the train and heard its rumbling as it approached the crossing. And the Court

---

the part of one seeking to recover for an injury so received, will prevent a recovery, it is not correct to say that it is incumbent upon him to prove such care and caution. The want of such care or contributory negligence, as it is termed, is a defence to be proved by the other side." *R.R. Co. v. Gladmon*, 82 U.S. 401, 406 (1873). Under the prevailing jurisdictional rules at that time, that Supreme Court decision was binding on federal courts as a matter of "federal common law," but state courts remained free to develop their own rules of common law, such as burden-of-proof rules, for example, for their respective state jurisdictions.

went on to explain that even if it were to assume that Dr. Pickard had *not* heard the train approaching, he would have been negligent in driving onto the crossing "in total ignorance" of the approach of a train. With that retort, the Court cut the legs out from under the State's claim on behalf of Dr. Pickard's widow and children, and never had to reach the question of the defendant's negligence in not having sounded a whistle or rung a bell as a warning at the crossing.

As noted above, Dr. Pickard's case is especially significant in historical perspective because the Court there began systematically to limit the role of juries in railroad crossing cases. The Court did that by establishing special rules of law for determining whether the injured party was guilty of contributory negligence. Those special rules, which gave concrete definition to the more general standard of "ordinary care," were then routinely utilized by the Court in deciding whether to set aside jury verdicts in favor of plaintiffs.

Thus, for example, in Dr. Pickard's case, the Court established the rule that, generally speaking, one who is struck by a train at a crossing is "*prima facie* guilty of negligence; and, in the absence of satisfactory excuse, his negligence must be regarded as established." To prevent juries from deciding with finality what excuse might be "satisfactory," the Court developed another rule. Under that rule, it was immaterial that the train did not sound a warning bell or whistle because a traveler who would drive onto a crossing in "total ignorance" of the approach of a train "must have been exceedingly negligent in the use of his eyes and his ears." With these rules, the Court put the injured party in a box from which it was extremely difficult to escape. If the traveler saw or heard the train approaching, he was guilty of contributory negligence in attempting the crossing. If the traveler did not see or hear the train approaching, he was exceedingly negligent in the use of his eyes and ears.

Coincident with its announcement of these rules, the Court in Dr. Pickard's case also began to substitute its judgment for that of juries on matters that had traditionally been considered to be core functions of juries, such as judgments concerning the credibility of witnesses, the weight to be given to their testimony, and the inferences to be drawn therefrom. For example, although the Court, being a court of appeals, had not heard or seen the witnesses testifying at trial, the Court nevertheless remarked, "The evidence seems to us to preponderate most overwhelmingly in favor of the fact that the bell was rung and the whistle sounded."

These developments represented major changes from the way the Court had done business in the past. The abrupt and substantial nature of these changes, ushered in by the Court's decision in Dr. Pickard's case, is brought into clearest focus by comparing that 1884 decision with the Court's decision only two years before in *Plummer v. Eastern Railroad Co.* (1882).[129] In that case, Mr. and Mrs. Plummer obtained favorable jury verdicts on their claims that the injuries they suffered in a railroad crossing accident were caused by the negligence of the defendant railroad company. The railroad company appealed to the Maine Court, arguing that those verdicts should be set aside on the basis of the plaintiffs' contributory negligence. Specifically, the railroad company contended that the Plummers should have stopped and looked in both directions before they crossed the tracks.

In contrast with the Court's disposition of Dr. Pickard's case, however, the Court in Mr. and Mrs. Plummer's case rejected the railroad company's appeal. Writing for a unanimous Court, Chief Justice John Appleton explained that the question of whether or not Mr. and Mrs. Plummer were guilty of contributory negligence in driving across the track when the train approached the crossing was a question for the jury, and not for the Court, to decide:

> The jury found [the plaintiff and his wife] were in the exercise of ordinary and common care. Is that verdict so manifestly erroneous that it should be set aside. It is true that the plaintiff was bound to exercise his sight to avoid danger, but he was not bound to use the greatest possible diligence. He was bound to exercise such care as a prudent man approaching such a place would ordinarily use for the protection of life. It is uncertain to what extent he could see the cars through the intervening obstructions. His attention was called to the

---

[129] 73 Me. 591 (1882).

danger and he and his wife looked to see if there was a train in view. The obstructions may have prevented their seeing. Seeing nothing, hearing no warning of danger through the negligence of the defendants, in attempting to cross, the plaintiff was injured. Under the circumstances of the case, it was for the jury to determine whether [the plaintiff] exercised the care the law requires. The jury saw and heard the witnesses; they examined the premises and with the best means of judging have arrived at a conclusion, which is not so manifestly erroneous as to demand our interference.[130]

In further contrast with the Court's decision in Dr. Pickard's case, we find in Appleton's earlier opinion in Mr. and Mrs. Plummer's case no attempt to lay down hard and fast rules to limit the scope of jury discretion on the question of contributory negligence. As Appleton explained in the *Plummer* case, "The fact that a person who, in attempting to cross a railroad, does not at the instant of stepping on it, look to ascertain if a train is approaching, is not conclusive of a due want of care on his part." Nor do we find any attempt at second-guessing the judgment of the jury. As Appleton pointedly noted, the jury "saw and heard the witnesses."

Also worth noting is the sharp difference in tone between Appleton's 1882 opinion for the Court in the *Plummer* case and Justice Walton's opinion for the Court two years later in Dr. Pickard's case. Appleton places the reader in the carriage with Mr. and Mrs. Plummer as they approached the crossing in the last few seconds before the impending collision. Using excerpts of conversation from the trial transcript, Appleton paints a picture that allows the reader to appreciate the rapidly evolving situation exactly as Mr. and Mrs. Plummer experienced it. The tone he strikes reflects a human understanding of the situation:

> It is true the plaintiff did not stop and listen, but he states that as they drove "most down to the station," his wife asked if there were any cars coming, to which he replied no, not from

---

[130] *Id*. at 594.

Boston, "unless there was extra trains, and he (I) was looking for the train." To the inquiry which way? his reply was, "from Portland, and I looked towards Boston and I did not see any train coming from any direction." The wife testifies that she asked her husband if there were any cars coming, to which he answered in the negative, giving as a reason that the train had not time to get out so that another could come from Oakhill; that she looked Portland way and then the other way and the train was close upon them—that she had looked away from Portland before this, through the opening to see if she could see any. The plaintiff and his wife looking in both directions hearing no sounds of cars, whistle or bell, and with vision somewhat obstructed by buildings and trees, attempted to cross, and in that attempt were injured.[131]

In contrast, Justice Walton's opinion in Dr. Pickard's case has an air of detached superiority to it. Granted, the Court believed that Dr. Pickard's carelessness was the cause of the accident, and, granted also that courts are under no obligation to sugar-coat their decisions, yet I find myself imagining Mrs. Pickard's feelings on reading, and probably re-reading, the Court's musings on the last few seconds of her husband's life: "[I]f he drove on to that crossing in total ignorance of the approach of a train; then the conclusion seems to us inevitable that he must have been exceedingly negligent in the use of his eyes and his ears." It would seem that under the tragic circumstances of this case, the Court might have found words to support its decision without sounding so mockingly judgmental.

The Court's deferential approach to jury verdicts, illustrated by Appleton's decision in the *Plummer* case, was destined to be soon swept aside by the Court's more assertive oversight of jury verdicts in railroad crossing cases, a development that began with Dr. Pickard's case. Indeed, as soon as the ink was dry on Appleton's

---

[131] *Id.* at 593-94.

opinion in *Plummer*, that case became a dead letter—the Court never mentioned it again.[132]

Albert Lesan's Case

A few months after its decision in Dr. Pickard's case, the Court decided another railroad crossing case, *Lesan v. Maine Central Railroad Co.* (1885).[133] This case involved Albert Lesan's claim for damages for personal injuries and damage to his carriage resulting from a collision at the Bridge Street crossing in the city of Belfast on February 17, 1882. Lesan claimed that the defendant railroad company was negligent in not having stationed a flagman at that crossing. The jury agreed and issued its verdict in his favor. On the defendant's appeal, however, the Court vacated that verdict on the ground that Lesan had failed to prove that his own negligence was not a contributing factor in the collision. As the result of that ruling, which completely disposed of Lesan's claim, the issue of the negligence of the railroad company in not having a flagman at the crossing became a moot point. In vacating Lesan's jury award, the Court not only removed the issue of the railroad company's negligence from the case, it also substituted its judgment for that of the jury on disputed issues of fact. Disagreeing with the jury's

---

[132] At this juncture, it is interesting to note the significant change that occurred in the composition of the Maine Court between 1882, when the Court issued its decision in *Plummer*, and 1884, when the Court decided Dr. Pickard's case. Chief Justice Appleton, who authored the Court's 1882 decision in *Plummer*, which deferred to the judgment of the jury on the question of contributory negligence, retired from the Court in the following year, September 19, 1883, after thirty-one years on the Court. Appleton's successor as Chief Justice was John A. Peters. In view of the considerable influence Appleton had on the Court during his long tenure, as well as the considerable influence Peters would himself have as Chief Justice from September 20, 1883, until his resignation on January 1, 1900, this change in leadership on the Court likely played a significant role in the Court's adoption of a more assertive approach to overseeing jury verdicts in railroad crossing cases, beginning with its 1884 decision in Dr. Pickard's case. With Appleton's retirement, the "Appleton Court" was history. A new Court—the "Peters Court"—now held the reins of judicial power.

[133] 77 Me. 85 (1885).

verdict, the Court stated, "Our very strong belief is, that the absence of whistling or bell-ringing or of signaling of any kind played no material part in causing the accident."

Other Cases of Note

Albert Lesan's case was only one of several cases in which the early Maine Court, over the years following its 1884 decision in Dr. Pickard's case, set aside plaintiffs' jury verdicts in railroad crossing cases despite evidence that the railroad companies were negligent in failing to provide warnings and in running their trains at excessive speed. So that the reader can approximate the experience I had in leafing through the reports of these cases as they were decided over the years—the cumulative impact of what in retrospect seems a lopsided jurisprudence that overtly favored railroad corporations—it seems appropriate to at least briefly mention some of those cases here.[134]

In *State v. Maine Central Railroad Co.* (1885),[135] the Court set aside a jury verdict against the Maine Central Railroad for having negligently caused the death of one Henry McBenner on June 17, 1884, in a collision between McBenner's dump-cart and a train at the Greenville Street crossing in the city of Hallowell. Disagreeing with the jury, the Court found that McBenner's own negligence had contributed to cause the collision. In setting aside the verdict, the Court noted that if, as the State contended, the train was running at a higher rate of speed than allowed by law, that violation "might subject [the railroad company] to the penalty prescribed by statute." In view of the Court's finding regarding McBenner's contributory negligence, however, the

---

[134] It should also be noted here that during those same years, the Maine Court did uphold jury verdicts in favor of plaintiffs in some railroad crossing cases. *See, e.g., Hooper v. Boston & Me. R.R. Co.,* 81 Me. 260, 17 A. 64 (1889) (concluding that under the particular circumstances involved, the jury could have properly found that the plaintiff was justified in relying on open gates at a crossing where gates had long been maintained); *York v. Me. Cent. R.R. Co.,* 84 Me. 117, 24 A. 790 (1891) (concluding that the jury could have properly found that the deceased was not guilty of contributory negligence in a collision caused by the rear division of a freight train making a "flying switch" at a grade crossing).

[135] 77 Me. 538, 1 A. 673 (1885).

defendant's speeding violation was deemed to have no bearing on the question of the defendant's liability for McBenner's death.

In *Chase v. Maine Central Railroad Co.* (1885),[136] the Court set aside a jury verdict in favor of the personal representative of the decedent who died when he was struck by one of the defendant's trains while riding in a horse-drawn sleigh. The collision occurred at a private crossing in the town of Richmond on February 24, 1882. There were no witnesses to the accident. In an attempt to prove that the decedent was not guilty of contributory negligence, the plaintiff presented the testimony of several neighbors regarding the decedent's general character for carefulness. When the case reached the Maine Court on the railroad company's appeal, however, the Court said that such testimony should not have been allowed because it was not directly probative of the decedent's use of due care in attempting to cross the track at the moment the train was coming.[137] The Court also ruled that the trial judge had erred in instructing the jury that in evaluating the issue, the jury could consider the natural instincts of people to preserve themselves from injury. The Court found that instruction improper because, as the Court stated, the instinct for self-preservation "does not operate on the minds of men until they can clearly see that they are endangered by their carelessness."

Following a second trial of this case, which again resulted in a verdict in favor of the plaintiff, the Court, disagreeing with the jury, found the deceased guilty of contributory negligence and set that

---

[136] 77 Me. 62 (1885).

[137] The Court's ruling to that effect was out of step with decisions of other courts. As a leading treatise on the law of negligence, published in 1913, noted, "In the few courts which require the plaintiff to prove affirmatively the exercise of due care [on his part], it is nevertheless universally held that such proof need not be direct, but may be inferred from circumstances.... Evidence that the injured person was careful and prudent, and that he had been careful on other occasions, is not competent to disprove contributory negligence, where he is living; but if he is dead, such evidence is admissible, especially if no eye-witnesses can be found." After citing several court decisions in support of the last proposition, the authors cite the Maine Court's decision in *Chase* as the only authority to the contrary. *See* Shearman & Redfield, *The Law of Negligence*, § 111, n. 358.

verdict aside as well.[138] Having decided the case on that basis, the Court did not have to address the question of whether the defendant should have provided warning of its approaching train. Instead, the Court used the occasion to enunciate additional "look and listen" rules for determining the question of contributory negligence in railroad crossing cases:

> The rule is now firmly established in this State, as well as by courts generally, that it is negligence *per se* for a person to cross a railroad track without first looking and listening for a coming train. If his view is unobstructed, he may have no occasion to listen. But if his view is obstructed, then it is his duty to listen, and to listen carefully. And if one is injured at a railroad crossing by a passing train or locomotive, which might have been seen if he had looked, or heard if he had listened, presumptively he is guilty of contributory negligence; and if this presumption is not repelled, a recovery for the injury can not be had.[139]

In *Allen v. Maine Central Railroad Co.* (1889),[140] the Court set aside the plaintiff's verdict for damages for the loss of his hand in a railroad crossing collision at the Pearl Street crossing in the city of Bath on August 20, 1888. The Court vacated that verdict despite the fact that the train was running at an unlawful rate of speed. The Court explained: "It is no excuse for [the plaintiff] that the train was running at an unlawful rate of speed. Negligence of both parties may have contributed to the disaster; but the common law, in such cases, gives neither damages for his injury arising from joint fault."

Romeo v. Boston & Maine Railroad Co. (1895)[141] was a suit for injuries sustained by the plaintiff, Marjorie Romeo, a young woman

---

[138] *Chase v. Me. Cent. R.R. Co.*, 78 Me. 346, 5 A. 771 (1886).

[139] *Id.* at 353, 5 A. at 771-72.

[140] 82 Me. 111, 19 A. 105 (1889).

[141] 87 Me. 540, 33 A. 24 (1895). Although this case did not involve a jury verdict, it is mentioned in this series of cases because it shows how rigorously the early Maine Court applied its *per se* rules of contributory negligence in railroad crossing cases.

of nineteen years of age, who was struck by a train while walking across the tracks at the Main Street crossing in the city of Biddeford at about nine o'clock in the evening on July 17, 1893. The parties agreed to submit the case to the Court on the basis of the evidence submitted by the plaintiff, with the understanding that if the Court believed her evidence was sufficient to justify a trial, the matter would be referred for trial; otherwise, the matter would be dismissed. The Court dismissed the case on the basis of its rule that "it is negligence *per se* for a person to cross a railroad track without first looking and listening for a coming train." In view of the Court's conclusion that the plaintiff was guilty of contributory negligence in not looking or listening for an approaching train, the Court considered it immaterial that the train was running at a speed of thirty to thirty-five miles per hour in a compact part of Biddeford where the speed limit for trains was set by statute at six miles per hour, unless there was either a gate or a flagman at the crossing. The fact that there was neither a functional gate (the arms of the gate had been left open) nor a flagman at that location was for the same reason deemed irrelevant to Ms. Romeo's case.

In *Giberson v. Bangor & Aroostook Railroad Co.* (1896),[142] the Court set aside a jury verdict in favor of Elizabeth Giberson in her suit to recover damages in connection with the death of James Giberson that resulted when the horse-drawn sleigh in which he was riding was struck by the saloon car of a train that was being backed over the roadway. The accident occurred on February 27, 1895, in the town of Mars Hill. Instead of deferring to the judgment of the jury, the Court summarily dismissed the plaintiff's claim with the remark that "[t]here was the usual conflict of evidence as to the speed of the train in backing up, and as to whether the locomotive whistle or bell was sounded as a warning." Rejecting the testimony of Mr. Giberson's passenger, to the effect that none of the three men on the sled had heard the approaching train, the Court remarked that it did not appear that any of them "listened" for any sound of a train.

---

[142] 89 Me. 337, 36 A. 400 (1896).

In *Day v. Boston & Maine Railroad* (1902),[143] the Court set aside a jury verdict in favor of the plaintiff, Lottie Day, in her suit against the defendant railroad corporation for having, by its negligence, caused the death of her husband, Edwin Day. Edwin Day died in a collision between the horse-drawn hay-rack in which he was riding and a train, which occurred at the Junkin's railroad crossing in the town of North Berwick on the morning of July 21, 1899. Even though the Court noted that there was evidence that the train was operating at an excessive rate of speed and no bell was rung or whistle blown, the Court set aside Mrs. Day's verdict on the ground that there was no evidence that her late husband (who, of course, was not available to testify) made any effort to see or hear the approaching train. Once again, the Court never reached the question of the defendant's negligence, because the case was disposed of on the ground that the plaintiff had failed to prove that her late husband had not been guilty of contributory negligence.

Following a second trial of this case, the trial judge ordered a verdict for the defendant at the close of the testimony. On Mrs. Day's appeal, the Maine Court affirmed that ruling.[144] The Court noted that if, as the plaintiff's evidence showed, the train was approaching the crossing at a speed of at least fifty miles per hour, or 73 feet per second, in a compact part of the town where the speed of trains was limited by law to six miles per hour, without flagmen at the crossing, and without giving the required warnings of its approach, the personnel in charge of the train "were guilty of gross and culpable recklessness which would justly have subjected them to the severest censure." But of course that did nothing to compensate Mrs. Day for the loss of her husband. In short, the Court dismissed Mrs. Day's suit on the basis of what it considered to be her husband's carelessness in attempting to cross the tracks at the crossing even though the Court acknowledged that there was evidence from which a jury might have concluded that the defendant was guilty of gross and culpable recklessness in the way it ran its train.

---

[143] 96 Me. 207, 52 A. 771 (1902).

[144] *Day v. Boston & Me. R.R.*, 97 Me. 528, 55 A. 420 (1903).

That same evidence might also have justified the jury's concluding that, under the circumstances, Mr. Day's over-estimation of
the distance of the train, or his miscalculation of its speed as it
approached the crossing, was not unreasonable. But Justice William
Penn Whitehouse, who wrote the opinion for the Court, rejected that
notion out of hand:

> The inference from all this testimony considered in the light of
> the undisputed situations, is almost irresistible that Mr. Day
> either did see, or hear, the approaching train but over-
> estimating its distance or miscalculating its speed, with an
> absence of caution which is incomprehensible, inconsiderately
> and rashly undertook to cross the track in front of the train
> instead of waiting for it to pass.[145]

In *McCarthy v. Bangor and Aroostook R.R. Co.* (1914),[146] the Court
set aside a verdict in favor of the plaintiff, a boy of fourteen years,
who was struck and severely injured in a collision between the milk
cart he was driving and one of the defendant's trains. The collision
occurred as the plaintiff was crossing the railroad tracks in the town
of Van Buren on September 29, 1910. The plaintiff maintained that
the crossing was "a blind and dangerous one," and that the defendants had failed to sound the whistle and ring the bell as the train
approached. Although the Court agreed that it would have been
negligence on the part of the defendant for it to have failed to provide warning of the approaching train, the Court found it unnecessary to look into that question because the Court concluded that the
plaintiff's evidence was inadequate to overcome the presumption of
his negligence. The Court stated that it did not believe the plaintiff's
testimony or that of his companion to the effect that they did not hear
the train: "We think the story is not credible, except upon the contin-
gency of preventing noises, of which there is no evidence."

At no time throughout this line of cases does the Court seem to
have had any reservations about its taking these cases from the jury.

---

[145] *Id.* at 533, 55 A. at 422.

[146] 112 Me. 1, 90 A. 490 (1914).

On the contrary, the Court expressed its belief that it was doing a good thing in substituting its judgment for that of the jury. Evidencing the distrust it had for juries, the Court even went so far as to remark that the tendency of courts "to multiply the instances in which the court will take negligence cases from the jury and decide them as matters of law" represented an "advancement of the law."[147] The patience of the Court was clearly being tested by juries who found the Court's harsh doctrine of contributory negligence difficult to square with their ideas of justice. But a Court's distrust of juries in negligence or any other category of cases hardly seems sufficient justification for a court's taking on fact-finding functions that are exclusively the responsibility of juries under the Constitutions of Maine and the United States.

With the benefit of hindsight, the early Maine Court's distrust of juries in railroad crossing cases seems especially unjustified, considering the unfairness of the Court's own contributory negligence rules. From the Court's perspective, however, jurors were supposed to decide cases in accordance with the law, regardless of whether they felt the law was unfair.

While as a general rule that may be the responsibility of juries, that general rule can be severely strained—indeed, the judicial process as a whole can be severely strained—where the rules of law

---

[147] *Lesan v. Me. Cent. R.R. Co.,* 77 Me. 85, 91 (1885). It is interesting to note that in characterizing that development as an "advancement of the law," Chief Justice Peters, who wrote the Court's opinion in *Lesan,* was supporting a point of view that had been expressed by Oliver Wendell Holmes in his book, *The Common Law,* which was published in 1881, only four years before the Court's decision in *Lesan.* In that volume, Holmes stated that an experienced trial judge "ought gradually to acquire a fund of experience which enables him to represent the common sense of the community in ordinary instances far better than an average jury. He should be able to lead and to instruct them in detail, even where he thinks it desirable, on the whole, to take their opinion. Furthermore, the sphere in which he is able to rule without taking their opinion at all should be continually growing." Oliver Wendell Holmes, Jr., *The Common Law* (Boston: Little, Brown & Co., 1881), 124. That view of the respective roles of judge and jury was not, however, universally accepted by the courts, as the New Hampshire cases discussed below illustrate.

that juries are expected to apply fall short of minimal standards of fairness. In retrospect, that seems to have been the situation that occurred as the result of the Court's insistence that juries apply the Court's special "look and listen" rules for determining the question of contributory negligence. No matter how many "per se" and "prima facie" rules of that kind the Court established, the underlying doctrine of contributory negligence was itself so transparently unfair that juries, not surprisingly, resisted the Court's attempt to tie their hands—as the numerous jury verdicts in favor of plaintiffs in the cases discussed above attest.

As a practical matter, many of those verdicts probably represented a jury-room compromise in which the jury reduced the amount of damages that might have been awarded in proportion to the extent it believed the plaintiff's negligence contributed to the collision. Thus, in effect, and many years before the Maine Legislature in the last half of the twentieth century replaced the common law doctrine of contributory negligence with a "comparative negligence" statute, these juries made up of ordinary Maine citizens were themselves probably applying comparative negligence principles by reducing damages proportionally to the relative fault of the plaintiff rather than by treating any amount of contributory negligence as a complete bar to the recovery of any damages whatsoever. In that respect, these Maine juries, with their keen sense of fairness, were decades ahead of the Court and the Legislature.

The Court seldom attempted to justify its railroad crossing jurisprudence in terms of right and justice. And when the Court did attempt to do so, it was not very convincing. For example, in the *Lesan* case, the Court explained that at a railroad crossing, the traveler and the railroad have "equal rights," but that "the traveler must stop for the train." In an attempt to put these rules in their best light, the Court explained that while on the one hand it is the responsibility of the traveler to stop for the train, it is the corresponding duty of the railroad to warn the traveler to keep out of the way. It is for that purpose, the Court said, that the requirements of "signals and gates and the like" have been established. As we have seen, however, the negligent failure of a railroad corporation to provide such warning devices often provided no basis for liability because unless the plaintiff could prove that he or she was entirely without fault, the plaintiff would lose, regardless of the negligence or even recklessness of the railroad corporation. It therefore does not seem unfair to say that in the final analysis the Court's attempt to present its railroad crossing jurisprudence in terms of equal rights and duties was more rhetoric than substance.

Presumably, the Maine Court believed that its railroad crossing jurisprudence was ultimately in the best interest of the citizens of the State of Maine—that what was good for railroads was generally good for the economy and that what was good for the economy was generally good for the community as a whole. What that rationale overlooked, however, is that it did little to encourage railroad corporations to operate their trains more safely.

Because the early Maine Court's railroad crossing jurisprudence today seems to have been so overbalanced in favor of railroad companies, it would be somewhat reassuring, in terms of our confidence in the fairness of the Court at that time, to be able to conclude that the Court was simply bound by precedent and could not easily change rules it inherited. And that is partly true. The Maine Court that decided the cases discussed above inherited the doctrine of contributory negligence from decisions of the Maine Court in earlier years. But as we have seen, the Court's decision to accord less deference to jury judgments in railroad crossing cases than it had in the past, beginning with its decision in Dr. Pickard's case in 1884, was a deliberate departure from tradition and precedent. And at every point where the Court might have ameliorated the inequity of the doctrine of contributory negligence—such as by easing the plaintiff's burden of proof in cases where the injured party died in the collision; by allowing evidence of the decedent's character for carefulness in cases where death ensued; by allowing the jury to consider the instinct for self-preservation in deciding whether the decedent exercised due care; or by recognizing that a person's miscalculation of the speed of a train does not necessarily equate with fault—the Court took the opposite course. Our Court simply seems to have been very hard-nosed about all of this.

To appreciate how far our Court had gone in that direction, it might be useful to take a look at two decisions of the highest court of Maine's neighboring state, New Hampshire, during the same time frame of the Maine cases discussed above.

New Hampshire's Jurisprudence—A Different View

In contrast with the position taken by the Maine Court, the New Hampshire Court, in *Smith v. Boston & Maine Railroad* (1899),[148] explained that it did not believe it wise for courts to lay down special "look and listen" rules in order to restrict the scope of jury discretion in deciding questions of contributory negligence. In that case, the New Hampshire Court rejected the railroad company's contention that the trial judge should have specifically instructed the jury that it was the duty of one approaching a crossing "to look or listen for a train." Supporting the trial judge's jury instructions, which were couched in more general terms—"to take such precautions to learn of the approach of trains as men of ordinary prudence would take in like circumstances"—the New Hampshire Court stated, in an eloquent tribute to the jury system:

> The law does not adopt particular circumstances as standards for measuring the degree of care required to amount to ordinary care. The circumstances in negligence cases are too numerous and variable to allow of this course. The rule must be so general that it may be applied to the circumstances of any case.... A jury, composed as it is, of twelve impartial men drawn from different walks in life, is as capable of correctly determining such a question, as a court composed of a less number of men whose training, occupation, and experience have not been so favorable for fitting them to form a sound judgment on the question. It certainly must be as apparent to

---

[148] 70 N.H. 53, 47 A. 290 (1899). This case involved the death of a man who was killed when a train struck him as he traveled on his horse over the tracks at a railroad crossing. The New Hampshire Court rejected the railroad company's appeal from a jury verdict in favor of the plaintiff, the personal representative of the decedent's estate.

jurymen as to members of the court that a person of average prudence will, under most circumstances, look or listen for a train when about to pass over a grade crossing. There is no more likelihood that a jury will be swayed by prejudice or passion in cases of this kind than in many other cases. If the defendants' views were adopted, it would take this class of cases out from the operation of the general rule governing negligence cases. It would also conflict with the general spirit of the law of the state. There is no sufficient reason for making such an exception.[149]

The New Hampshire Court's willingness to trust in the wisdom of juries, as illustrated by this passage, seems poles apart from the Maine Court's evident lack of confidence in juries, as shown by its decisions in the cases discussed in this chapter.[150]

Compared with the Maine Court, the New Hampshire Court also seems to have had a more realistic understanding of the difficulty of estimating the speed of an oncoming train. As we have seen from Justice Whitehouse's remarks in Mrs. Day's case, there was no slack in the Maine Court's jurisprudence for an error of judgment in estimating the speed of an oncoming train, even one that was moving along the tracks at a grossly excessive rate of speed. The New Hampshire Court, in contrast, took a decidedly different view. Writing for the New Hampshire Court in *Huntress v. Boston & Maine Railroad* (1890),[151] Chief Justice Charles Doe explained that a traveler's miscalculation of the speed of a train might be said to be based on

---

[149] *Id.* at 85, 47 A. at 293.

[150] One study of nineteenth-century New Hampshire railroad crossing cases notes that "[o]f the fourteen intersection cases in New Hampshire during the nineteenth century, plaintiffs emerged victorious in every one." *See* Gary T. Schwartz, "Tort Law and the Economy in Nineteenth-Century America: A Reinterpretation," 90 *Yale Law Review* 1717, 1745 (1981). As the Maine cases discussed above show, that record was certainly not duplicated in Maine.

[151] 66 N.H. 185, 34 A. 154 (1890). In this case, the New Hampshire Court affirmed a verdict in favor of the plaintiff in his suit against the railroad company for his wife's death, which was caused when the carriage in which she was riding with her mother was struck by a train at a railroad crossing.

"an inadequate understanding of the risk," but that did not necessarily constitute contributory negligence or "fault":

> A person of ordinary prudence, exercising the caution and vigilance which the law has adopted as the test of duty, might make an extremely hazardous attempt to cross a railroad in front of a train. From the mere fact of great danger, it does not necessarily follow that he exposed himself recklessly and consciously. When there is no evidence of insanity, intoxication, or suicidal purpose, and no evidence on the question of his care, except the instinct provided for the preservation of animal life, it may be inferred from this circumstantial proof that, for some reason consistent with ordinary care and freedom from the fault on his part, his attempt to cross was due to his inadequate understanding of the risk. In the full possession and vigorous use of his faculties, without even a momentary absence or preoccupation of mind, with his intelligence alert and diligently applied to the question of waiting for the train to pass, he might act upon an error of judgment in regard to the speed of the train and the time that would elapse before its arrival. There is reason to believe a mistake on this point is the cause of many accidents. A large portion of the community have such knowledge of the danger of crossing a street in front of a horse team moving at a moderate gait as is necessary in determining whether safety requires them to wait for the team to pass. But high rates of speed create a degree of danger that is not generally realized by those who have no special means of information on the subject.[152]

Legislative Reform

Despite the injustice of the doctrine of contributory negligence, that doctrine remained in effect in Maine until 1965, when it was replaced by a "comparative negligence" statute enacted by the Maine Legislature. That statute did away with the Court's contributory

---

[152] *Id.* at 190, 34 A. at 156.

negligence rule under which any amount of contributory negligence on the part of the plaintiff was a complete bar to the plaintiff's claim.[153] Under the comparative negligence statute, damages are apportioned on the basis of the jury's judgment concerning the amount of fault of the plaintiff compared with that of the defendant; and contributory negligence on the part of the plaintiff does not prevent the plaintiff from being awarded damages, provided the jury finds the plaintiff less at fault than the defendant.

Reform of the Court's rule that required the plaintiff to prove his freedom from contributory negligence was similarly a long time in coming. In 1913, the Maine Legislature shifted the burden of proving the decedent's contributory negligence to the defendant in wrongful death cases.[154] Many more years, however, would pass before the Maine Court itself, in 1974, citing "principles of fundamental fairness," decided that the defendant should bear the burden of proving the plaintiff's contributory fault in personal injury cases as well.[155]

All of this of course came years too late to be of any help to Dr. Pickard's widow and children, to Albert Lesan, or to any of the other injured parties or surviving family members in the cases discussed above. In their time, they and many others like them had no choice but to accept the consequences of court-made rules of contributory negligence that today are almost universally considered to have been unjust and unfair.[156]

---

[153] An Act Relating to Comparative Negligence, Me. P.L. 1965, ch. 424, *now codified at* 14 M.R.S.A. § 156 (2003).

[154] An Act to Change the Burden of Proof in Certain Negligence Cases, Me. P.L. 1913, ch. 27.

[155] *Crocker v. Coombs,* 328 A.2d 389 (Me. 1974).

[156] In looking back over the long history of those rules in Maine, it is interesting to note that at an early day in its history, the Maine Court gave at least a moment's thought to the idea that a court might itself develop comparative negligence rules that would ameliorate the harshness of the doctrine of contributory negligence by apportioning damages where there was fault on both sides. But it seems that no sooner had the thought occurred than it was dismissed, the Court remarking that "the common law does not attempt to apportion the loss in such cases." *Kennard v. Burton,* 25 Me. 39, 50 (1845).

WOMEN AND THE LAW

At this point in our travels through the early years of Maine law, we find ourselves in what seems to be a thicket of competing legal principles and attitudes. Old rules and traditions from the past were being challenged by concepts that were new. For the first hundred years of Maine's history as a separate state, until the ratification of the Nineteenth Amendment in 1920, women in Maine were denied the right to vote as a matter of official state policy. Maine's Constitution, as originally enacted, expressly limited the right to vote to every qualified "male citizen." By force of that provision, women were prohibited from exercising the most basic aspect of citizenship. Moreover, under ancient rules of the common law, which Maine inherited at its founding, married women, in contrast with single women and married men, were considered as having no individual identity of their own. Throughout this time, a tension existed between these conditions and the emerging realization that they could not be squared with the principle of equality of rights under the law.

Under the old common law, a woman's separate legal existence was regarded as suspended and merged into that of her husband for the duration of her marriage. By operation of law, her husband automatically acquired ownership of all her personal property and the use of her real estate. She was not allowed to acquire or dispose of property. Nor could she enter into a contract or bring a lawsuit. Indeed, under the old rules of the common law, she could do virtually nothing of any legal significance in her own name at all. As the Maine Court once put it, under that model of marriage, "Her disabilities were about complete."[157] In return for those disabilities, which the wife by law was required to endure, her husband was made responsible for her conduct and support. Looking back at the rules of law that prevailed when Maine became a state, the Court has more recently summed up the legal status of married women at that time as follows:

> In the eyes of the common law upon marriage a husband and wife became one person and that person was the husband. A married woman of any age was held incapable of entering into binding contractual relations and of acquiring or disposing of property. Upon marriage her husband took over all her personal property and the use of her real estate for his life and became responsible for her support, her debts and her torts.[158]

As early decisions of the Maine Court show, the Court was in no hurry to modify rules that for centuries had served as the foundation for institutions of such central importance to the stability of society as marriage and family life. Strongly supportive of those institutions, and firmly rooted in common law traditions it inherited from the distant past, the early Maine Court played a decidedly conservative role regarding legal issues of particular concern to women. The Court's conservative treatment of those issues during its first hundred years stands out sharply against the backdrop of the political movement to advance the rights of women that took place during that time—a movement that would eventually result in women obtaining the right to vote. Against that backdrop, our Court seems to have been comfortable with its role as a guardian of the social order it had inherited from the past.

The Court demonstrated its interest in preserving the traditional social order in several ways: by limiting the circumstances in which one spouse could testify against the other; by conservatively

---

[157] *Abbott v. Abbott,* 67 Me. 304, 306 (1877), *overruled on other grounds by MacDonald v. MacDonald,* 412 A.2d 71 (Me. 1980).

[158] *Mellott v. Sullivan Ford Sales,* 236 A.2d 68, 70 (Me. 1967).

construing statutes that granted married women property rights and the right to bring lawsuits to protect those rights; by refusing to allow either spouse, even after divorce, to sue the other for torts committed while they were married; by preserving the traditional structure of marriage; and by its majority (5-3) opinion in 1874, to the effect that women could not be judges in Maine.

Limiting the Circumstances in Which One Spouse May Testify Against the Other

Under common law rules that dated back to medieval days, husband and wife were generally prohibited from testifying as witnesses against each other in any legal proceeding. Although that prohibition was phrased in gender-neutral terms, its practical impact must have been most keenly felt by the wife, for under other principles of the common law, she was completely subject to the control and authority of her husband. If she could never testify against him in any legal forum whatever, his domination would be complete. As a limited concession, courts in England carved out a narrow exception to the general rule, permitting the wife to testify against her husband in criminal cases where her husband was accused of an act of violence against her.

On the basis of those precedents, the Maine Court, in one of its earliest decisions, allowed the wife to testify against her husband in a criminal prosecution where her husband was charged with having physically assaulted her. In that case, known simply as *Soule's Case* (1828),[159] the charge was aggravated assault and battery. The Court first noted that, as a general rule, for "reasons of policy" one spouse may not testify against the other. In this case, however, the Court permitted the wife's testimony under the exception mentioned above. Chief Justice Mellen explained the rationale supporting that exception as follows:

> It is well known that, as a general principle, husband and wife are not legal witnesses against each other. Reasons of policy

---

[159] 5 Me. 407 (1828).

forbid it.… From the general rule some exceptions have been
established, founded on the necessity of the case: for instance,
if a wife could not be admitted to testify against the husband
as to threatened or executed violence and abuse upon her
person, he could play the tyrant and the brute at his pleasure,
and with perfect security beat, wound, and torture her at
times and in places when and where no witnesses could be
present, nor assistance be obtained. Reasons of policy do not
certainly extend so far as, in such cases, to disqualify her from
being a witness against him.… It is difficult to perceive any
sound reason why she should not be [allowed to testify] in
such cases, where other proof can be seldom presumed to
exist or be obtainable.[160]

Mellen also explained that to the extent the general rule
prohibiting one spouse from testifying against the other was based
on the importance of preserving peace in the household, that
rationale falls by the wayside where marital unity and domestic
peace have already been destroyed:

So far as the general incompetency of the wife [to testify] is
founded on the idea that her testimony, if received, would
tend to destroy domestic peace, and introduce discord,
animosity, and confusion in its place, the principle loses its
influence when that peace has already become wearisome to a
passionate, despotic and perhaps intoxicated husband, who
has done all his power to render the wife unhappy and
destroy all mutual affection.[161]

It is difficult to find fault with Mellen's reasoning on that score.
If domestic peace has already been destroyed, why not allow one
spouse to testify against the other? Or, was the general rule
prohibiting one spouse from testifying against the other based on
some consideration other than the importance of preventing
domestic discord? And if it was, what was that consideration? In

---

[160] *Id.* at 407-08.

[161] *Id.* at 408.

making the point that the general rule was difficult to justify where there was no marital peace to preserve, Mellen showed himself to be a jurist who believed it important to take a candid look at the reasons behind old rules of law instead of simply passing those rules along, unthinkingly, to the next generation. However, in a case decided just ten years after *Soule's Case*—and, incidentally, after Mellen's term of service on the Court had come to an end—the Court made it clear that it was not interested in examining the rationale for the general rule disqualifying husband and wife from testifying against each other. In *State v. Burlingham* (1838),[162] the Court narrowly defined the scope of the exception it had recognized in *Soule's Case* and indicated that it was not inclined to allow any additional exceptions.

The question at issue in *Burlingham* was whether Julia Rines could testify for the prosecution in a criminal case in which her husband, Stover Rines, and others were charged with having engaged in a criminal conspiracy to falsely accuse her of the crime of adultery. The trial judge allowed Julia to testify in the conspiracy trial, and Stover, together with the other defendants, was found guilty of the crime of conspiracy, as alleged. On appeal, the defendants argued that Julia should not have been permitted to testify for the prosecution because she was the wife of one of the defendants. The defendants relied on the general rule that husband and wife could not be witnesses against each other. In reply, the Attorney General, representing the State, maintained that the rationale for the exception pursuant to which the wife testified in *Soule's Case* was equally applicable here. Calling the Court's attention to the dire consequences, for Julia, of the conspiracy in which her husband was allegedly involved, the Attorney General explained:

> This is a conspiracy to convict her of a crime [adultery] which would take away her liberty, and render her infamous. On principle then there is more reason for permitting her to testify, than where mere personal violence is threatened. It is a new case and should be decided on principle.[163]

---

[162] 15 Me. 104 (1838).

[163] *Id.* at 105.

The Attorney General also pointed out that, just as the wife's testimony was necessary in *Soule's Case*, Julia's testimony was absolutely necessary here. Noting that without her testimony, none of the defendants could be convicted, the Attorney General said that "humanity requires" that her testimony be allowed to stand.

The Court, however, was not persuaded. It decided that this case was covered by the general rule prohibiting one spouse from testifying against the other and not by the exception to that rule. Limiting the scope of that exception to cases involving personal violence, the Court declared that "in criminal prosecutions, the admissibility of the husband or wife [as a witness against the other] must be confined to cases seeking security of the peace, and cases of personal violence." Because this was not such a case, the Court set aside the defendants' convictions on the ground that Julia should not have been allowed to testify as a witness for the prosecution inasmuch as her husband was one of the defendants.

In his opinion for the Court, Justice Nicholas Emery avoided any discussion of the merits of the Attorney General's contentions. Instead, he invoked the ancient common law doctrine that "husband and wife are one person, and that person is the husband," as if the recitation of that doctrine resolved the matter:

> [T]he whole theory [of the rules of the common law concerning husband and wife] is a slavish one compared even with the civil law. The merging of her name in that of her husband is emblematic of the fate of all her legal rights. The torch of hymen serves but to light the pile on which those rights are offered up. The legal theory is, that marriage makes the husband and wife one person, and that person is the husband, that there may be an indissoluble union of interest between the parties. On this ground, and to prevent connubial harmony and confidence from being disturbed, it is a general rule of law, that neither the husband nor wife can in any case, civil or criminal, be a witness for or against each other....[164]

---

[164] *Id.* at 106.

By invoking that doctrine as the basis for its decision—and by refraining from offering a reasoned response to the Attorney General's arguments in favor of allowing Julia to testify—the Court was indicating that it had no desire to modify, or even consider modifying, common law rules that were based on that doctrine. The fact that the doctrine was "slavish" did not trouble the Court. As the above-quoted passage indicates, as of 1838, when *Burlingham* was decided, the Court did not feel that the slavishness of that doctrine detracted from its authority as a precept of law in any way. Indeed, as that passage shows, the Court referred to the doctrine as "slavish" in the same breath that it cited it as the basis for its decision refusing to allow Julia to testify.

In the eyes of the early Maine Court, the ancient doctrine that husband and wife were one person, and that person was the husband, was the bedrock on which the traditional social order and all the old rules of the common law concerning husband and wife were based. From that perspective, any court that undertook to alter those rules to correct flaws that it might perceive in them ran the risk of doing harm to the institution of marriage, which the Court regarded as the basis of civil society. The Court had inherited the "one person" doctrine from a long line of judicial decisions extending back to the distant past, and the Court saw no value to be gained by tinkering with rules based on that doctrine.[165]

---

[165] Ultimately, some thirty-five years later, in 1873, the Legislature enacted a statute allowing either spouse, with or without the consent of the other, to testify against the other in civil and criminal proceedings. An act relating to recognizances and testimony, Me. P.L. 1873, ch. 137, §§ 4, 5; *see State v. Benner*, 284 A.2d 91 (Me. 1971) (discussing statutory history). That statute, in effect, rescinded the common law rule that had prevented husband and wife from testifying against each other in civil and criminal cases. A similar fate befell the early Maine Court's strongly held view that husband and wife should not be allowed to testify in their own divorce proceedings. In *Dwelly v. Dwelly*, 46 Me. 377 (1859), the Court decided that the trial judge had erred in allowing the wife in that divorce case to testify over the objection of her husband. The Court described the common law rule preventing husband and wife from testifying against each other as having "its foundation in those principles of public policy

Strictly Construing Statutes Granting Rights to Married Women

During the nineteenth century, the Maine Legislature largely did away with the old discriminatory rules of the common law that from time immemorial had denied married women basic property rights. The Legislature accomplished that monumental feat by enacting a series of statutes, which one by one, on a piecemeal basis, granted married women property rights of their own. The first statute of major importance in that series was a law passed in 1844, entitled, "An Act to secure to married women their rights in property."[166] In addition to providing that a married woman may acquire and own property in her own name, that statute also rescinded the old common law rule that ownership of all the personal property that the wife possessed at the time of her marriage automatically passed to her husband the instant they became married.[167] To make these newly granted property rights meaningful, and to allow for their protection, the Legislature also granted married women the right to bring lawsuits in their own names, as if they were unmarried.

---

which lie at the basis, not only of social life, but of civil society." Yet, evidently the Legislature did not share that view. Only four years later, the Legislature enacted a statute allowing either of the parties in a divorce case to testify, with or without the consent of the other. An act relating to divorce, Me. P.L. 1863, ch. 211, § 4; *see Bond v. Bond*, 127 Me. 117, 141 A. 833 (1928) (discussing statutory history).

[166] Me. P.L. 1844, ch. 117.

[167] Where the marriage took place before the effective date of that statute, the Court continued to apply that old common law rule. Thus, in *Carleton v. Lovejoy*, 54 Me. 445 (1867), the Court rejected Margaret Carleton's claim to certain articles of furniture and a dress, which had been given to her by her sister shortly before she died. Although Margaret's sister had acquired those items before her marriage, her husband automatically became the owner of them when he married her, and he continued to be the lawful owner of them. Consequently, Margaret's sister had no ownership interest in those items when, shortly before she died, she purported to give them to Margaret. In another case decided on the basis of the same old rule, the Court decided that ownership of a gold watch the husband had given to his wife before their marriage automatically reverted to him when she married him; therefore, the watch was property that was subject to the claims of his creditors—the wife's ownership of the watch lasted only until the day of her wedding. *Tllexan v. Wilson*, 43 Me. 186 (1857).

Despite the remedial purpose of these statutes, the early Maine Court viewed those enactments with a cautious eye. Because these statutes contradicted ancient rules of the common law, the Court thought it wise to interpret these statutes conservatively. As the Court frequently put it, because these statutes were "in derogation of the common law," they should be construed "strictly." The Court's conservative interpretation of these statutes is graphically demonstrated by its decisions limiting the right of a married woman to bring a lawsuit in her own name and by its decision that a married woman could not form a business partnership with her husband.

In *Smith v. Gorman* (1856),[168] a married woman sued her husband for damages for having wrongfully absconded with some items of her own personal property. She based her right to bring that suit on an 1848 statute that allowed any married woman, for the protection and enforcement of her rights to her own property, to bring suit "in her own name, in the same manner as if she were unmarried, or [to] prosecute or defend such suit jointly with her husband."[169] Under old common law rules that had existed for centuries before this statute was enacted, neither the husband nor the wife could sue the other, nor could the wife bring a lawsuit in her own name. Those rules were based on the theory that husband and wife were one person in the eyes of the law, and that person was the husband.[170] Because the 1848 statute was "in derogation of" those rules of the common law, the Court construed that statute strictly. In other words, as the Court stated, "The statute is in derogation of the common law, and is not to be construed as giving the wife a right of action against the husband, unless it results from the express terms of the statute, or from necessary implication."

As construed by the Court, the 1848 statute allowed the wife to bring a lawsuit in her own name only in those cases where she could have brought suit jointly with her husband; because she could not

---

[168] 41 Me. 405 (1856).

[169] Me. P.L. 1848, ch. 73.

[170] *See Abbott v. Abbott*, 67 Me. 304 (1877) (discussing those rules).

bring a suit jointly with her husband against her husband (for he would then be suing himself), it followed that she could not bring a suit in her own name against him. As the Court saw it, while the statute allowed a married woman to sue a third party, it did not go so far as to make an exception to the common law rule prohibiting either spouse from suing the other. In the absence of language more clearly indicating that the Legislature intended to allow a married woman to sue her husband, the Court was not going to assume that the Legislature intended that result.

On the basis of the same strict statutory analysis, the Court also decided that married women could not bring "breach of contract" suits against their husbands. For example, in *Crowther v. Crowther* (1868),[171] the Court decided that a married woman who had loaned her husband $1,075, in exchange for a promissory note by which he agreed in writing to repay that sum with interest, could not sue him to collect the amount owed. Here again, the Court construed the 1848 statute as permitting a married woman to sue a third party, but not her husband. Consequently, as long as she and her husband continued to be married, she could not sue him to collect the amount he owed her.

From the point of view of married women, this must have been an unsatisfactory result. The Legislature had granted married women property rights of their own. The Legislature had also authorized married women to bring suits in their own names, as if unmarried, in order to protect those rights. Yet, curiously, as the result of the Court's strict construction of those statutes, a woman who loaned money to her husband in exchange for his promise to repay that sum

---

[171] 55 Me. 358 (1868). It should be noted that in *Moulton v. Moulton*, 309 A.2d 224 (Me. 1973), the Maine Court declared that to the extent its decision in *Crowther v. Crowther* was based on "the common law mystique that husband and wife are a single legal person," that decision was no longer an authoritative precedent. As the Court stated in *Moulton*, at 228, "The common law doctrine of unity in marriage has been so eroded during the years by positive legislation that in modern times the status of the spouses has been practically equalized and the unity of marriage concept remains more theory than fact." (quoting *Roberts v. American Chain & Cable Co.*, 259 A.2d 43, 48 (Me. 1969)).

had only a theoretical right to enforce that promise as long as she and her husband remained married.

The question remained whether, if she were to divorce him, she could then sue him to collect the amount owed. That question was answered two years after its decision in *Crowther*, when the Court decided that she could. In *Webster v. Webster* (1870),[172] the Court decided that after divorce a woman could sue her former husband on a promissory note he had given her in exchange for money he borrowed from her while they were married. As the Court explained its reasoning, the wife, as the result of the married women's property rights statutes, had a valid property interest in the promissory note while she was married to her husband; but because of the old rules of the common law, she could not sue him on that note while she was married to him. Her right to enforce that promise through litigation was suspended as long as her marriage lasted. Once she obtained a divorce, however, that obstacle to her right to enforce the note was removed, and she could then sue her former husband to collect the amount he owed her.

It is ironic that this outcome—which could be read as providing an inducement for the wife to seek a divorce in order to protect her property rights—ultimately stemmed from the Court's interest in preserving the common law concept of the unity of husband and wife in marriage. For it was the Court's interest in preserving that common law concept that led the Court to construe the married women's property rights statutes conservatively, instead of liberally, in the first place; and it was the Court's conservative construction of those statutes that led it to decide that, although a married woman had a valid property interest in a promissory note given to her by her husband, she could not enforce that note as long as she remained married to him.

Looking back at these developments, that result may seem strange today, but such ironies were probably inevitable in a climate in which the Court and the Legislature were addressing issues at the

---

[172] 58 Me. 139 (1870).

interface between ancient rules of the common law and "modern" statutes that for the first time in history granted married women separate rights of their own.

The early Maine Court's policy of construing married women's property rights statutes conservatively is also illustrated by its decision in *Haggett v. Hurley* (1898),[173] where the Court decided that, despite the many statutes that had by then been enacted to secure the separate property rights of married women, those statutes did not go so far as to allow a married woman to form a business partnership with her husband. In reaching that result, the Court noted that an "incongruity" existed between the equality of rights that characterized the relationship between business partners and a husband's status as "the head of the family with marital authority," which continued to characterize the relationship between husband and wife. With that incongruity in mind, the Court concluded that until the Legislature more explicitly indicated that it intended to allow a woman to form a business partnership with her husband—a change in the law the Court called "almost revolutionary"—it would not assume that such was the Legislature's intent.

Preventing Tort Claims by One Spouse Against the Other

As we have seen, the early Maine Court consistently upheld the common law principle that prohibited either spouse from bringing a lawsuit against the other. Even after the Legislature had granted married women the right to bring suits in their own names in order to protect their newly obtained property rights, the Court refused to read those statutes as allowing a married woman to bring a suit against her husband for that purpose. Against that background, the Court, in *Abbott v. Abbott* (1877),[174] addressed the question whether the plaintiff, Cynthia Abbott, after her divorce from her husband, Ransom Abbott, should be allowed to sue him for various intentional

---

[173] 91 Me. 542, 40 A. 561 (1898). The Court's decision contains an exhaustive list of those statutes.

[174] 67 Me. 304 (1877).

torts[175] he allegedly committed while they were married. In her complaint, Cynthia alleged that, among other things, Ransom, acting together with certain other defendants, had assaulted her, falsely accused her of being "a crazy and insane person," and caused her to be "inhumanly bound and put in irons and conveyed to the insane asylum or hospital [at Augusta]," where she was "imprisoned as an insane person... against her will and to the great injury of her health and comfort." The report of the case indicates that Cynthia escaped from that facility a few days later. The trial judge referred the case to the Court for it to determine whether the case would be allowed to proceed to trial. The Court dismissed the complaint.

Explaining its rejection of Cynthia's claims, the Court first noted that suits between spouses were not permitted by the common law because the common law regarded husband and wife as "one person." Being one person, neither could sue the other. The Court then took that rule one step further by declaring that for the same reason—the presumed unity of husband and wife—a wrong done by one spouse to the other could *never* materialize into a claim upon which the injured spouse could bring suit. It therefore followed, the Court explained, that after divorce, Cynthia could not sue her former husband for torts he committed while they were married.[176] The Court also said that it believed that a married woman who was injured by her husband's wrongful acts "has remedy enough"—by the criminal prosecution of her husband; by the availability of the writ of habeas corpus, if she were unlawfully confined; and by an

---

[175] A "tort" can generally be defined as a wrongful act committed against the person or property of another, as distinguished from a breach of contract.

[176] The Court also dismissed the plaintiff's claims against the co-defendants who had allegedly acted in concert with her former husband in committing the torts alleged. The Court explained the test of their liability was whether they could have been sued by the plaintiff at the time when the torts were committed. The Court reasoned that those co-defendants could not have been sued by the plaintiff in her own name at that time because under rules of the common law, which applied at that time, a married woman was not permitted to bring a tort suit in her own name. Nor, as of that time, could she have brought this suit jointly with her husband because he would then have been, in effect, suing himself, considering that the co-defendants, "merely aided and assisted him."

award of alimony, if she were to obtain a divorce—without the additional remedy of a civil suit against him for monetary damages.

What is perhaps the most remarkable aspect of the Court's decision in *Abbott* is the breadth of the rule the Court adopted in that case. Under that rule, neither spouse could *ever* sue the other for *any* tort, including intentional torts, committed while they were married. The Court described that rule in the broadest of terms: "So to speak, marriage acts as a perpetually operating discharge of all wrongs between man and wife, committed by one upon the other." And, the Court added, quoting from a decision of the North Carolina Court, "it is better to draw the curtain, shut out the public gaze, and leave the parties to forget and forgive." Presumably, the Court here meant, "better for all concerned." But from Cynthia Abbott's perspective, that rhetoric must have been a bitter pill to swallow.[177]

Here again, as was the case with other common law rules concerning husbands and wives, it bears noting that, even though the Court indicated that the rule it adopted in *Abbott* applied equally to married men and married women alike—"marriage acts as a perpetually operating discharge of all wrongs between man and wife, committed by one upon the other"—that rule must have been particularly frustrating for married women in view of the subordinate position they continued to occupy within the institution of marriage at that time. For as previously noted, in a case decided twenty-one years after *Abbott*, the Court itself observed that notwithstanding the many statutes that had been enacted during the nineteenth century to secure rights for married women, the husband still remained "the head of the family with marital authority."[178]

---

[177] It should be noted that in a case decided more than a century later, the Maine Court overruled its decision in *Abbott v. Abbott*, noting that a "paternalistic apprehension of domestic discord" should not be allowed to "overbalance the fundamental unfairness in depriving any person of the right to have legal redress for a wrong actually suffered." *MacDonald v. MacDonald*, 412 A.2d 71, 73 (Me. 1980) (quoting *Bedell v. Reagan*, 159 Me. 292, 297, 192 A.2d 24, 26 (1963) and *Moulton v. Moulton*, 309 A.2d 224, 229 (Me. 1973)).

[178] *Haggett v. Hurley*, 91 Me. 542, 40 A. 561 (1898).

In establishing the rule that neither spouse could ever sue the other for a tort committed while they were married, the Court in *Abbott* probably believed that its adoption of that rule would help to preserve the stability of marriages by preventing them from being torn apart by lawsuits and threats of litigation by one spouse against the other. But, as the next case we will consider shows, good intentions do not necessarily guarantee results that are fair.

In *Libby v. Berry* (1883),[179] the plaintiff, Sarah Libby, after obtaining a divorce from her husband, James Given, and after resuming her maiden name, sued the defendant, Thaddeus Berry, for injuring her, impairing her health, and causing her to suffer "intense pain of body and mind" by using "an instrument whose name is to the plaintiff unknown," internally, in an illegal attempt to cause her to have an abortion against her will and consent. As described in the case report, Sarah also alleged that her then husband, Given, was "then and there present, compelling and coercing her to endure the use of said instrument." After Sarah testified to those acts, the parties agreed to refer the case to the Maine Court to determine whether the case would be allowed to proceed to trial. The Court ordered the case dismissed.

In rejecting Sarah's suit against Berry, the Court explained that, based on its conservative interpretation of a recently enacted statute permitting married women to bring lawsuits for the redress of injuries caused by torts, that statute did not go so far as to allow a married woman to sue her husband for a tort committed against her; and neither did it allow her to sue those who, in the Court's words, "act with the husband and under his direction in doing such a wrong." By that reasoning, Sarah, who was a married woman when the assault was committed, could not have sued Berry at that time because as the Court saw it, Berry had acted as an "agent," under the direction of her former husband, in committing the assault. And for the same reason, the precedent of *Abbott v. Abbott*, which prevented Sarah from suing her former husband after her divorce, for an assault

---

[179] 74 Me. 286 (1883).

committed while she was married, also prevented Sarah from suing Berry after her divorce for his role in the assault.

In sum, Sarah, by her testimony the victim of a grossly invasive assault, intentionally committed by a party who was neither her spouse nor her former spouse, was turned away by the Court by a convoluted process of reasoning that resulted in the Court's granting her alleged assailant immunity from liability for damages. Although at each step of that process the Court may have been motivated by its interest in protecting marriages from the destabilizing effects of litigation, it is hard to see how the outcome of this case promoted the stability of marriages in any way. If anything, this case would seem to teach the lesson that, even at a time when married women were gaining property rights of their own, a woman might stand a better chance of obtaining justice if she were to remain single instead of getting married. Under the circumstances, the Court's rejection of Sarah's claim might aptly be described as the triumph of formalism over fairness—and that is perhaps the most charitable description the Court's decision deserves.

Preserving the Traditional Structure of Marriage

As the nineteenth century drew to a close, our Court continued to support the traditional common law model of marriage even though by that time the common law disabilities of married women had been largely removed by statutes enacted by the Legislature. Thus, in *Haggett v. Hurley* (1898),[180] the Court explained that despite the rights married women had obtained by those statutes, the institution of marriage had not yet become an equal partnership: "The husband was still left the head of the family with the duty of support and the right to direct family life."

At that same point in history, however, the Court apparently felt the need to offer a more benign rationale for the old common law

---

[180] In this case, discussed earlier in this chapter, the Court decided that Maine statutes that had conferred property rights on married women did not go as far as to allow a married woman to form a business partnership with her husband.

rules defining marriage than it had offered only eight years earlier in *Cummings v. Everett* (1890).[181] In that earlier case, in what appears to have been a burst of judicial candor, the Court explained that those old rules had been adopted by the courts, not so much for the protection of the wife, but to secure the power and authority of the husband:

> The disabilities of [married women under the common law] however, were not so much imposed for the protection of the wife, as for the advantage of the husband.... We do not forget that Blackstone in his optimism, says that the disabilities of the wife are intended for the most part for her protection and benefit, "so great a favorite is the female sex of the law of England," but one need not read very far in the books of the common law to learn that the power and authority of the husband were of far more concern to the law, than the protection and benefit of the wife.[182]

In contrast with that earlier explanation, the Court in *Haggett* explained that the old common law rules defining marriage had been established not "to exploit the female sex," but "to insure the preservation and unity of the family":

> There was of course for this [common law] rule [that excluded married women from business matters] a reason which seemed sufficient for centuries. There is no warrant for saying that this reason was in the harshness or selfishness of the male sex, or in any desire to exploit the female sex.... The reason appears to be in the almost instinctive desire to insure the unity,—the singleness of the family.
>
> ...To insure the unity and preservation of the family, there seemed to be thought necessary a complete identity of interests and a single head with control and power. The

---

[181] 82 Me. 260, 19 A. 456 (1890). In this case, the Court decided that a statute allowing suits against married women did not override the common law rule that prohibited suits based on contracts made by minors under the age of twenty-one.

[182] *Id.* at 262, 19 A. at 456.

husband was made that head and given the power, and in return was made responsible for the maintenance and conduct of the wife. To prevent any clashing of interests between husband and wife, to prevent any divisions or separations in the family, the wife was disqualified during coverture [marriage] from having any business interests and from subjecting her personal estate to the claims of creditors. Such at least was the common law.[183]

As these remarks suggest, the Court at the end of the nineteenth century was struggling to develop a currently acceptable explanation for old common law rules that supported the institution of marriage in its traditional form, with husband as head and wife occupying a subordinate position. But times were changing. The subordinate status of women in marriage had been ensured for centuries past by rules of the common law that had denied married women property rights and treated them as if they were children. But as married women gained rights of their own, the legal framework on which their subordinate status had been based began to fall apart, in spite of the Court's efforts to shore up that framework with reassuring words of justification. The concept of equality of rights under the law was gaining increasing traction, and over the years the Court's patriarchal model of marriage would become increasingly difficult to justify as a precept of law.

Court Majority (5-3) Opines That Women Cannot be Judges in Maine

In 1874, the Maine Court faced the question whether women could be judges in the state of Maine. This question was brought to the Court by the Governor's Executive Council, which sought an advisory ruling from the Court with respect to two questions: whether a woman, appointed to be a justice of the peace, could

---

[183] *Haggett*, 91 Me. at 549-50, 40 A. at 563. Interestingly, the Court's opinion in *Haggett* was written by the same Justice, Lucilius A. Emery, who wrote the Court's earlier opinion in *Cummings v. Everett*.

perform the acts of that office, and whether a married or unmarried woman could be appointed to the office of justice of the peace. In considering these questions, the Court split into three camps.[184]

Five of the Justices, including Chief Justice John Appleton, were of the opinion that under Maine's Constitution and laws, a woman could not be a justice of the peace or perform the duties of that office. At the same time, however, those Justices concluded that the Legislature could authorize the appointment of married or unmarried women to administer oaths, take acknowledgements of deeds, and solemnize marriages.[185] Justices Charles W. Walton and William G. Barrows submitted a dissenting opinion. Justice Jonathan G. Dickerson also dissented in a separate opinion.

To the majority of the judges on the Court, it was very clear that under the Maine Constitution, women could not be judicial officers. Although the Constitution said nothing at all about the matter, these Justices believed that their view was supported by the history of the formation of the state. They pointed out that under the Act of Separation from Massachusetts, the authority to vote on separation and to elect delegates to vote on a constitution was limited to qualified (meaning male) inhabitants of the District of Maine. In addition, they noted that the vote on the adoption of Maine's Constitution was limited to males. "It thus appears," they said, "that the constitution of the State was the work of its male citizens." Moreover, they stated, "By the constitution, the whole political power of the State is vested in its male citizens." Under these circumstances, these Justices, constituting a 5-3 majority of the Court, concluded that if there had been any intention on the part of the framers of the Constitution to

---

[184] *See Opinion of the Justices*, 62 Me. 596 (1874). Article VI, Section 3 of Maine's Constitution requires the Justices of the Supreme Judicial Court to issue advisory opinions under specified circumstances when requested by the Governor, Senate, or House of Representatives. Prior to being amended in 1964, that provision also provided for the issuance of advisory opinions by the Justices to the Governor's Executive Council. The Executive Council was eliminated by a constitutional amendment in 1975. *See* Me. Const. Res. 1975, ch. 4.

[185] Joining Chief Justice Appleton in that majority opinion were Justices Jonas Cutting, Charles Danforth, William Wirt Virgin, and John A. Peters.

transfer political power to women, that intention would have been made manifest in appropriate language. Finding no such intention disclosed, they concluded:

> Having regard, then, to the rules of the common law as to the rights of women married and unmarried, as then existing; to the history of the past; to the universal and unbroken practical construction given to the constitution of this State, and to that of the Commonwealth of Massachusetts upon which that of this State was modelled; we are led to the inevitable conclusion that it was never in the contemplation or intention of those forming our constitution, that the offices thereby created should be filled by those who could take no part in its original formation, and to whom no political power was intrusted for the organization of the government then about to be established under its provisions, or for its continued existence and preservation when established.[186]

In their dissenting opinion, Justice Walton and Justice Barrows made the point that the right to vote and the right to hold office are two distinct matters. Because the Constitution did not prohibit the appointment of women to the office of justice of the peace, the Legislature in their view was authorized to enact a law authorizing

---

[186] *Id.* at 598. In 1871, the Supreme Judicial Court of Massachusetts similarly concluded that under that state's constitution, a woman could not be appointed to the office of justice of the peace. *Opinion of the Justices*, 107 Mass. 604 (1871). That court's unanimous opinion summarily disposed of the issue in a single paragraph:

> "By the Constitution of the Commonwealth, the office of justice of the peace is a judicial office, and must be exercised by the officer in person, and a woman, whether married or unmarried, cannot be appointed to such an office. The law of Massachusetts at the time of the adoption of the Constitution, the whole frame and purport of the instrument itself, and the universal understanding and unbroken practical construction for the greater part of a century afterwards, all support this conclusion, and are inconsistent with any other. It follows that, if a woman should be formally appointed and commissioned as a justice of the peace she would have no constitutional or legal authority to exercise any of the functions appertaining to that office."

the appointment of women to that office. In that regard, they noted that "there is not so much as a masculine pronoun [in the Constitution] to hang an objection on." These dissenting Justices also made the compelling point that the majority view of the matter was based "not on any expressed intention of the framers of the constitution that women should not hold office, but upon a presumed absence of intention that they should." Noting that "[t]his seems to us a dangerous doctrine," they went on to say:

> It is nothing less than holding that the legislature cannot enact a law unless it appears affirmatively that the framers of the constitution intended that such a law should be enacted. We cannot concur in such a doctrine. It would put a stop to all progress. We understand the correct rule to be the reverse of that; namely, that the legislature may enact any law they think proper, unless it appears affirmatively that the framers of the constitution intended that such a law should not be passed.[187]

Perhaps nowhere have the shortcomings of the "original-intent school" of constitutional interpretation been better expressed.[188]

The separate dissenting opinion of Justice Jonathan Dickerson is the most interesting of the three opinions written in this matter. That opinion, years ahead of the then prevailing judicial mindset, surely ranks as one of the great prophetic judicial opinions concerning the rights of women. Justice Dickerson's observations concerning the rightful place of women in society and the duty of the Court under the Maine and U.S. Constitutions to secure for women a status equal to that of men stand out in bold relief against the tradition-bound

---

[187] *Opinion of the Justices*, 62 Me. at 599-600.

[188] The dissenting opinion of Justices Walton and Barrows was praised by Justice David J. Brewer of the Kansas Supreme Court in *Wright v. Noell*, 16 Kan. 601, 606 (1876) ("[W]e cannot do better than to quote from the dissenting opinion of Justices Walton and Barrows of the supreme court of Maine."). The Kansas Court there decided that women were eligible to fill the elected office of County Superintendent of Public Instruction. Justice Brewer later became a Justice of the U.S. Supreme Court.

jurisprudence of the majority of the members of the Maine Court in the year 1874. Indeed, almost one hundred years would pass before the U.S. Supreme Court finally adopted Justice Dickerson's views concerning the rights of women.[189] The following quotations from Justice Dickerson's opinion give some idea of the strength of this jurist's convictions and his passionate sense of justice and equality for all citizens, without regard to race or sex:

> [The office of justice of the peace] is a public office with judicial functions which are clearly within the sphere of woman's capacity.
>
> ....
>
> ...The ability of women to elicit, quicken and purify the activities of humanity, is one of the most important factors in modern civilization. Wise statesmanship and enlightened jurisprudence alike seek to enlarge the scope of such instrumentalities, without regard to race, color, sex or previous condition of servitude, either of race or sex.
>
> By ancient usage women were regarded as inferior beings, and treated as the servants or slaves of men: married women were subject to personal chastisement from their

---

[189] *See Reed v. Reed*, 404 U.S. 71 (1971). In *Reed*, the U.S. Supreme Court decided that an Idaho statute granting a gender-based preference to male relatives of the deceased in the appointment of an administrator of an estate was "the very kind of arbitrary legislative choice forbidden by the Equal Protection Clause of the Fourteenth Amendment." As the Supreme Court has observed, *Reed* was the first case in which it ruled in favor of a woman who complained that her state had denied her equal protection of its laws. *United States v. Virginia*, 518 U.S. 515 (1996) (holding that exclusion of women from admission to Virginia Military Institute, a state military college, violated the Equal Protection Clause of the Fourteenth Amendment). In *Virginia*, the Supreme Court also stated: "Since *Reed*, the Court has repeatedly recognized that neither federal nor state government acts compatibly with the equal protection principle when a law or official policy denies to women, simply because they are women, full citizenship stature— equal opportunity to aspire, achieve, participate in and contribute to society based on their individual talents and capacities." *Id*. at 532. *See also Craig v. Boren*, 429 U.S. 190 (1976) (explaining that to withstand judicial scrutiny, gender-based statutory classifications must be substantially related to the achievement of important governmental objectives and cannot be justified by increasingly outdated gender stereotypes).

husbands without any adequate right of redress; the church denied all women the right of speech in the sanctuary; and even the common law gave the husband all the wife's personal property upon marriage, and, also, that which should subsequently fall to her during coverture; her legal identity became merged in her husband, so that in fact her person, property, earnings and children belonged to him; the husband and the wife were one, and the husband was the one.... To deny women the right to hold office upon the ground of usage would be to set back the clock of time and substitute reaction for progress.

This, however, is not merely a question of usage, but of constitutional right. The exclusion of one half of the people of the State from participation in the administration of the laws, by the dominant half, however long continued, neither implies, nor confers the right to enforce such exclusion. A usage originating in contravention of the constitution, does not become obligatory by lapse of time. The constitution and not usage is the touchstone of civil and political rights.

....

...It should not be forgotten that we live under the fourteenth amendment, and not under the Dred Scott decision, if we would avoid falling into the error of following the doctrine in that case, instead of obeying the supreme law of the land.

....

It by no means follows, that women are ineligible to the office in question, because by the act of separation [from Massachusetts] they were not permitted to take part in the formation of the constitution, and, by the organic law itself, were excluded from voting upon its adoption. I have always understood, and still understand, that the convention that formed the constitution of this State, was an independent body, and perfectly free to propose a framework of government upon a broader and more liberal basis than that of the parent commonwealth....

....

What is there, it may be not inaptly asked, in judicial offices, and other offices named in the constitution, that invests them with such importance and sanctity, inherently, or because they happen to be thus mentioned, that none but male citizens can hold them?...

....

The eligibility of women to office does not depend upon the common law or the usages, laws and constructions of the commonwealth of Massachusetts, prior to the adoption of the constitution, unless they are specifically made a part of it, and it is not pretended that they are for this purpose. The meaning and intent of the framers of the constitution are not to be learned from such recondite sources, but are to be ascertained from their own language, interpreted by the tribunal they established for this purpose, in accordance with the objects and purposes of the great charter of liberty, equality, justice and progress, which those masters of political science framed.

....

...The precedent of outlawing freedmen, because, by such a rule of construction, their race had no rights that the dominant race was bound to respect, is no less repugnant to the judicial than the philanthropic mind, and deserves to be shunned as a perversion of the law, rather than followed as authority....

....

It will not answer to strain, subordinate and dwarf the constitution of this State. That instrument does not bind the people to the perpetual observance of pre-existing customs, usages, constructions and laws which form no part of it, but it rather emancipates them from the exclusiveness, monopolies, inequalities and injustices, if any there be, that arise therefrom. Aside from the single discrimination in respect to suffrage, in certain specified cases, the constitution does not determine the rights of the people, according to caste, color or sex, but leaves them free, within specified limitations, to secure the objects stated in its preamble in the best possible manner. The plain people need no judicial handbook to enable them to learn their rights under the organic law of their government; it is so plain, in this respect, that he that runs may read and understand his rights.

There is, in fine, one brief and conclusive answer to the questions propounded to the members of the court; it is, that the burden is upon those who deny the right of women to hold the office in question, to show affirmatively that the constitution prohibits them from so doing. This they certainly have not done. There being no constitutional inhibition, the right to hold that office attaches alike to both female and male citizens.[190]

I have taken the liberty of quoting at length from Justice Dickerson's dissent because his own words best convey the strength of his convictions regarding the fundamental issues of justice and equality involved in this advisory-opinion proceeding. Justice Dickerson's outlook on these issues is particularly noteworthy because the prevailing sense of the judiciary at that time (1874) was overwhelmingly in the opposite direction. As we have already seen, the Massachusetts Court in 1871 dismissed such a claim, summarily. Ten years later, that court also decided that women could not be attorneys in Massachusetts.[191]

Similarly, the U.S. Supreme Court itself, in 1873, decided that the decision of the Illinois Court to deny a woman admission to the bar of that state did not violate the Privileges and Immunities Clause of the Fourteenth Amendment to the U.S. Constitution.[192] In a concurring opinion in that case, Justice Joseph Bradley offered his perspective on the proper place of women in society:

Man is, or should be, woman's protector and defender. The natural and proper timidity and delicacy which belongs to the female sex evidently unfits it for many of the occupations of civil life. The constitution of the family organization, which is founded in the divine ordinance, as well as in the nature of

---

[190] *Opinion of the Justices*, 62 Me. at 600-07.

[191] *Lelia J. Robinson's Case*, 131 Mass. 376 (1881).

[192] *Bradwell v. Illinois*, 83 U.S. 130 (1873).

things, indicates the domestic sphere as that which properly belongs to the domain and functions of womanhood. The harmony, not to say identity, of interests and views which belong, or should belong, to the family institution is repugnant to the idea of a woman adopting a distinct and independent career from that of her husband....

...The paramount destiny and mission of woman are to fulfil the noble and benign offices of wife and mother. This is the law of the Creator.[193]

When I first came upon Justice Dickerson's dissenting opinion in which he proclaimed the right of women to be appointed to judicial office and to occupy a status in the eyes of the law equal to that of men, I was immensely struck by the power of his rhetoric. The more I have thought about that opinion, the more impressed I am with Justice Dickerson's courage in staking out and forcefully stating the position he did in the face of the contrary opinion of the majority of the members of the Maine Court, who must have regarded his views with disdain. Yet the judgment of history has ultimately supported Dickerson's prophetic vision that the Constitution "does not determine the rights of the people, according to caste, color or sex."

In the history of the law, dissenting opinions have frequently played an important role. For one thing, they force the dissenter's colleagues on the bench to reassess their position in light of the dissenter's contrary judicial voice. Through that process, both the reasoning and the result of the opinion that ultimately emerges as the majority opinion of the court will often be improved. Dissenting opinions can also serve the helpful purpose of providing a reference point upon which jurists in future cases may build a legal rationale that might, but for a previous dissenting opinion, never have even been considered at all. In addition, dissenting opinions that call the majority to task for having "gotten it wrong" on one point or another can be the inspiration for later legislative reform.

---

[193] *Id.* at 141.

In view of the positive results that may come from dissenting opinions, it is interesting to note that dissenting opinions were seldom issued by Justices of the Maine Court during its first hundred years. The Justices probably felt that dissenting opinions might be taken as an indication that the law was unsettled and as detracting from the authority of the Court. The Court might also have felt that its ability to maintain the respect of the populace would be enhanced by its speaking in unison instead of speaking in many differing voices.[194]

Fortunately, Justice Dickerson must have been one of those who believed that the publication of dissents was both justified and desirable. His dissenting opinion, written in 1874, on the question of whether women were entitled to hold judicial office will for all time stand as an eloquent reminder of the irrepressible forces of justice and equality of rights on which this nation was founded, for which our Civil War was fought by the North, and on which our nation's distinctive worth ultimately depends. Indeed, it does not seem overstatement to suggest that Justice Dickerson's dissenting opinion in this matter deserves to be regarded by history as resting comfortably in that select company of distinguished dissenting opinions that rank among the most significant judicial utterances in the history of American law.

One such distinguished dissent, considered by many to be the greatest of all dissenting opinions ever uttered by a judge in America, was U.S. Supreme Court Justice John Marshall Harlan's dissenting opinion in *Plessy v. Ferguson* (1896).[195] Dissenting from the Supreme Court's "separate but equal" doctrine expounded in that case, Justice

---

[194] This may have been how Chief Justice John A. Peters felt about this matter. As Justice Lucilius Emery remarked, referring to Peters: "He encouraged the utmost freedom of dissent in consultation, though he deprecated the publication of dissents. In this he differed from some justices, notably of the United States Supreme Court, who hold that occasional publications of dissents are justified and even desirable." *See* Remarks of Justice Emery at memorial proceedings for Chief Justice Peters in Bangor, June 14, 1904, 99 Me. 541, 569 (1905).

[195] 163 U.S. 537, 552 (1896).

Harlan stated, in words reminiscent of Justice Dickerson's dissent written some twenty-two years earlier:

> But in view of the Constitution, in the eye of the law, there is in this country no superior, dominant, ruling class of citizens. There is no caste here. Our Constitution is color-blind, and neither knows nor tolerates classes among citizens. In respect of civil rights, all citizens are equal before the law. The humblest is the peer of the most powerful.[196]

Discovering Justice Dickerson's opinion was for me an experience akin to coming across an artist's masterpiece long hidden in an attic closet. Having found and dusted off this dissent, we have the opportunity to look upon the craftsmanship of a long-since deceased, and now obscure, Justice of the Maine Court, to reflect on his words, and to recall with gratitude the courage and foresight he displayed in speaking so forcibly for rights that at the time were far from being generally recognized, but which today the citizens of Maine take for granted and enjoy.

Following the ratification of the Nineteenth Amendment to the U.S. Constitution in 1920, the issue of whether women could be appointed to judicial office came before the Maine Court once again.[197] Reexamining the issue in 1921 in light of that Amendment, the Court concluded that if there was any doubt as to whether the majority opinion of the Court in 1874 was correct at the time it was written, the adoption of the Nineteenth Amendment resolved any such doubt in favor of the constitutional permissibility of the appointment of women to the office of justice of the peace.[198]

Despite this development, it was not until 1973 that a woman was appointed to be a judge in the State of Maine. In that year, Harriet Putnam Henry, Maine's first woman judge, was appointed to

---

[196] *Id.* at 559.

[197] The Nineteenth Amendment declares, "The right of citizens of the United States to vote shall not be denied or abridged by the United States or by any State on account of sex."

[198] *Opinion of the Justices*, 119 Me. 603, 113 A. 614 (1921).

the bench of the Maine District Court by Governor Kenneth M. Curtis. That it took so long for Maine to appoint its first woman judge shows the strength and tenacity of long-held stereotypical views of the proper roles of women and others in our society.

In reviewing the development of Maine law regarding the rights of women, one cannot help but be struck by the similarity between that long, drawn-out process and the current political debate concerning "gay rights" in Maine. Just as in 1874 it was absolutely unthinkable to a majority of our Court that a woman could be a judge, so too, today it is for many unthinkable that the law would ever permit a gay couple to become married. Yet, in reviewing the development of women's rights under the law in Maine, we have seen that once it became generally understood that equality of rights under the law is the foundational principle on which our nation stands, custom and tradition proved inadequate to justify a jurisprudence that had treated blacks and women as inferior to whites and men. Similarly, in all likelihood, our laws in time will ensure equality of legal rights for gays and allow them all benefits of marriage. As our own Justice Dickerson more than a hundred years ago reminded us, "The Constitution does not determine the rights of the people according to caste, color or sex."

EMPLOYEE INJURIES

We come now to the story of the early Maine Court's treatment of claims by employees against their employers for injuries sustained on the job. Long before modern workers' compensation legislation existed, our Court, along with other American courts, decided to adopt rules of law that directly favored employers at the expense of injured employees. As a result of these rules—contributory negligence, assumption of risk, and the fellow servant rule—large numbers of claims by injured employees were thrown out, leaving those employees without any meaningful legal remedy despite the existence of unsafe working conditions for which their employers were responsible. Consequently, injured workers and their families—those least able to afford it—were in large measure left to bear the human and financial costs of the industrial accidents that occurred.[199]

---

[199] Although the injured worker would, in cases involving injuries resulting from the negligence of a co-worker, have a valid claim against that co-worker, *Atkins v. Field*, 89 Me. 281, 36 A. 375 (1896), this was not really a *meaningful* legal remedy because it was unlikely that a co-worker, earning modest wages at best, could adequately compensate the victim fully for the injuries sustained. How different employers actually dealt with sickness and injury among employees at this time in Maine's history was inconsistent, depending on the policy of the employer. As Charles A. Scontras describes, "Some employers deducted wages when employees were out, some raised donations in the place of work, while others continued to pay workers for a brief period of time. Sometimes employers would continue wages while making provision for medical expenses for a period of time. Still others might remit rent monies or pay workers on the basis of need and circumstances, etc." Charles A. Scontras, *Organized Labor in Maine: Twentieth Century Origins* (Orono: University of Maine, 1985), 63-64. *See also*, Charles A. Scontras, *Collective Efforts Among Maine Workers: Beginnings and Foundations, 1820-1880* (Orono: University of Maine, 1994), 262.

The long line of workplace injury cases in Maine begins in 1857, but in order to understand the full story, we must venture back to 1842, when Lemuel Shaw, the extraordinarily influential Chief Justice of the Massachusetts Supreme Judicial Court, wrote the opinion for that court in *Farwell v. Boston & Worcester Rail Road Corp.*[200] Shaw's opinion in that case was one of the most significant state court decisions in the history of American law. It provided the legal framework upon which the Maine Court and almost every other court in the country eventually relied in deciding workplace injury claims over a period of many years. A brief examination of Shaw's opinion is necessary here because it was that opinion that ultimately led the early Maine Court down a long road of employee injury decisions that seem extremely unfair to injured employees, as we look back on those cases today.[201]

Massachusetts Chief Justice Shaw and the Fellow Servant Rule

The *Farwell* case involved a claim for damages brought by Nicholas Farwell, a train engineer, against his employer, a railroad company, after his right hand was crushed and destroyed when the train he was operating went off the tracks. Farwell's injuries were the direct result of the negligence of another employee of the same railroad company, a switchman, who had set a switch in the wrong direction. The Massachusetts Court rejected Farwell's claim.

In his opinion for the Massachusetts Court, Shaw first noted that if Farwell had been a third party not employed by the railroad company, Farwell could have sued the company for damages under the well-established principle of *respondeat superior*. That Latin

---

[200] 45 Mass. 49 (1842).

[201] Shaw's decision in the *Farwell* case has been the subject of much scholarly commentary. *See, e.g.,* Lawrence M. Friedman, *A History of American Law*, 3rd ed. (New York: Simon & Schuster, 2005), 224-25, 354. For a particularly insightful critique, see Leonard W. Levy, *The Law of the Commonwealth and Chief Justice Shaw* (Cambridge: Harvard University Press, 1957). For a comprehensive examination of the development of the fellow servant rule, see Comment, "The Creation of a Common Law Rule: The Fellow Servant Rule, 1837-1860," 132 *University of Pennsylvania Law Review* 579 (1984).

maxim, meaning "let the master answer," holds the employer liable for an employee's wrongful acts committed within the scope of employment. As Shaw stated,

> This rule is obviously founded on the great principle of social duty, that every man, in the management of his own affairs, whether by himself or by his agents or servants, shall so conduct them as not to injure another; and if he does not, and another thereby sustains damage, he shall answer for it.[202]

Shaw, however, then proceeded to carve out an exception to that "great principle of social duty" by relieving employers from liability in that category of cases involving injuries their employees suffered as a result of the negligence of their co-workers. This exception soon came to be known as the "fellow servant rule."

Shaw attempted to justify the fellow servant rule by invoking what he called "considerations of justice and policy." As for considerations of justice, Shaw reasoned that there exists between an employee and his employer an "implied contract," whereby the employee "takes upon himself the natural and ordinary risks and perils incident to the performance of such services, and in legal presumption, the compensation is adjusted accordingly." Shaw observed that employees can guard against co-worker negligence as effectively as employers can. He then concluded that injury caused by the negligence of a co-worker was simply one of those "ordinary risks and perils" that every employee assumes in exchange for his compensation. With these words, Shaw established that an employee injured by the negligence of a co-worker has no claim against the employer because, by accepting employment for the wages paid, the employee has impliedly agreed to assume all "ordinary" risks of employment, including the risk of injury caused by the negligence of a co-worker.

As for considerations of policy, Shaw maintained that his rule would promote the safety of employees because they are in a

---

[202] *Farwell*, 45 Mass. at 55-56.

position to oversee the conduct of each other, to report employee carelessness, and to "leave the service" if the employer does not correct the situation. As Shaw stated this:

> Where several persons are employed in the conduct of one common enterprise or undertaking, and the safety of each depends much on the care and skill with which each other shall perform his appropriate duty, each is an observer of the conduct of the others, can give notice of any misconduct, incapacity or neglect of duty, and leave the service, if the common employer will not take such precautions, and employ such agents as the safety of the whole party may require. By these means, the safety of each will be much more effectually secured, than could be done by a resort to the common employer for indemnity in case of loss by the negligence of each other.[203]

Although Shaw confidently asserted that these considerations justified the fellow servant rule, his reasoning cannot be squared with reality. Beginning with Shaw's "considerations of justice," the notion that wages are "adjusted" to compensate for the risk of injury is simply a "legal fiction"—an artificial construct that has no basis in fact. In the first place, the disparity in bargaining power between employers and individual employees makes a mockery of any suggestion that compensation is in fact adjusted to reflect degrees of risk of injury. And secondly, it seems absurd on its face to suggest that an employee's wage rate has in fact been set at a level that will fairly compensate him for whatever injuries he sustains as the result of co-worker negligence, regardless of the extent of those injuries, and even if such negligence causes his death. As for Shaw's suggestion that an employee can guard against co-worker negligence as effectively as an employer might, Shaw failed to note that an ordinary worker does not have hiring or disciplinary authority and therefore cannot weed out unreliable workers as an employer is able to do.

---

[203] *Id.* at 59.

The reasoning underlying Shaw's "considerations of policy" fares no better when evaluated in light of everyday experience. To begin with, employee safety would clearly seem to be more effectively secured by a rule that would hold the employer responsible for employee injuries caused by the negligence of other employees than would be the case under the contrary rule advanced by Shaw. If an employer knows that he could be liable for injuries to employees caused by the negligence of other employees, would not the employer, in concert with his supervisory employees, have every incentive to take effective action, by proper supervision and by maintaining a safe workplace, to prevent such negligence in the first place?[204] Shaw's rule provided none of that incentive, and the notion that a co-worker having no authority over another worker can more effectively police that other worker's conduct makes no discernable sense at all.

Shaw's suggestion that in situations where the employer may fail to take adequate steps to remedy a hazardous work environment the complaining employee can "leave the service" is hardly an answer to that employee's safety concerns. With the departure of that employee, the employer would be free to continue to maintain an unsafe workplace, and the complaining employee would be out of a job. Being an intelligent jurist in touch with the realities of industrial development, Shaw must have known that an employee would have little incentive to complain about another employee's conduct when the complaining employee could be fired by his employer and "blacklisted" by other employers for having had the audacity to

---

[204] Compare U.S. Supreme Court Justice Story's discussion of the rationale for holding the owners of a ship liable for medical expenses incurred by sick crew members during a voyage: "On the other hand, if these expenses are a charge upon the ship, the interest of the owner will be immediately connected with that of the seamen. The master will watch over their health with vigilance and fidelity. He will take the best methods, as well to prevent diseases, as to ensure a speedy recovery from them. He will never be tempted to abandon the sick to their forlorn fate; but his duty, combining with the interest of his owner, will lead him to succor their distress, and shed a cheering kindness over the anxious hours of suffering and despondency." *Harden v. Gordon*, 11 F. Cas. 480 (C.C.D. Me. 1823) (No. 6,047).

bring safety concerns to the attention of management. There were no "whistleblower" statutes to protect employees in those days.

Yet another shortcoming of the purported "policy" rationale for Shaw's fellow servant rule is the notion that employees are in a position effectively to oversee the conduct of each other. As a practical matter, that notion is completely inapplicable where employees work in separate departments or locations—the very situation in the *Farwell* case, where a train engineer was injured when his train left the tracks as the result of a switchman's negligence. Shaw must have realized that with the advent of railroads and the growth of large industrial organizations, situations such as that, in which the injured worker would never have had any contact at all with the negligent co-worker, would become increasingly common.

In summary, it is indeed difficult to see how Shaw could have believed that his fellow servant rule would promote safety in the workplace. Despite Shaw's best efforts to justify his rule by asserting that the safety of employees "will be much more effectually secured" by that rule than by the rule of *respondeat superior*,[205] those efforts fall short; for as we have seen, at bottom that rule was supported by nothing but legal fictions and Shaw's assertions that it made sense. Shorn of the linguistic tinsel Shaw draped upon it, and from the perspective of history, Shaw's fellow servant rule is revealed for what, in practical effect, it turned out to be—a generous gift from the Massachusetts judiciary to commerce and industry, a gift of immunity from liability for vast numbers of employee injury claims.[206]

---

[205] *Farwell*, 45 Mass. at 59.

[206] In looking back at the doctrine of assumption of risk "against the background of one hundred years of master-servant tort doctrine," the U.S. Supreme Court itself has noted that "[a]ssumption of risk is a judicially created rule which was developed in response to the general impulse of common law courts at the beginning of this period to insulate the employer as much as possible from bearing the 'human overhead' which is an inevitable part of the cost—to someone—of the doing of industrialized business. The general purpose behind this development in the common law seems to have been to give maximum freedom to expanding industry." *Tiller v. Atl. Coast Line R.R. Co.*, 318 U.S. 54, 59 (1943).

The Fellow Servant Rule Comes to Maine

Despite the apparent flaws in Shaw's reasoning, the fellow servant rule quickly caught on among other courts, and eventually arrived in Maine when, in 1857, the Maine Court decided *Carle v. Bangor & Piscataquis Canal & Railroad Co.*[207] In that case, Robert Carle, an employee of the defendant railroad company, sued his employer for injuries caused by the negligence of a co-worker. His claim was dismissed by the trial court, which relied on the fellow servant rule. Carle appealed to the Maine Supreme Judicial Court.

Carle's appeal was the first case in which the Maine Court considered the fellow servant rule. Under those circumstances, and considering the far-reaching implications of that rule, it would seem only reasonable for the Court to have examined the purported rationale for that rule and to have taken the opportunity to set forth the reasons why that rule should, or should not, become law in Maine. But the Court evidently was not inclined to analyze the merits of the fellow servant rule. The Court summarily affirmed the dismissal of Carle's claim on the basis of the reasoning in Shaw's opinion for the Massachusetts Court in the *Farwell* case, noting that courts in England and New York had also approved the fellow servant rule.[208]

In thus disposing of Carle's case, the Maine Court made the astonishing statement that employees "are *presumed* to have arranged their compensation with their eyes open, and to have assumed the relation [of employee] with all its ordinary dangers and risks, without any remedy against the corporation for such injuries as may be incident to the service they have engaged to perform." With no discussion of how that "presumption" related to the reality of the employer-employee relationship, the Court then stated that some of

---

[207] 43 Me. 269 (1857).

[208] Several years later, the Maine Court reaffirmed its approval of Shaw's reasoning in *State v. Me. Cent. R.R. Co.*, 60 Me. 490, 493 (1872) (reciting, almost verbatim, Shaw's reasoning regarding the employee's responsibility, as opposed to the company's, for ensuring workplace safety by being "an observer of the conduct" of other workers).

the cases that have addressed the question "*assert* that the ordinary risks and perils assumed [by employees] include those arising from the negligence of other fellow servants." The words, "presumed" and "assert," have been emphasized because those words indicate that the early Maine Court itself may have understood that the fellow servant rule was based on nothing more than presumptions and assertions that were contrived to buttress conclusions that lacked a realistic foundation.

Toward the close of the Maine Court's brief decision in Carle's ill-fated appeal, we come to what, with the benefit of hindsight, seems to be one of the most disappointing statements ever uttered by our Court. Referring to the fellow servant rule, our Court there stated:

> Such a rule is supposed to induce greater caution on the part of servants, and thus to conduce to the general safety, and the public good, and we are satisfied with the reasons, the justice, and the policy upon which it rests.[209]

With those words, and without any explanation of why it was "satisfied with the reasons, the justice, and the policy upon which [the fellow servant rule] rests," our Court adopted a rule of law for the State of Maine, which for many years was to be utilized as a devastatingly effective basis for denying employees and their families compensation for injuries and death resulting from industrial accidents. Through the lens of hindsight, it seems that much anguish might have been avoided if the Court had taken the time to consider more fully the weakness of the rationale for, and the inequitable consequences of, the rule it was adopting.

The fact that the Maine Court did not believe it necessary to explain *why* it was satisfied with "the reasons, the justice, and the policy" of Shaw's *Farwell* opinion suggests that the authority of that Massachusetts decision as a judicial precedent was at least as influential with the Court as the reasoning on which it was based.

---

[209] *Carle,* 43 Me. at 272.

Evidently, the Maine Court was eager to adopt a methodology for dealing with workplace injury claims, and the *Farwell* case conveniently provided a ready-made set of rules designed for that very purpose. In "tempting" circumstances such as that, it seems especially important for a state court to remember that, just as a state legislature could not justify a law it enacts merely on the ground that other state legislatures have enacted similar statutes, a state court should not adopt rules of law merely because other state courts have adopted similar rules. To do so would be nothing less than the abdication of the judicial function vested in that court by the constitution of the state that established it.

The Maine Court, of course, was not required to adopt the assumption of risk and fellow servant rules simply because the Massachusetts Court proclaimed those rules in the *Farwell* case. The "implied contract" that Shaw read into the employer-employee relationship was not the only way in which the mutual rights and duties of those parties could have been defined. For example, instead of adopting Shaw's rules, the Maine Court might have decided that there was no good reason why the general rule of *respondeat superior* should not apply to employee injury claims, just as it applied to injury claims asserted by third parties. Or, for another example, the Court might have concluded that in cases involving employee injury claims, the employer should be held to a heightened standard of care for the safety of employees, as the employer's counterpart to the employee's duty of loyalty to the employer. If one were to imagine terms for an implied contract between employer and employee, there would seem to be no reason why either of those alternatives is inherently any less reasonable than the harsh terms of the imaginary pro-employer employment contract Shaw chose to imply. By adopting Shaw's analysis, without further explanation, we have no way of knowing whether the Maine Court in *Carle* considered either of these alternatives, or others. As a result, the Court's ruling in that case suffers from a taint of arbitrariness that still clings to the decision despite the passing of the years.

As the cases discussed below illustrate, the Court's adoption of the doctrine of assumption of risk, the fellow servant rule, and the doctrine of contributory negligence, in combination, made it extremely difficult for employees to obtain any monetary remedy from their employers for injuries incurred in the workplace.[210]

Angele Podvin's Case[211]

Angele Podvin operated a spinning machine in the Pepperell Manufacturing Company's cotton mill in the city of Biddeford. At the time of her accident, she was fifty-nine years old and had been working with the spinning machine for fifteen years. One of Podvin's duties was to clean up around the machine and remove any fallen bobbins in the vicinity of the machine. As the Court explained, two revolving metal cones connected with shafts ran horizontally under the spindles on the machine. The lower cone was within two inches of the floor. The upper cone was twenty-four and a half inches above and directly over the lower cone. The small end of the upper cone was connected to a shaft by a metal collar held in place by "set-screws" that protruded five-eighths of an inch above the collar. When in operation, that cone revolved at the speed of 280 revolutions per minute.

One day, while Podvin was reaching down between the two revolving cones to pick up a bobbin that had fallen to the floor, her hair became entangled in the set-screws on the upper cone, and in the words of the Court, "her scalp [was] torn from her head." Podvin sued her employer, Pepperell, on the ground that the spinning machine was unsafe and dangerous because of the protruding set-

---

[210] These cases are only a small sample of the numerous workplace injury cases in which the Maine Court set aside verdicts for the plaintiffs. It should be noted, however, that in some cases the Court sided with the injured employee, as, for example, in cases where the injuries resulted from defects in machinery or unsafe working conditions that were known to the employer but not the injured employee. *See, e.g., Frye v. Bath Gas & Elec. Co.*, 94 Me. 17, 46 A. 804 (1900) (unsafe working conditions); *Kolasen v. Great Northern Paper Co.*, 115 Me. 367, 98 A. 1029 (1916) (unsafe machinery). *See generally Buzzell v. Laconia Mfg. Co.*, 48 Me. 113 (1861) (distinguishing claims based on negligence of fellow laborers from claims based on the employer's own negligence).

[211] *Podvin v. Pepperell Mfg. Co.*, 104 Me. 561, 72 A. 618 (1908).

screws. The jury rendered a verdict in her favor. That verdict, however, was set aside by the Court on appeal.

The issue presented on appeal was whether the risk that the plaintiff might be hurt by the revolving set-screws was a risk borne by the employer or a risk assumed by the employee. Podvin maintained that the risk was upon the employer because it failed to have the set-screws countersunk. The Court, however, flatly rejected that contention. The Court concluded that the risk of injury was a risk that was assumed by Podvin because the set-screws were "open to observation." An employee, the Court said, assumes the risk of injury "not only from those features of the machine called to his attention, but also from those open to observation." The Court further limited the scope of the legal duties of employers by establishing the following rule:

> It is not the legal duty of an employer of labor upon machines to provide and use the safest possible, or even the safest, known machines. There must be no weakness, no want of repair, no dangerous feature not visible to an observing operative or made known to him, and such as the employer should have known. If such a machine be provided the employer has done his full legal duty in that respect. He can otherwise use machines of such pattern, detail of construction, and roughness of finish as he prefers, leaving to the operative free choice to operate it or not as he prefers.[212]

The Court concluded its decision in favor of Podvin's employer with the following observation: "The danger to a woman from allowing her hair to become entangled in set-screws revolving as these were is too obvious for comment." One would think that if that danger was that obvious, the Court would have decided the case in Podvin's favor. Particularly where, as was the case here, a safer kind of set-screw was then in common use, one would think that the Court would have decided that the employer had a legal duty to countersink the projecting set-screws so that they could not injure

---

[212] *Id.* at 564, 72 A. at 619.

employees. But the Court evidently did not see it as its job to require employers to take even that small step in the interest of promoting workplace safety. The Court, in addition, seems to have had no understanding or appreciation of how fatigue resulting from over-work, repetitive manual labor, unrelieved attention to detail, and the constant noise generated in a cotton mill, would affect reasonably careful employees.[213]

This and many other similar decisions issued by our Court over a period of many years afforded little incentive for employers to improve the safety of the machinery in and about their workplaces. Even more disturbingly, these decisions resulted in an "Alice in Wonderland" state of affairs in which the more grossly and notor-iously hazardous a machine was, the less likely an employee injured by its operation would be able to establish any claim against his or her employer. As long as the Court could conclude that a dangerous aspect of a machine was "visible," the employer was completely immune from liability.

Lewanna Wiley's Case[214]

On July 17, 1906, Lewanna Wiley, a fifty-five-year-old woman, was employed in a laundry in Sanford. While running a tablecloth

---

[213] *See* Charles Scontras & Yves Frenette, "Control at the Workplace," in *Maine: The Pine Tree State from Prehistory to Present*, ed., Richard W. Judd, Edwin A. Churchill & Joel W. Eastman (Orono: University of Maine Press, 1995), 463 ("Workers labored in multistoried factories that lacked fire escapes, with machines that lacked safeguards, or in rooms where ventilation was so poor that the cry for fresh air could be heard with monotonous regularity. Cotton factories were known for their deafening noise, inadequate lighting, and high summer temperatures. Heat prostration was common. The high humidity necessary to keep the threads pliable often caused bronchitis, and cotton dust choked the lungs. Accidents were common.... Female textile operatives, who customarily exchanged street clothes for lighter garments in the mills, often had to disrobe behind the looms and spinning frames. They were given a storage box near their place of work, but this left their street clothes damp and cold when they donned them again. If workers were fortunate enough to have access to a toilet, it was often uncovered and uncared for.").

[214] *Wiley v. Batchelder*, 105 Me. 536, 75 A. 47 (1909).

through an ironing mangle, Wiley's left hand got caught in the mangle, resulting in the amputation of the first and second fingers. The machine had no guard or protection bar to prevent an employee's fingers from being drawn into it. It was the duty of the employee operating the mangle to keep material smooth by holding it on the feed board leading to the mangle "and in some instances to retain her hold upon the corners of [the material] until it was within an inch of the point of contact with the upper rollers." Despite that dangerous situation, the Court approved the dismissal of Wiley's claim against her employer.

The basis for the Court's rejection of her claim was that the danger of the machine was so manifest and understood by her that she must be deemed to have assumed the risk of the employment to which she thus "understandingly consented." Here, as in Angele Podvin's case, the Court excused the failure of the employer to provide a reasonably safe machine on the ground that the risk of harm was apparent to the employee. By that reasoning, the Court gave lip service to the principle that an employer should provide machinery that is reasonably safe, while at the same time it emasculated that principle by declaring that it could be trumped whenever the part of a machine that presented a risk of danger could be seen by the employee operating it.

Lewanna Wiley's case is also particularly interesting because it shows how the Court attempted to justify its rule that the employee assumes the risk of injury from visible hazards of machinery. The Court emphasized the point that trial judges in Maine and courts in other states had frequently applied that same rule, clearing employers from any responsibility in cases involving injuries resulting from the operation of unguarded or imperfectly guarded laundry mangles. The Court referred to those cases as supporting its decision in Ms. Wiley's case, but in retrospect that seems a blatant misuse of precedent.

As was the case with the set-screws in Angele Podvin's case, one would think that the frequency of injuries and litigation resulting from unguarded laundry mangles would have caused the Court to reassess the wisdom of its rule that in effect granted employers immunity from liability in that category of cases—particularly inasmuch as the Court knew that guard rails that could prevent injuries like those sustained by Wiley were available at that time. But the Court simply did not see this category of cases in that light. Indeed, referring to the operation of an unguarded mangle, the Court simply stated that the work could be "more easily and rapidly done without any guard rail or protecting rod, and that this method of operating it was accordingly preferred by the operatives as well as by the proprietors."[215]

The Court's reliance on decisions of other courts in cases involving unguarded laundry mangles is also disturbing because the hapless circumstances of the injured employees in those cases graphically show how deaf the Court had become to pleas for justice on behalf of injured victims of industrial progress. Again, with the benefit of hindsight, it is hard to see why the Court was not embarrassed by relying on the court decisions it did. Among those decisions, which concerned unguarded laundry mangles, were a Massachusetts Court decision that rejected a claim brought by "a French girl nineteen years of age [whose] hand [was] caught by the revolving rolls of a steam mangle upon which she had been at work for three weeks"; a New York Court decision that rejected a similar claim brought by a girl "between fourteen and fifteen years of age [who] at the time of the injury had worked on the machine about six weeks"; and a Kansas Court of Appeals decision that rejected a similar claim brought by "a girl seventeen years of age [who] had been at work on the unguarded machine for a day and a half when her hand was caught between the cylinders and injured."[216]

It is also interesting to note that in relying on these decisions that involved injuries to minors, the Court seems to have overlooked the point that the assumption of risk doctrine, on which most of these decisions rested, was ultimately based on what Massachusetts Chief

---

[215] *Id.* at 538, 75 A. at 48.

[216] *See id.* at 540-42, 75 A. at 48-49 (citing *Gaudet v. Stansfield*, 182 Mass. 451, 65 N.E. 850 (1903); *Hickey v. Taaffe*, 105 N.Y. 26, 12 N.E. 286 (1887); and *Greef v. Brown*, 7 Kan. App. 394, 51 P. 926 (1898)).

Justice Shaw, in the *Farwell* case, described as an "implied contract," by which each employee assumes risks in the workplace, including the risk of injuries caused by the negligent conduct of co-workers. It is difficult to understand, and the Court never explained, how that implied contract could apply to minors, who were (and are) incapable of entering into binding contracts as a matter of law. The next case illustrates this point.

Julia Cote's Case[217]

This case involved a claim by a fourteen-year-old girl, Julia Cote, whose hand was severed at the wrist by the cutting blades of a planer used for manufacturing wooden skewer sticks. Vacating a jury award in her favor, the Court held that Cote's claim against her employer was barred by her own negligence. In addition, the Court decided that even if it could be said that the accident had been caused by the negligence of Cote's co-worker, one Louis LaPointe, a fifteen-year-old boy who was working on the planer with her, the employer could not be liable for Cote's injury because of the fellow servant rule. In considering the application of the fellow servant rule, the Court never explained how Cote, a minor, who was only thirteen years old when she was hired, could be deemed to have impliedly agreed to assume the risk of being injured by a co-worker's negligence.[218] Nor, interestingly and incidentally, did the Court

---

[217] *Cote v. Jay Mfg. Co.*, 115 Me. 300, 98 A. 817 (1916).

[218] Julia Cote's case was not the only case in which the early Maine Court applied the doctrine of assumption of risk to minors who were not capable of entering into binding contracts as a matter of law. *See also, e.g., Bak v. Lewiston Bleachery & Dye Works*, 112 Me. 270, 91 A. 977 (1914) (seventeen-year-old boy who had lived in this country for only four months, whose hand got caught between two unguarded iron rolls that were part of a starching machine, was deemed to have assumed the risk of injury); *Bessey v. Newichawanick Co.*, 94 Me. 61, 46 A. 806 (1900) (seventeen-year-old boy scalded in dye-room of woolen mill was deemed to have assumed the risk); *Cunningham v. Bath Iron Works*, 92 Me. 501, 43 A. 106 (1899) (seventeen-year-old boy whose arms were mangled in unguarded cog-wheels used in process of cutting iron and steel, resulting in his death, was deemed to have assumed the risk).

consider it relevant that Cote and LaPointe had both been initially employed by Jay Manufacturing when they were under the age of fourteen, in violation of the state's then-applicable child labor law. That statute, the Court asserted, was "not involved here because both the plaintiff and LaPointe had passed their fourteenth birthday when the accident happened, the plaintiff by nine days and LaPointe by more than a year."

We seem here to have reached a point in our ramble through the early years of Maine law where we need to pause and take a rest. The cumulative impact of these cases that involved gruesome accidents is painful and difficult to bear. We long for fresher air. So here, as we take a moment to consider the sorry circumstances of these Maine children who, many years ago, were injured while at work, let us take a moment to reflect on "The Golf Links," a simple verse penned by the American poet, Sarah Norcliffe Cleghorn:[219]

The Golf Links

The golf links lie so near the mill
That almost every day
The laboring children can look out
And see the men at play.

Silas Potter's Case[220]

At issue in this case, which concerned the fellow servant rule, was the legal sufficiency of a complaint filed by the administrator of Mr. Potter's estate against the Maine Central Railroad Company. That complaint alleged that on December 11, 1875, Silas H. Potter was operating a hand-car as a section-man employed by the Maine Central Railroad Company; that as a section-man, Potter was responsible for seeing that the track between Waterville and West

---

[219] Sarah Norcliffe Cleghorn (1876-1959) was active in many reform movements, including women's suffrage and opposition to child labor.

[220] *Blake v. Me. Cent. R.R. Co.*, 70 Me. 60 (1879).

Waterville was in good repair and suitable for the running of trains;
and that without any notice to Potter, who was in the exercise of due
care, the railroad company negligently, recklessly, and willfully
dispatched and operated a locomotive engine and attached car over
the track on which Potter was moving in his hand-car and in the
same direction that he was moving, with the result that the locomotive struck the hand-car "then and there instantly crushing a hole
in the skull of said Potter, and then and there inflicting upon him
mortal and fatal wounds and injuries, whereof the said
Potter...died." The complaint also alleged that the defendant had
been grossly negligent and careless in appointing unsuitable
employees to manage the running of the locomotive that struck
Potter's hand-car.

Although the Court concluded that these allegations were
sufficient to allow the complaint to proceed to a trial, the Court's
decision shows how broadly the Court applied its fellow servant
rule. As we have seen, one purported justification for that rule was
that it promoted safety because it gave employees the incentive to
police the conduct of their fellow employees. In Mr. Potter's case, the
Court applied that rule in circumstances in which that rationale was
plainly inapplicable.

First, the Court noted that the fellow servant rule would bar an
injured employee's claim against an employer even though the
employee who caused the injury was engaged in a different kind of
work and even if that employee was a supervisor with authority to
direct the conduct of the injured employee. The Court thereby
extended the reach of the fellow servant rule to situations far beyond
the category of cases (co-employees, working side by side) on the
basis of which Massachusetts Chief Justice Shaw had originally tried
to justify it.

Silas Potter, a section man, riding in a hand-car, was hardly in a
position to police the conduct of the employees who were responsible for the management of the locomotive that struck and killed
him. Yet, because those employees were deemed to have been
Potter's fellow servants, proof that Potter suffered fatal injuries as the
direct result of the negligence of those employees would not, by

itself, suffice to establish the company's liability even though Potter was not in the slightest degree negligent himself.

As the Court explained, the plaintiff, in addition, would have to prove that the company knew or ought to have known that those responsible for the management of its locomotive were incompetent to perform that job. In that regard, the Court also explained that, although at the time an employer hired an employee, the employer was obliged to ascertain that the employee was of good character and properly qualified, thereafter, "good character and proper qualifications once possessed may be presumed to continue, and the master may rely on that presumption until notice of a change."[221] In short, although the Court did not completely close the door on the plaintiff's claim, the Court's ruling did not leave the plaintiff much daylight.

The Court's expansive application of the fellow servant rule left employees, who were expected to obey their supervisor's orders, in an especially vulnerable position, as shown by the circumstances of Maurice Lawler's case, discussed below.

Maurice Lawler's Case[222]

Maurice Lawler, an employee of the Androscoggin Railroad Company, was permanently disabled when a large bank of stone, gravel, and frozen earth fell on him while he was working to repair a washed-out culvert along the railroad's line in the city of Lewiston on January 3, 1870. Lawler's supervisors were alleged to have known full well the dangers the overhanging embankment posed; yet they nevertheless ordered him to go into the excavation site to work. After the trial court threw out Lawler's complaint against the railroad company, Lawler appealed his case to the Maine Court, which quickly disposed of the matter in the railroad company's favor.

The Court began by stating that the fellow servant rule was by then "well settled" in Maine and "pretty universally recognized" in

---

[221] *Id.* at 60.

[222] *Lawler v. Androscoggin R.R. Co.*, 62 Me. 463 (1873).

most jurisdictions in the United States. It then continued by upholding the broad interpretation of the fellow servant rule—that it
was immaterial whether or not the co-worker was "engaged in a
different department of the same general service or exercising a
higher grade of authority." Under that approach, it made no difference to the Court that the fellow servants in question were
Lawler's supervisors or that they had ordered Lawler to go down
into the excavation site, knowing the perilous situation that existed,
even though Lawler was himself not aware of the danger presented.
Absent a showing that the railroad company had negligently hired
the supervisors, Lawler had no claim for his injuries.

While giving a nod to workplace safety concerns—"When a
master employs a servant on a work of a dangerous character, he is
bound to all reasonable precautions for the safety of his workmen"—
the Court fell back on the principle that "the negligence of a fellow
servant is regarded as an ordinary risk," and affirmed the dismissal
of Lawler's case. Without any consideration of the perspective of the
injured worker, who, according to his complaint, had been ordered
into harm's way by the negligence of his supervisors, the Court
rigidly applied the broad fellow servant rule it had adopted and
thereby prevented Lawler from getting a trial of his case in court.[223]

---

[223] The Court followed this decision in subsequent cases, including one where
Chief Justice Peters summed up the holding as follows: "In [Lawler], the injury
was caused by the plaintiff going into a culvert to repair it, when it was
dangerous to do so, the service being expressly ordered of the injured party by
the road master of the defendant corporation; and it was held that the plaintiff in
that case could not recover." Doughty v. Penobscot Log Driving Co., 76 Me. 143, 148
(1884). The Court also treated supervisors as fellow servants of employees where
it was the negligent act of the supervisor that directly caused the injuries. See,
e.g., Conley v. City of Portland, 78 Me. 217, 3 A. 658 (1886) (employee suffered fatal
injuries when earth fell in on him while constructing a sewer on Adams Street in
the city of Portland on August 31, 1883; case was dismissed and no trial was
allowed even if it could be proved that his injuries were "caused by the
carelessness of the one who had the oversight and direction of the work"). In
1909, the Maine Legislature enacted "An Act relating to the employment of
Labor," which, among other things, addressed the matter of defective machinery
and made employers liable for injuries sustained by their employees as the result

In addition to proving the negligence of the employer and contending with the fellow servant rule and the doctrines of assumption of risk and contributory negligence, injured employees and their families who sought redress from employers in the early years of Maine law had to bear the added burden of proving that neither negligence of the injured employee nor that of a co-employee was to any extent a factor in the injury, regardless of the degree of the employer's negligence.[224] In a word, as the next two cases graphically demonstrate, the road to recovery of damages in workplace injury cases was full of legal obstacles.

Howard Bessey's Case[225]

Howard Bessey was seventeen years old when he fell into a vat of boiling hot dye and was scalded while working in the dye room of a woolen mill in the town of South Berwick. The Maine Court rejected Bessey's claim against his employer. Bessey's claim was based on the contention that his employer had knowingly provided unsafe and defective machinery and appliances and had failed to instruct him in the use and dangers thereof. The Court, however, concluded that the hazards of the job were known to Bessey, and, in the Court's view, that was sufficient basis for rejecting his claim. The Court described in detail the circumstances in the mill's dye-house that resulted in Bessey's scalding:

> The dye-house contained four kettles or vats, each six feet long and five wide, and two feet and seven inches in height above a planking which circled each vat at the floor. The plank, eight or ten inches wide, were laid flatly on the floor and were "beveled off" from the vat. Each vat, having clamps upon it, required the hole in the floor where it was to be set to be a little larger than the vat would be without such

---

of the negligence of employees whose "sole or principal duty was that of superintendence." Me. P.L. 1909, ch. 258.

[224] *See Murinelli v. T. Stuart & Son Co.*, 117 Me. 87, 92, 102 A. 824, 826 (1918).

[225] *Bessey v. Newichawanick Co.*, 94 Me. 61, 46 A. 806 (1900).

attachments, leaving an open space around the vat, and the
plank used to stop up the opening.

There was an open frame, a structure fitted with slats,
designed to be sunk into the vat, upon which wool and
blankets were loaded, sometimes the one and sometimes the
other, and then lowered into the vat to be dyed. The frame
was fitted with a hoisting gear, so that it could be swung over
and then lowered into the vat containing boiling hot dye, and
raised up out of the vat when the process of dyeing became
completed.

In order to raise the frame out of the vat the two men in
attendance had to do some coupling of hooks with rings
connected with the gearing, which necessitated their leaning
over the sides of the vat, while facing each other, to a point
near the centre of the vat; and the plaintiff while performing
his part of such an act, somehow fell into the vat, and before
he could be rescued by his co-worker and another person at
work in the same room, was severely scalded and injured
thereby.[226]

It would be difficult to imagine a more hazardous working environment than this, especially considering that the footing around these
vats containing boiling hot dye was slippery and wet. Yet even these
extreme perils and the horror of this boy's injuries were insufficient
to persuade the Court to reconsider the injustice of its arbitrary rule
that made employees assume all risk of injury from visibly
dangerous machinery and appliances while at work.

On the contrary, with each such case, the Court seems to have
become increasingly firm in its resistance to employee injury claims
and increasingly impatient with claimants who questioned the
Court's rulings in this area of the law. For example, in rejecting
Howard Bessey's claim, the Court also relied on its contributory
negligence rule that required the plaintiff to bear the burden of proving that his own negligence was in no respect a contributing cause of
his injuries. Despite the grossly dangerous work environment with

---

[226] *Id.* at 66, 46 A. at 807.

which Howard Bessey had to contend, and despite the horrific injuries he suffered when he fell into the vat of boiling hot dye, the Court seems to have gone out of its way to add insult to injury by concluding its decision with the humiliating observation that "the case fails to show that the plaintiff's heedlessness was not the great cause of the accident."

Mark Cunningham's Case

The tragic case of *Cunningham v. Bath Iron Works* (1899)[227] involved gruesome injuries that proved fatal to Mark Cunningham, a seventeen–year-old boy who had only recently been hired as a helper at Bath Iron Works. In the course of his employment, on June 6, 1896, Cunningham's arms were drawn into unguarded revolving cog-wheels used in the process of cutting pieces of iron and steel, resulting in his death later that day. A jury returned a verdict in favor of Cunningham's mother, the administrator of his estate. On the employer's appeal, however, the Court vacated that verdict on several grounds, including the grounds that the employer's failure to cover or shield the cog-wheels did not amount to negligence because the cog-wheels were exposed to "plain view"; the employer was not required to warn Cunningham about the danger connected with the revolving cog-wheels because he could see and comprehend the danger himself; Cunningham assumed the risks of his job; and the evidence failed to show, affirmatively, that Cunningham was in the exercise of due care, even though Cunningham died as the result of the accident and was therefore not able to provide any evidence in that regard.

Reading through the long line of cases in which the early Maine Court routinely applied those old common law rules, one listens in vain for even one judicial voice of dissent from the Court's jurisprudence that was then so stacked against injured employees and

---

[227] 92 Me. 501, 43 A. 106 (1899).

their families.[228] The absence of any significant dissent on the Maine Court in its decisions that rejected injury claims brought by employees against their employers is especially notable in view of the fact that a few judges in other states readily perceived and pointed out the injustice of rules, such as the assumption of risk and fellow servant rules, that were for many years consistently and rigorously applied by the Maine Court.

Some Contrary Judicial Views From Other States

For example, in an 1851 Ohio case involving a railroad engineer who was scalded and otherwise seriously injured in a train collision caused by the failure of his fellow employees to notify him of a schedule change, Justice William P. Caldwell of the Ohio Court clearly pointed out the weaknesses of the reasoning that underlay the fellow servant rule.[229] First, he observed that the rationale underlying the general rule of *respondeat superior* is "founded on the principles of justice between man and man," and that, as to that rule, "[t]here must be some good reason for taking any case without its application." Caldwell concluded that court decisions adopting the fellow servant rule were "contrary to the general principles of law and justice" and should therefore not be followed as precedents. Rejecting Massachusetts Chief Justice Shaw's "implied contract" theory, Caldwell stated:

> So far as an implied contract, in reference to the business, will be presumed, it will be on the hypothesis that the business is to be properly managed. [An employee] can not be presumed to have contracted in reference to injuries inflicted on him by negligence—by wrongful acts. An express stipulation would at least be necessary to make it a part of the contract. The employer has paid [the injured employee] no money for the

---

[228] On occasion, a member of the Court would go so far as to say that he "does not concur." *See Murinelli*, 117 Me. at 94, 102 A. at 827 (Hanson, J., dissenting).

[229] *Little Miami R.R. Co. v. Stevens*, 20 Ohio 415 (1851); *see also Chicago, Milwaukee & St. Paul Ry. Co. v. Ross*, 112 U.S. 377 (1884) (discussing cases).

right to break his legs, or, as in this case, to empty on him the contents of a boiler of scalding water.[230]

Caldwell also explained why he believed Shaw's "policy" rationale for the fellow servant rule made no sense:

> It is contended, however, on the part of the company, that public policy forbids the right of a party to bring suit against his employer for an injury by another in the same employ, because it is supposed that it will lead to carelessness on the part of those employed, when they know that they can recover for any damage that they may receive. In answer to this, it may be remarked that it is only where the person has been careful himself, that any right of action accrues in any case. Besides, we do not think it likely that persons would be careless of their lives and persons or property, merely because they might have a right of action to recover for what damage they might prove they had sustained…. We think the policy is clearly on the other side. It is a matter of universal observation that in any extensive business, where many persons are employed, the care and prudence of the employer is the surest guaranty against mismanagement of any kind. The employer would, we think, be much more likely to be careless of the persons of those in his employ, since his own safety is not endangered by any accident, when he would understand that he was not pecuniarily liable for the careless conduct of his agents. Indeed, we think that those who have others in their employ are under peculiar obligations to them to provide for their safety and comfort, and we think they should at least be held legally responsible to them as much as to a stranger.[231]

Only a few years later, two other justices of the Ohio Supreme Court weighed in on the inherent flaws of the fellow servant rule.

---

[230] *Little Miami R.R. Co.*, 20 Ohio at 432-33.

[231] *Id.* at 434.

Justice Rufus P. Ranney quoted at length from a Scottish opinion that
had rejected the rule:

> "I have rarely come upon any principle that seems less
> reconcilable to legal reason. I can conceive some reasonings
> for exempting the employer from liability altogether, but not
> one for exempting him only when those who act for him
> injure one of themselves. It rather seems to me that these are
> the very persons who have the strongest claim upon him for
> reparation, because they incur danger on his account, and
> certainly are not understood, by our law, to come under any
> engagement to take these risks on themselves."[232]

Justice Robert B. Warden took Shaw on directly, echoing Justice
Caldwell's earlier criticism of Shaw's "implied contract" theory:

> The notion of Chief Justice Shaw, that the contract of service
> includes an undertaking by the servant of all risks, whether of
> unavoidable accident or of damages arising from the
> negligence of other servants, is certainly an ingenious
> invention.... But the rate of compensation in dangerous
> employments, and the well known motives of inclination or
> necessity which cause men to undertake them, are against
> such a supposition. No such agreement or understanding is
> ever had, or ought ever to be countenanced by the law. It
> would be so against reason and conscience as to be void.[233]

Similarly, the opinions of justices on the Indiana, Wisconsin,
and Kentucky courts show that the above-mentioned Ohio justices
were not alone in believing that the fellow servant rule was unjust
and not founded upon reasonable justifications. Justice Andrew
Davison of the Indiana Court, in rejecting the idea that the fellow
servant rule could apply where employees worked in completely

---

[232] *Cleveland, Columbus & Cincinnati R.R. Co. v. Keary*, 3 Ohio St. 201, 214-15 (1854)
(quoting Scottish judge Lord Cockburn).

[233] *Id.* at 225.

different departments, also rejected the implied contract theory that was the basis of Shaw's *Farwell* opinion:

> True, there is authority for the position that "when a party contracts to perform services, he takes into account the dangers and perils incident to the employment"; but this can only be intended to mean such "dangers and perils" as necessarily attend the business when conducted with ordinary care and prudence. He can not be presumed to have contracted in reference to injuries inflicted on him by negligence.[234]

Likewise, Justice Byron Paine of the Wisconsin Court, after weighing the cases dealing with the fellow servant rule and the purported justifications advanced for its adoption, upheld the general principle of *respondeat superior* in employee injury cases: "We are satisfied, therefore, that the general principles of the common law sustain this liability [of the employer], and that those cases which have attempted to establish an exception do not rest upon solid ground."[235]

Finally, Judge George Robertson of the Kentucky Court put his disagreement with the majority of American courts concerning the fellow servant rule succinctly enough in 1865: "[T]his anomalous rule, even as sometimes qualified, is, in our opinion, inconsistent with principle, analogy, and public policy, and is unsupported by any good or consistent reason."[236]

Legislative Response

Eventually, in 1915, the Maine Legislature enacted a workers' compensation statute that completely overhauled the system of adjudicating workplace injury claims. For claims by injured employees against their employers, that statute eliminated the three

---

[234] *Fitzpatrick v. New Albany & Salem R.R. Co.*, 7 Ind. 347, 350 (1856).

[235] *Chamberlain v. Milwaukee & Mississippi R.R. Co.*, 11 Wis. 238, 257-58 (1860), *overruled by Moseley v. Chamberlain*, 18 Wis. 700 (1861).

[236] *Louisville & Nashville R.R. Co. v. Collins*, 63 Ky. 114, 117 (1865).

common law defenses—contributory negligence, assumption of risk, and the fellow servant rule—that had long been applied by the Maine Court and relied on by employers in stifling such claims.[237] Under the statute's system of strict liability, an injured worker was required to prove only that his injury had been caused by an accident that arose out of and in the course of his employment.[238] Proof of employer negligence was no longer required. In place of judicial proceedings for recovery of damages, the statute established an administrative system to hear claims, thus eliminating juries from the process. The statute also established monetary caps that limited the amount of compensation injured workers could receive. As the Maine Court would later explain, "The Workers' Compensation Act is premised on the recognition that accidents are inevitable incidents of modern industry and that the burden should not be borne by the employee.... The Act relieves the victims of industrial accidents of the adverse consequences of personal injury and resulting unemployment by shifting the burden from the individual and ultimately to society at large."[239]

Although for the most part the early Maine Court seems to have had little sympathy for the plight of injured workers whose cases came before it, the Maine Legislature, at least by the time of legislative debate leading up to the enactment of Maine's first workers' compensation statute, appears to have been more aware of the harsh realities of life in Maine's industrial workplaces. In 1913, in remarks supporting that legislation, Senate President (later, Governor) Carl E.

---

[237] An Act Relative to Compensation to Employees for Personal Injuries, Me. P.L. 1915, ch. 295. That statute was administered by the Maine Industrial Accident Commission. Prior to the Maine Legislature's enactment of that statute, the U.S. Congress, in 1906, enacted the Federal Employers' Liability Act (FELA) (re-enacted in 1908), which concerned the liability of railroad companies for injuries of their employees. For those cases, the FELA retained the requirement of proof of employer negligence, but abolished the defense of the fellow servant rule, limited (and by subsequent amendment, abolished) the defense of assumption of risk, and substituted comparative negligence for the strict rule of contributory negligence. See Tiller v. Atl. Coast Line R.R. Co., 318 U.S. 54 (1943).

[238] See, e.g., Westman's Case, 118 Me. 133, 106 A. 532 (1919).

[239] Lindsay v. Great Northern Paper Co., 532 A.2d 151, 153 (Me. 1987).

Milliken, of the town of Island Falls in Aroostook County, put a human face on the matter:

> Now I say this bill is the climax of this human welfare program of this Legislature, because, important as the other features of that program are, I believe this to be the most important and to have the most vital effect upon the life, the average life of the average man throughout this State. The heroes of the old days in the advance of civilization were those who went forth to battle, in brilliant uniforms and with flashing banners and the blare of music. The heroes of civilization in these days are those who work, the toilers in the various branches of industry. And as it was true in the old days that the march of civilization was attended with fearful cost and loss of life and limb upon the battlefield, so it is true now that in the natural course of business and industry there is a terrible toll taken every year of human life and of human limb, and a terrible toll is paid in the aggregate of human suffering that is caused by the modern industry that is necessary to the life of us all. Many a poor fellow caught and mangled by whirling shaft or flying belt has looked his last upon this world in the surroundings that have become common to him through his daily toil, surrounded, perhaps, by his rough mates that work by his side, and in addition to the physical anguish of that last hour has had to bear the mental sorrow brought to him by the thought of what was to become of those at home who were dependent upon his daily toil for their daily bread. It is to remedy, so far as legislative action can do it, the necessity for that mental anguish in the case of those stricken down in the progress of modern industry that this bill is introduced here.[240]

Looking back at these developments, it is interesting to speculate on how the course of history would have differed if the Maine Court had initially decided not to adopt Shaw's fellow servant rule and the assumption of risk doctrine of which it was a part. In

---

[240] Remarks of Mr. Milliken of Aroostook, Me. Legis. Rec. 1136 (1913).

that event, employers at the outset would certainly have had to shoulder significantly increased costs in paying employee injury claims. But, correspondingly, workplace safety over time would have been improved as employers took steps to reduce the risks of injury. And the number of workplace injuries would have been reduced because employers would have had more incentive to prevent employee injuries. If the early Maine Court ever weighed these considerations, its reported decisions were silent in that regard. Nor did the Court in its written decisions ever suggest that this was an area of law that in fairness to all concerned called for a legislative solution. Instead of any reasoned analysis of the grounds for, and the economic consequences of, its workplace safety jurisprudence, all the Court left for posterity under that heading is a disappointing record of rulings that rested on nothing more than the fictions that were originally crafted by Massachusetts Chief Justice Shaw in the *Farwell* case.

Regrettably, we must conclude that this chapter in the history of the early development of Maine law stands as an example of how easy it is for a court to take a turn that sets it on a course that with each passing year becomes increasingly established and more difficult for the court to change, while over the same span of time the injustice of that course becomes increasingly apparent.[241]

---

[241] The U.S. Supreme Court has observed that in the nineteenth century English courts had worked themselves into a similar corner: "As English courts lived with the assumption of risk doctrine they discovered that the theory they had created had become morally unacceptable but of such legal force that it could not be repudiated." *Tiller v. Atl. Coast Line R.R. Co.*, 318 U.S. 54, 60 (1943).

WRONGFUL DEATH CLAIMS

Our ramble through the early years of Maine law now takes us through the uneven terrain that marks our Court's first encounters with wrongful death claims. Wrongful death claims can be generally described as claims against a person or corporation for monetary damages for having caused a person's death by intentional, reckless, or negligent conduct. A typical case would be a claim by a widow who lost her husband and sole means of support when her husband was killed as the result of the negligent conduct of another person or corporation.

Initially, following the lead of the Massachusetts Court, the Maine Court decided that wrongful death claims were not allowed by the common law. That decision resulted in the anomaly that a defendant could be held liable for injuring a person, but not for killing a person. To rectify that injustice, the Maine Legislature, in 1891, enacted a statute that allowed wrongful death claims. Thereafter, however, the Court severely limited the scope of that wrongful death statute by deciding that it would apply only to cases in which the deceased died "immediately." That decision resulted in another anomaly: a wrongful death claim could be brought under the statute if the deceased died "immediately," but not if he died a few minutes later. Ultimately, decades later, in 1943, the Legislature amended the statute to correct that injustice.

Before discussing the wrongful death statute and the Court's restrictive interpretation of that statute, it would be appropriate first to look at the way in which the common law rule prohibiting wrongful death actions came to Maine.

Wrongful Death Claims Under the Common Law

The Maine Court first considered the matter of wrongful death claims in the case of *Nickerson v. Harriman* (1854).[242] In that case, a father sued the owner of a ship for damages after the defendant transported his son, who was a minor under the age of twenty-one, out of state without the father's permission in violation of a Maine statute that provided the penalty of a fine for such conduct and also allowed a suit for damages to be brought by the parent. The plaintiff's son died soon after the ship's arrival at its outward-bound port. The trial judge had instructed the jury that the plaintiff's damages could include the value of his son's services up until the time he would have reached the age of twenty-one.

On the ship owner's appeal, the Court found that the judge's jury instructions were defective because they allowed the jury to award damages to the father for the value of his son's services subsequent to his death, that is, for the period between his death and the time he would have reached the age of twenty-one. The Court began by stating that damages for loss of life are not permitted by the common law: "By the common law no value is ever put upon human life, to be recovered by way of damages in an action." For that proposition, the Court cited an 1848 decision of the Massachusetts Court in the case of *Carey v. Berkshire Railroad Co.*[243] and an English case dating from 1808 in which the trial judge had instructed the jury that "in a civil Court, the death of a human being could not be complained of as an injury."[244] The Maine Court then reasoned that "[i]f, when death is the direct and immediate consequence of a wrongful or negligent act, compensation is not recoverable, still less can it be, when at the most, it is but an indirect or remote and uncertain result." In other words, the Court reasoned that if the father could not have recovered damages for the death of his son in the event that his son had been killed by the willful or negligent act of the ship owner, the father certainly should not be

---

[242] 38 Me. 277 (1854).

[243] 55 Mass. (1 Cush.) 475 (1848).

[244] *Baker v. Bolton*, 1 Camp. 493, 170 Eng. Rep. 1033 (1808).

allowed to recover damages for the loss of his son's services after his death where there was no showing that the ship owner was at fault in his son's death. With that analysis, the Court determined that no damages could be awarded to the father for the loss of his son's services resulting from his son's death.

The first Maine case that directly presented the issue of whether wrongful death claims would be allowed in Maine was *Lyons v. Woodward* (1860).[245] Betsey Lyons, the widow of Jeremiah Lyons, sued Jeremiah's employer for damages on account of Jeremiah's death, which had been caused by the explosion of a defective steam boiler in the defendant's mill in Bangor. The boiler allegedly lacked a safety plug that was required by law and that would have permitted the safe escape of steam. Betsey sought damages for loss of support for herself and her children, who had been wholly dependent on Jeremiah. Although to present-day ears the result sounds harsh indeed, the Maine Court summarily rejected Betsey's claim on the ground that wrongful death actions were not allowed by the common law. As the Court stated, "At common law, no cause of action accrues to the plaintiff to recover damages for the injury set forth in her declaration." The Court rested its decision to that effect on its 1854 decision in the *Nickerson* case and the same Massachusetts case, *Carey v. Berkshire Railroad Co.*, to which it had referred in *Nickerson*.

In adopting the rule that wrongful death claims were not permitted by the common law, neither the Maine Court nor the Massachusetts Court explained how that rule could be justified as a matter of common sense, reason, or justice. As the U.S. Supreme Court in more recent years has observed, American courts that adopted that rule from England "failed to produce any satisfactory justification for applying the rule in this country."[246] That failing is all

---

[245] 49 Me. 29 (1860).

[246] *Moragne v. States Marine Lines, Inc.*, 398 U.S. 375, 385 (1970). As the Supreme Court noted in this case, the rule prohibiting wrongful death actions was probably originally based on the ancient English "felony-merger" rule, which originated in feudal times and which never applied in America at all. Under that antiquated English rule, a civil action could not be brought in a case in which death was wrongfully caused because any property of the offender that might have been

the more striking because on its face that rule seems so absurd. Indeed, it is difficult to imagine a more irrational rule of law than one that would provide a remedy in damages in cases of injury, but not in cases of death. Commenting on the injustice of that result, the U.S. Supreme Court has said:

> One would expect, upon an inquiry into the sources of the common-law rule, to find a clear and compelling justification for what seems a striking departure from the result dictated by elementary principles in the law of remedies. Where existing law imposes a primary duty, violations of which are compensable if they cause injury, nothing in ordinary notions of justice suggests that a violation should be nonactionable simply because it was serious enough to cause death. On the contrary, that rule has been criticized ever since its inception, and described in such terms as "barbarous."[247]

Although the Maine Court left us no reasoned analysis for its decision in *Lyons v. Woodward* to adopt the common law rule prohibiting wrongful death claims, the Court probably believed that its reliance on the precedent of the Massachusetts Court's decision in *Carey* was sufficient justification for its decision to reject Betsey Lyons' claim. In addition, the Court may well have believed that the Legislature, rather than the Court, was the body best suited to determine the circumstances under which wrongful death claims might be

---

available for the benefit of the heirs of the deceased would revert to the Crown as the result of the offender's crime. In *Moragne*, the Supreme Court also noted that some early American courts, including, notably, federal courts in admiralty cases, took issue with the common law rule prohibiting wrongful death claims. Interestingly, one such court was the U.S. District Court for the District of Maine. *See Plummer v. Webb*, 19 F. Cas. 894 (D. Me. 1825) (No. 11,234) (Ware, J.) (noting that "[i]t is not easily perceived upon what principles of natural right" that rule can be justified); *see also Cutting v. Seabury*, 6 F. Cas. 1083 (D. Mass. 1860) (No. 3,521) (Sprague, J.) ("I cannot consider it as settled, that no action can be maintained for the death of a human being."). The court's decision in *Cutting* contains a particularly good discussion of the issue.

[247] *Moragne*, 398 U.S. at 381.

allowed in Maine.[248] In that regard, the Court knew that the English Parliament had enacted a wrongful death statute in 1846.[249] And the Court no doubt also knew that in 1848 the Maine Legislature had enacted a limited wrongful death statute that applied to railroad and steamship companies.[250]

On the basis of these considerations, we can speculate that the Maine Court probably felt it had ample justification for deciding not to allow wrongful death claims in Maine. Nevertheless, the Court's categorical rejection of Betsey Lyons' claim, summarily and without any reasoned explanation, is still troubling. Inasmuch as that case was the first Maine case that definitively established that wrongful death claims were not allowed by the common law, it would seem that the public was entitled to some rational justification for that ruling. Had the Court become so remote and aloof from the cares of ordinary citizens that it felt no need to explain its decisions to them? And wasn't Betsey Lyons at least entitled to a reasoned explanation as to why she and her children should be left to fend for themselves while her late husband's employer escaped without any liability? Couldn't the Court have provided her something more in the way of explanation than the following cold and formal rescript with which it rejected her claim?

> At common law, no cause of action accrues to the plaintiff to recover damages for the injury set forth in her declaration. On this point, the decisions in [*Carey*] and [*Nickerson*], and authorities there cited, are conclusive.[251]

---

[248] We know that the Massachusetts Court felt that way. In *Carey*, the Massachusetts Court said that "[i]f such a law [allowing wrongful death claims] would be expedient for us, it is for the legislature to make it." *Carey*, 55 Mass. at 480.

[249] The Court specifically mentioned that statute, commonly known as "Lord Campbell's Act," in its decision in *Nickerson v. Harriman*, 38 Me. 277 (1854).

[250] *See* Me. P.L. 1848, ch. 70, § 2.

[251] *Lyons*, 49 Me. at 29-30.

In contrast with the Maine Court's formalistic disposition of Betsey Lyons' claim, courts today would generally be much more likely to explain the rationale for their decisions, especially in cases involving important issues they have not previously decided. The media and the public expect courts to give reasons for their decisions, and, in turn, courts seem to have become more conscious of their responsibility to explain the reasons for their decisions, even though such explanation may not be, strictly speaking, required. In several respects, this has been a positive development: it forces courts to focus on the reasons that justify their decisions; it makes courts more aware of the practical effects of their decisions on the lives of individual citizens in all walks of life; and it avoids the perception of arbitrariness that results when decisions are handed down without explanation. At the same time, however, this increased sense of responsibility to the public, if taken too far, could result in the courts becoming so responsive to the public that their independence from public opinion could be compromised. Suffice it to say that the Maine Court, in the manner in which it disposed of Betsey Lyons' claim, was not at risk of crossing that line.

Maine's Wrongful Death Legislation and the Court's Response Thereto

As we have seen, the Maine Court's decision that wrongful death claims were not permitted by the common law resulted in the anomaly that a wrongdoer could be liable for damages for injuring a person, but not for killing a person. To correct the injustice of that result, the Maine Legislature, in 1891, enacted a general wrongful death statute that applied "whenever" the death of a person was caused by "wrongful act, neglect or default."[252] Under that statute, the deceased's personal representative (executor or administrator) could bring a civil action (wrongful death claim) against the wrong-doer, and the jury could award damages, not to exceed $5,000, to

---

[252] An Act to give a right of action for injuries causing Death, Me. P.L. 1891, ch. 124.

compensate the widow and children for their loss of financial support resulting from the death of the deceased.[253] This progressive development, however, was soon significantly thwarted by the Maine Court.

In a remarkable exercise of judicial "law making," the Maine Court, in *Sawyer v. Perry* (1895),[254] decided that Maine's wrongful death statute would apply only to cases in which the injured person died "immediately."[255] The Court read that limitation into the statute despite the broad language of the statute and even though the statute contained no terms suggesting that it should be limited that way. Applying that test in *Sawyer v. Perry*, the Court rejected a widow's claim for damages under the wrongful death statute because her husband had lived for "about an hour" after his injury, and therefore he had not died "immediately."

The Court attempted to justify its restrictive reading of the wrongful death statute by suggesting that the Legislature could not have intended "to duplicate the wrong-doer's liability, and subject him to two actions for a single injury." One of the two actions the Court had in mind was an action by the deceased's personal representative to recover damages for the pain and suffering endured by the deceased between the time of his injury and the time of his ensuing death.[256] The other action the Court had in mind was an action by the personal

---

[253] The statute was amended in 1929 by adding "widowers" to the persons for whose benefit wrongful death actions could be brought. Me. P.L. 1929, ch.1.

[254] 88 Me. 42, 33 A. 660 (1895).

[255] The Court had similarly construed an earlier wrongful death statute that applied to deaths caused by the negligence of railroad corporations. *See State v. Me. Cent. R.R. Co.,* 60 Me. 490 (1872) and *State v. Grand Trunk Ry.,* 61 Me. 114 (1873). In *State v. Me. Cent. R.R. Co.,* 90 Me. 267, 38 A. 158 (1897), the Court held that the passage of the 1891 wrongful death statute abrogated and superseded that earlier wrongful death statute.

[256] Under Maine's "survival statute," personal injury suits that the deceased might have brought while alive were deemed to survive his death and, thereafter, could be prosecuted by his personal representative. *See Hooper v. Gorham,* 45 Me. 209 (1858); *see also Anderson v. Wetter,* 103 Me. 257, 267, 69 A. 105, 109 (1907) (noting personal representative's "right of action to recover for conscious suffering up to the time of death").

representative to recover damages under the wrongful death statute for a widow's loss of financial support. The Court was determined to prevent both of those claims from being prosecuted in connection with a single death.

To achieve that result, the Court limited the application of the wrongful death statute to cases where death occurred "immediately."[257] In those cases, a claim could be brought against the wrong-doer under the wrongful death statute. On the other hand, in cases where death did not occur immediately, no such action could be brought, but the deceased's personal representative could sue the wrongdoer for damages for the deceased's pain and suffering between the time of injury and the time of death.

Beyond its concern that the wrongful death statute not be permitted to "duplicate the wrong-doer's liability, and subject him to two actions for a single injury," the Court never explained why, as a matter of reason and logic, the availability of a claim for damages for the deceased's pain and suffering should preclude a claim for damages for a widow's loss of support. The Court may have been concerned that, as a practical matter, juries might award excessive damages if both claims were allowed, but it is difficult to see how that worry would justify disallowing an entire category of legitimate claims under the wrongful death statute.

Moreover, with the benefit of hindsight, we can see that the Court's restrictive interpretation of the wrongful death statute was flawed from the outset. The premise on which that interpretation was based—that otherwise, there could be "two actions for a single injury"—mischaracterized the situation. The enactment of the wrongful death statute did not present the prospect of there being two actions for a *single injury*. Rather, the enactment of that statute simply presented the prospect of there being two actions for *two separate injuries*—the pain and suffering sustained by the deceased, and the

---

[257] In a subsequent case, the Court defined "immediately" as including cases where the deceased was rendered totally unconscious from the moment of the accident and continuing until death. *Perkins v. Oxford Paper Co.*, 104 Me. 109, 71 A. 476 (1908).

loss of support sustained by his widow—in the case of a *single death*. And, as a conceptual matter, no duplication of damages could result by allowing prosecution of both of those claims because damages for the deceased's pain and suffering prior to death are separate and distinct from damages for a widow's loss of support as the result of the deceased's death.[258]

In addition, the unfairness of the Court's restrictive reading of the wrongful death statute was readily apparent. If the deceased maintained consciousness for only a matter of minutes after an accident, the surviving spouse and children would have no remedy at all for damages for loss of support under the wrongful death statute. As we have seen, in *Sawyer v. Perry*, a death that occurred "about an hour" after an injury did not meet the Court's test of immediacy. And in another case, *Conley v. Portland Gas Light Co.* (1902),[259] the

---

[258] In a case decided by the U.S. Court of Appeals for the First Circuit in 1940, the court made that very point. *Farrington v. Stoddard*, 115 F.2d 96, 101 (1st Cir. 1940). There, in deciding that a judgment against the defendant in a suit under Maine's wrongful death statute did not preclude a subsequent suit against the defendant to recover damages for property damage and medical expenses incurred by the deceased prior to his death, the court stated: "No duplication of damages results, because under the survival statute recovery is limited to damages for conscious pain and suffering and for pecuniary losses cast upon the victim prior to his death; whereas under the death statute damages not to exceed $10,000 [the then statutory maximum] are assessed with reference to pecuniary injuries resulting from such death to the persons for whose benefit the action is brought."

Interestingly, the prevailing party in the *Farrington* case, the plaintiff-appellant, was represented by a young attorney, the late Sidney W. Wernick of Portland, Maine, who eventually served as a Justice on the Maine Supreme Judicial Court (1970-1981). Wernick's advocacy in that case, and the scholarly articles he wrote at that time, urging legislative reform of Maine's wrongful death jurisprudence, *see* Sidney W. Wernick, "The Maine Law of Wrongful Death, Parts I and II," 5 *Peabody Law Review* 57 (1940), 5 *Peabody Law Review* 73 (1941), are a reminder of the importance of the role of lawyers in the administration of justice. As we shall see, legislative reform of Maine's wrongful death jurisprudence finally came to pass in 1943. However, had Wernick not taken the *Farrington* case to the First Circuit Court of Appeals, and had he not written those articles, who knows how many more years might have elapsed before the "immediate death" limitation of Maine's wrongful death statute would have been changed.

[259] 96 Me. 281, 52 A. 656 (1902).

Court dismissed a suit, brought for the benefit of the deceased's widow and children under the wrongful death statute, on the ground that death was not "immediate" because the deceased survived a gas explosion for a period of twenty minutes before he died.

In trying to understand the outlook of the Court in these cases, it is interesting to note that, throughout its analysis of the wrongful death statute, the Court looked at the statute exclusively through the eyes of defendants and potential defendants in wrongful death litigation. The Court never considered the statute from the perspective of the deceased's widow and children who, as the result of a wrong-doer's conduct, may have lost their sole means of financial support with the death of a husband and father. Had the Court looked at the statute through their eyes, the illogic and unfairness of limiting the statute to cases where death was immediate would have been difficult to ignore, and the Court in all likelihood would never have engrafted its "immediate death" limitation onto the statute in the first place. In addition, the Court might have suggested a judicial procedure that would have allowed a widow, as the administrator or executor of her husband's estate, to combine in a single proceeding her claim for her husband's pain and suffering and her claim for her loss of financial support, instead of having to bear the cost and inconvenience of prosecuting two separate claims in two separate proceedings.

But the Court never looked at the situation from the widow's viewpoint. Instead of suggesting a way in which the widow might be allowed to pursue both claims, and do so in a single proceeding, the Court solved the "problem" of the widow having two separate reme-dies for two separate injuries by simply eliminating one of those remedies.

That state of affairs continued until 1943, when the Legislature amended the wrongful death statute to allow wrongful death claims to be combined in a single proceeding with claims for damages for the deceased's pain and suffering, when death did not occur immediately.[260] As a practical matter, that legislation largely nullified

---

[260] An Act Relating to Conscious Suffering Preceding Death, Me. P.L. 1943, ch. 346.

the Court's "immediate death" limitation of the wrongful death statute, which, with the acquiescence of the Legislature, had persisted as a barrier to economic justice for surviving spouses and children for many years.

In retrospect, the Court's restrictive interpretation of Maine's wrongful death legislation late in the nineteenth century shows how far the Court at that time was willing to go in order to accommodate the interests of potential defendants in wrongful death litigation. Among the most prominent of those potential defendants, in view of the dangerous nature of their operations and their perceived ability to pay monetary damages, were railroad and industrial corporations, enterprises that were extremely important for the development of Maine's economy.

MAINE'S MORALITY LAWS

Maine's early "morality laws" were significant features of Maine's legal world in the nineteenth century. Those laws included prohibitions on wagering (betting) and doing business on Sunday. Our Court's experience with these prohibitions is a good example of the point that declaring certain activities illegal is one thing, but developing equitable and commonsensical rules for the enforcement of such commands is a different matter altogether. As the cases discussed below illustrate, in supporting these laws, our Court, ironically, sometimes found itself in the awkward position of issuing rulings that were difficult to reconcile with elementary principles of fairness and justice. Before turning to the matter of wagering, we will first take a look at the consequences of the way the Court treated transactions that had taken place on Sunday in violation of Maine's early "Lord's Day" statute.

Maine's Lord's Day Law

When Maine became a separate state in 1820, Maine inherited a Lord's Day statute from Massachusetts. Among other things, that law prohibited the doing of "any manner of labour, business, or work" on the Lord's Day, "works of necessity and charity only excepted."[261] The statute provided fines as a penalty for violation of its terms. The question of the effect of that law on transactions that took place on Sunday came before the Maine Court in a number of cases, three of which are mentioned here.

---

[261] *See* An Act Providing for the due observation of the Lord's day, Me. P.L. 1821, ch. 9, § 2.

The first of these cases, *Towle v. Larrabee* (1847),[262] involved the sale of a horse that took place on Sunday. The plaintiff, Mr. Towle, was the administrator of the seller's estate. Towle claimed that the buyer, Mr. Larrabee, owed the seller's estate fifty dollars on a promissory note that Larrabee had delivered to the seller in exchange for the seller's delivery of the horse to him. Towle's claim was based on the straightforward proposition that he was entitled to payment of the promissory note because Larrabee had possession of the horse but had not paid for it. In response, Larrabee contended that his promissory note was void and unenforceable because it had been signed and delivered on the Lord's Day.

In an opinion authored by Justice Ether Shepley, the Court first decided that the sale of the horse was prohibited by the broad scope of the "any manner of business" language of the Lord's Day statute. The sale was therefore illegal. The Court then dismissed Towle's claim, explaining that a court will not assist a party in enforcing a contract made in violation of the law. In prose that combined legal analysis with preaching, the Court explained its decision as follows:

> If the language of the [Lord's Day statute] be permitted to have a literal and fair exposition, it cannot be denied, that the transaction, upon which this action is founded, was a violation of law. And the law will not assist a party to enforce a contract made in violation of its provisions. There can be no excuse for any attempt to destroy, by a forced construction of the language, the effect of an enactment so suited to enable man to derive the benefit designed to be bestowed upon him by Providence, in the consecration of the Lord's day to the duty of doing good and of seeking endless happiness, in accordance with the precepts of the gospel of our Lord Jesus Christ.[263]

The Court evidently believed that the harsh result of its decision, from the seller's perspective, would be a deterrent to others

---

[262] 26 Me. 464 (1847).

[263] *Id.* at 469.

who might otherwise be inclined to do business on Sunday. But what the Court did not mention is that as the result of its refusal to assist the plaintiff, the buyer was allowed to keep the horse without having to pay for it. In effect, the Court applied the Lord's Day statute in a way that allowed Larrabee to "steal" the seller's horse.

Equally harsh, this time from the point of view of the purchaser of a horse, was the Court's decision in *Plaisted v. Palmer* (1874).[264] Mr. Plaisted bought a horse from Mr. Palmer on Sunday. Claiming that Palmer had unlawfully deceived him in that transaction, Plaisted sued Palmer in an attempt to rescind the deal and recover the purchase price. Consistent with its earlier decision in *Towle v. Larrabee*, however, the Court dismissed Plaisted's suit on the ground that the transaction had taken place on Sunday in violation of the Lord's Day statute. As the result of that ruling, Palmer was allowed to keep the proceeds of the sale and simply walk away from Plaisted's allegations that he was guilty of unlawful deceit.

Two years later, a similar situation came before the Maine Court in *Meader v. White* (1876).[265] This case involved a loan that Mr. Meader had made on Sunday to his brother-in-law, Mr. White. When White failed to repay the loan as agreed, Meader sued White for the amount of the loan. Not surprisingly, in view of its decisions in the *Towle* and *Plaisted* cases discussed above, the Maine Court dismissed Meader's claim on the ground that White's debt to him was unenforceable because it arose out of a transaction that had taken place on Sunday. By that ruling, the Court in effect rewarded the borrower's illegal activity (doing business on Sunday) with a judicial grant of immunity from the lender's claim.

By 1876, when the Maine Court decided *Meader v. White*, the third case in the trio of cases discussed above, it had become apparent to the Court itself that its hands-off approach to claims based on transactions that had taken place on Sunday had resulted in some "unfortunate" consequences. Speaking for the Court in *Meader*, Chief Justice Appleton stated that it is "an unfortunate condition of

---

[264] 63 Me. 576 (1874).

[265] 66 Me. 90 (1876).

the law when the violator of its commands is rewarded by it for such violation."[266] Appleton might well have added that it is an *especially* unfortunate condition of the law when, as between two parties to a transaction in violation of the Lord's Day statute, the one who is rewarded by the law for that violation—for example, the purchaser in *Towle*, the seller in *Plaisted*, the borrower in *Meader*—is not the innocent one, but the party who allegedly wronged the innocent one by cheating him or taking his property without paying for it. Yet even though the Court recognized that by its own unyielding jurisprudence it had boxed itself into a position that was difficult to justify, the Court offered no solution to remedy the situation.

Four years later, however, in 1880, the Legislature stepped in and enacted legislation to prevent the unjust consequences of the Court's Sunday-transaction decisions.[267] By that legislation, a party seeking to be relieved of liability on a contract on the basis that the contract had been entered into on Sunday would first have to return any cash or other consideration he received in the transaction. That legislation put an end to the rather obvious injustice of allowing a defendant to defeat a claim against him on the ground that it arose from an unlawful transaction, while at the same time he was holding onto benefits he had received in the transaction. In time, the Court itself acknowledged that this legislative reform was an improvement

---

[266] *Id.* at 92. Later, the Court would acknowledge this point even more directly, stating that the Lord's Day law "was found, in practice, to work a fraud, by allowing one party to a Sunday contract to retain his fruit of the transaction and to give the other party none...." *Bridges v. Bridges*, 93 Me. 557, 562, 45 A. 827, 828 (1900).

[267] An act in relation to Defenses in Actions involving Contracts made on Sunday, Me. P.L. 1880, ch. 194. In 1895, the Legislature also enacted a statute that provided that the Lord's Day statute shall not bar "any action for a tort or injury suffered on [Sunday]." An Act relating to actions for torts or injuries suffered on the Lord's day, Me. P.L. 1895, ch. 129. That statute was enacted in response to decisions of the Court to the effect that, for example, a person injured as the result of a defective carriage that had been rented by that person from the owner of the carriage on Sunday would not be allowed to sue the owner for damages for those injuries because the rental violated the Lord's Day statute. *See Bridges*, 93 Me. at 562-63, 45 A. at 828 (discussing these legislative reforms).

on its jurisprudence, describing that reform as "a wholesome doctrine, that will not allow a desecration of the Lord's Day to become a
cheat."[268]

We are left to speculate as to why the Court seems to have been
unwilling to initiate that improvement itself. It is not as though no
one had ever thought of a better way to deal with Sunday transactions. Indeed, as early as 1847, Justice Isaac F. Redfield of the
Vermont Supreme Court had clearly explained the illogic of a court's
trying to enforce the Lord's Day law through a hands-off approach
that would allow one of the parties to a transaction that took place on
Sunday to use that statute to cheat the other.[269] As Redfield there
stated:

> And it seems to the court, that, in the class of contracts now
> under consideration, there is a most urgent necessity so to
> administer this rule in regard to them, that it shall not be in
> the power of the reckless and irreligious to circumvent and
> defraud the unwary, under the guise of the sacredness of the
> time when their own injustice was perpetrated. We have little
> doubt such practices have already been attempted in some
> cases, and that it might become a not infrequent resort of
> those who desired to effectually cut off all remedy for their
> own fraud and dishonesty. If the general rule of holding
> contracts, made upon Sunday, void, is, also, to shield the
> contracting parties from the consequences of their frauds, and
> to allow the dishonest and abandoned to retain whatever they
> may be able to get possession of under such contracts, and at
> the same time release them from all liability upon their own
> contracts, then the rule itself will be productive of infinite
> mischief, and should be discarded at once.[270]

Consistent with that reasoning, the Vermont Court in that case
approved a procedure whereby the plaintiff, who had been cheated

---

[268] *Bridges*, 93 Me. at 562, 45 A. at 828.

[269] *Adams v. Gay*, 19 Vt. 358 (1847).

[270] *Id.* at 369.

by the defendant in a trade of horses that had taken place on Sunday, was allowed (having tendered the return of the horse he had received in that trade) to recover from the defendant the value of the horse he had traded to the defendant. In effect, the Vermont Court allowed the plaintiff to rescind, or undo, the trade, despite the fact that it had taken place on Sunday.

The Maine Court never discussed the merits of the Vermont Court's more flexible—and more equitable—approach to dealing with transactions that took place on Sunday. We know that the Maine Court was aware of Redfield's decision in *Adams v. Gay* because the Maine Court referred to that Vermont case in its 1874 decision in *Plaisted v. Palmer*, discussed above.[271] But the Maine Court mentioned that Vermont precedent there only to dismiss it because there were more precedents to the contrary from courts in other states. As the Maine Court put it, that Vermont case "may be regarded as almost a single authority the other way," as if that were sufficient reason to reject that precedent, without further ado.

The Maine Court's summary rejection of Redfield's decision in *Adams v. Gay*, and its unwillingness to discuss the matter further, could be read as indicating that the Court by that time had become so attached to the judicial doctrine of *stare decisis* that it was unwilling to reconsider its previous decisions in any respect, even when the deficiencies of those rulings had become glaringly apparent. Yet it seems at least as likely that the Court at that time continued to believe sincerely that its approach to the problem of Sunday contracts—by categorically depriving parties of the ability to enforce or seek relief from such contracts—would ultimately prove to be the most effective way to discourage such transactions and to uphold the values for which the Lord's Day statute stood.

From the vantage point of the present day, in which Sunday in America has lost much of its religious significance,[272] it is difficult to

---

[271] In *Plaisted v. Palmer*, the Court mistakenly referred to *Adams v. Gay*, 19 Vt. 358 (1847), as *Adams v. Dunklee*, 19 Vt. 382. *See Plaisted*, 63 Me. at 576.

[272] The U.S. Supreme Court itself has upheld the constitutionality of state Sunday-closing laws on the ground that, although they were undeniably

appreciate the strength of religious influences that affected judicial thinking in Maine on the topic of Sunday transactions during the last half of the nineteenth century. But the fact that the Court remained resolute in its hands-off approach to the problem of Sunday contracts, despite what it called the "unfortunate" consequences of that approach, suggests that those influences at that time must still have been very powerful indeed.

Illegal Wagers

Just as the Court placed a high priority on preserving the values of the Lord's Day statute, it also placed a high priority on doing what it could to prevent the evil of betting. In the present day and age, when gambling has become a significant national pastime and the State itself has for years been a major player in the business of gambling, it is not easy to imagine a time when betting of any kind was illegal in Maine. Yet that was the situation in the nineteenth century. In its first case involving the matter of betting, *Lewis v. Littlefield* (1839),[273] the Maine Court flatly declared that "all wagers" in Maine were "unlawful." In so ruling, the Court, as a matter of the common law of Maine, greatly expanded the scope of the then-existing statutory prohibition on betting, which was essentially limited to betting for money on the "side or hands of any person gaming."[274]

In two respects, *Lewis v Littlefield* is a particularly significant case in the early development of Maine law. First, it shows how a court's determination to prevent what it considers to be an evil can be so strong that common sense and simple justice get lost in the process. Second, the majority and dissenting opinions of the Court provide a classic illustration of two very different approaches to defining the scope and boundaries of legal rules.

---

religious in origin, they now serve the secular purpose of providing a day of rest disassociated from the everyday intensity of commercial activities. *See McGowan v. Maryland*, 366 U.S. 420 (1961).

[273] 15 Me. 233 (1839).

[274] *See* An Act to prevent Gaming for Money or other Property, Me. P.L. 1821, ch. 18, *amended by* Me. P.L. 1836, ch. 221.

The case of *Lewis v. Littlefield* concerned a bet between Mr. Lewis and another runner as to which of them would win a foot race to be run from the city of Saco to the city of Portland, Maine, a distance of approximately fifteen miles. Mr. Lewis and the other runner each deposited a sum of money with a stakeholder, one Charles Littlefield, who, it was agreed, would pay the stakes to the winner of the race. Complicating this arrangement was the fact that Littlefield was under the age of twenty-one and hence a minor in the eyes of the common law.[275] As events would unfold, Littlefield would rue the day he ever agreed to be the stakeholder in this arrangement.

After the race, Lewis, who lost, demanded that Littlefield return the money Lewis had deposited with him and not pay that money over to the winner. In accordance with the original understanding, however, Littlefield paid the money over to the winner. After Littlefield had done so, Lewis sued Littlefield to recover the sum of money he had deposited with him. Surprisingly, Lewis managed to win at trial in his case against Littlefield. On appeal, the Maine Court, also surprisingly, affirmed that judgment.

The three most important issues in this litigation were, first, whether the bet in question was unlawful; second, whether under any circumstances, and particularly the circumstances of this case, the losing party to a bet should be allowed to recover from the stakeholder the amount of money he had deposited with him; and third, whether the fact that the stakeholder was a minor should make any difference in the outcome.[276]

In an opinion written by Justice Ether Shepley, the Court summarily disposed of the first issue by declaring, as we have noted, that all bets were unlawful in Maine. Shepley quickly passed over the

---

[275] The common law uses the terms "minors," "infants," and "juveniles" interchangeably.

[276] The complexity of these issues in combination would make this case a law school professor's dream, one that would only be enhanced if the race or the bet had taken place on Sunday in violation of Maine's Lord's Day statute. We should perhaps be grateful that we need not concern ourselves with that additional complexity here. The Court's report of the case contains no mention of Sunday at all.

second issue, apparently because the stakeholder's attorney did not press the point. In a later case, the Court would explain that the reason for allowing the losing party to an illegal bet to recover from the stakeholder the amount the loser deposited with him before it was paid over to the winner was "to arrest the illegal proceeding, before it is consummated."[277]

Turning to the third issue presented by Littlefield's appeal—whether Littlefield's legal status as a minor protected him from liability in this case—Shepley immediately became bogged down in an abstract discussion of the essential nature of Lewis's claim. As Shepley saw it, the question of the essential nature of Lewis's claim was important because the common law protected minors from liability on contracts to which they were a party, but not from liability for wrongful acts (torts) that did not involve the breach of a contract.

Against that background, to avoid the shield of protection the law provided to minors in contract cases, Lewis tried to paint his claim against Littlefield as a tort claim, a claim for the "conversion" (meaning, "wrongful taking") of property. Littlefield, on the other hand, tried to paint Lewis's claim against him as a claim that arose out of a contractual relationship.

After citing a number of cases from other jurisdictions, none of which were directly on point, the Court decided to accept Lewis's "wrongful taking" description of his claim and dismissed Littlefield's appeal—even though Littlefield had "taken" nothing, and even though it seems more than a stretch to call Littlefield's payment to the winner, pursuant to the terms of the parties' agreement, "wrongful." Under these circumstances, it seems likely that the Court's disdain for the evil of betting and for anyone who would enable the

---

[277] *Stacy v. Foss*, 19 Me. 335 (1841). The Court there noted that, in contrast, once a stakeholder has paid the money over to the winner, the loser cannot recover from the winner because in the eyes of the law the loser and the winner are equally guilty of illegal conduct (betting), and in that situation the law will assist neither of them.

"consummation" of an illegal bet, played a significant role in the Court's ultimate disposition of this case.

When I first came across Shepley's opinion in this case, while I was leafing through reports of old Maine cases, the outcome of the case struck me as so unfair that I was surprised there was no dissenting opinion. Of the three parties concerned—Lewis, who lost the race; the other runner, who won the race; and Littlefield, the stakeholder, who was a minor and whose only "wrong" was paying the stakes to the winner, as originally agreed by all concerned—the moral and legal position of the loser of the race clearly seemed the least compelling of all. Yet, strangely, the loser of the race, who tried to back out of the deal after the race had been run, ended up the winner in court.

Because the outcome of *Lewis v. Littlefield* seemed so unjust, it came as a gratifying surprise to find a dissenting opinion, authored by Justice Nicholas Emery, in a volume of the Court's reported decisions published a year after the publication of Shepley's opinion.[278] Dissents are almost always reported simultaneously with majority opinions, but, as the Reporter of Decisions explained in a note accompanying Emery's dissent, Shepley's opinion had been issued at a time when Emery was not present, having then been engaged in holding the Court in another county.[279] It is regrettable that this happened because, as this case so clearly shows, the quality of a court's work product may well fall short unless the views of every member are taken into account.

Fortunately, Emery was so disturbed by the unfairness of Shepley's opinion that he took the time to compose what is one of the most compelling dissenting opinions in Maine's legal history. Getting directly to the unfairness of the Court's faulting the minor stakeholder, Emery began:

---

[278] *See* Emery's dissenting opinion at 17 Me. 40 (1840).

[279] The Reporter's note also explains that "when the case was published, the Reporter had not known, or did not recollect, that the opinion had not the assent of all the Court." *See* 17 Me. at 40.

> The very general instruction [to the jury at the trial of this case] that infancy is no bar to the maintenance of this suit, seems to me to draw with it consequences calculated to take from infants the protection which ought to be thrown around them. It is the case of a minor stakeholder, appointed by two persons of full age, of the sums of money, by those two persons placed in the hands of the infant, to be paid to the winner, in a foot race. Did not this necessarily include and raise a promise on the minor's part to pay over those sums to the winner? And was it not received by the minor under the faith and expectation that these depositors mutually promised and engaged to him that he should so act? And he paid it over agreeably to the original stipulation of the parties.[280]

Invoking the power of simple justice, Emery went on:

> Can justice be promoted by permitting the party who has led the infant into the predicament of a depository in a gambling transaction, to turn round, and by changing *the form of the action* [by describing his claim as a tort claim instead of a contract claim] hold the infant responsible for a mistake of judgment as to his own liability to hand over the property on a contingency which happened in exact conformity to the first direction of the plaintiff?[281]

In several respects, Emery's approach to deciding this case was markedly different from Shepley's. For Shepley, the case was simple: all bets are illegal because we say so, and the fact that Littlefield was a minor was immaterial because Lewis did not charge him with breach of contract. End of case. In contrast with the exceedingly narrow focus of Shepley's opinion, Emery's dissenting opinion opened the windows of a musty courthouse and let the refreshing breezes of justice in. Unlike Shepley's abstract and formalistic opinion, which was limited to an almost metaphysical attempt to divine the essential

---

[280] *Id.* at 40-41.

[281] *Id.* at 41.

nature of Lewis's claim, Emery's dissent conscientiously weighed the merits of the parties' competing contentions on the scales of justice.

Emery also looked at the case through the lens of the purpose behind the common law rule that protects minors from liability. For Shepley, the purpose of that rule was immaterial; all that was necessary in order to decide whether Littlefield was protected by that rule was to look at the characteristics of contract claims on the one hand and tort claims on the other and then decide whether the characteristics of Lewis's claim had more in common with the one or the other. If more in common with contract claims, Littlefield wins. If more in common with tort claims, Lewis prevails.

In contrast, Emery adopted an altogether different approach, an approach that was both more practical and more "modern." Instead of trying to answer the question of the applicability of the common law rule protecting minors by conducting a laboratory-like examin-ation of the essential nature of Lewis's claim, as Shepley endeavored to do, Emery looked first at the purpose of that rule. Noting that the purpose of that rule was to protect minors and save them from the consequences of their "rashness and folly," Emery concluded that the impossible situation in which Littlefield had been placed by Lewis and the other party to the bet—where he was damned if he paid the one or the other—was plainly a situation in which, as a minor, Littlefield deserved the protection that the common law allowed for minors. As Emery put it,

> This present [case] seems to me precisely the case, in which it is *the duty of the Court to apply the protection to the infant, and save him from the consequences of his rashness and folly in yielding to the solicitations of older men to become their stakeholder; and not permit the form of action to bring him into trouble for a mistake as to his rights, duties, and seeming liabilities.*[282]

As we conclude our digression through the tangle of Maine's early morality laws, we might take a moment to note that the

----

[282] *Id.* at 42.

difficulties our Court encountered in dealing with these laws many years ago continue to have much of importance to teach today. The unjust result of the case of *Lewis v. Littlefield* and the "unfortunate" consequences of the Court's early approach to the problem of Sunday contracts continue to serve as helpful reminders of the dangers of an ideologically-driven jurisprudence that allows one consideration of many—the sanctity of this or the evil of that—to so dominate a court's judgment that those considerations blot out even more compelling considerations of justice and equity.

ENSURING PUBLIC SAFETY

Many decisions issued by our Court in its early years reflect the importance the Court placed on ensuring public safety and discouraging acts of violence and other uncivil behavior. From one perspective, it is hardly remarkable that a court would support the cause of public safety. Isn't that what courts are expected to do? But these decisions are more significant than one might at first think. The larger significance of these decisions becomes clear when they are considered in light of the fundamental purposes of government. Those purposes, as described in the Preamble to Maine's Constitution, are "to establish justice, insure tranquility, provide for our mutual defense, promote our common welfare, and secure to ourselves and our posterity the blessings of liberty."[283] By any definition, those terms plainly include "ensuring public safety." The promotion of public safety is, therefore, not only a matter of judicial philosophy; it is also a constitutional foundation stone.

In deciding cases that came before it over the years, the Court adopted a number of principles and rules to protect the public from harm and to promote civil behavior on the part of the citizenry at

---

[283] The full text of the Preamble, as originally adopted, provided: "We the people of Maine, in order to establish justice, insure tranquility, provide for our mutual defence, promote our common welfare, and secure to ourselves and our posterity the blessings of liberty, acknowledging with grateful hearts the goodness of the Sovereign Ruler of the Universe in affording us an opportunity, so favorable to the design; and, imploring His aid and direction in its accomplishment, do agree to form ourselves into a free and independent State, by the style and title of the State of Maine, and do ordain and establish the following Constitution for the government of the same." In 1988 the Preamble was amended by changing "His" to "God's."

large. Some of those early cases and the principles for which they stand are noted here.

"Salus Populi Suprema Lex"

The importance of ensuring the safety and well-being of every member of the community is summed up in the ancient Latin maxim, *salus populi suprema lex* (the safety of the people is the supreme law).[284] In a constitutional republic such as ours, this maxim must of course be considered in the context of constitutional provisions that limit the authority of government and that consequently limit the scope of this maxim itself. Yet this maxim is often relevant in the adjudication of controversies involving personal rights that are protected by the Constitution. The Maine Court's decision in *Seavey v. Preble* (1874)[285] illustrates that point.

In *Seavey*, the owner of a house in which smallpox patients had been confined sued the city physician for damages for having advised and directed the removal of wallpaper from the walls of that house. The city physician had taken that action because of the risk that otherwise the smallpox might have spread. Medical opinion was divided on the question of the necessity for taking that precaution. The owner of the house obtained a favorable jury verdict against the city physician. On appeal, however, the Maine Court set that verdict aside on the basis of the maxim, *salus populi suprema lex*.

Writing for the Court, Justice Charles W. Walton noted, first, that the applicable statute required that "all possible care" be taken to prevent the spread of smallpox. He then explained that the law demands "the utmost vigilance" to prevent the spread of smallpox or other contagious diseases, and that to accomplish that end, rights of individual citizens may sometimes have to give way to the

---

[284] The significance of this maxim has long been recognized in the Western world. In his *Second Treatise of Government*, originally published in 1690, John Locke made the observation that "Salus populi suprema lex, is certainly so just and fundamental a rule, that he who sincerely follows it, cannot dangerously err." John Locke, *Second Treatise of Government* (1690), § 158.

[285] 64 Me. 120 (1874).

paramount interest in ensuring public safety. Citing the maxim, *salus populi suprema lex*, Walton put it this way:

> To accomplish this object persons may be seized and restrained of their liberty or ordered to leave the state; private houses may be converted into hospitals and made subject to hospital regulations; buildings may be broken open and infected articles seized and destroyed, and many other things done which under ordinary circumstances would be considered a gross outrage upon the rights of persons and property. This is allowed upon the same principle that houses are allowed to be torn down to stop a conflagration. *Salus populi suprema lex*—the safety of the people is the supreme law—is the governing principle in such cases.[286]

Walton then elaborated on the rationale for this maxim, using additional examples to help explain the range of circumstances in which it might properly be employed:

> Where the public health and human life are concerned the law requires the highest degree of care. It will not allow of experiments to see if a less degree of care will not answer. The keeper of a furious dog or a mad bull is not allowed to let them go at large to see whether they will bite or gore the neighbor's children. Nor is the dealer in nitro-glycerine allowed in the presence of his customers to see how hard a kick a can of it will bear without exploding. Nor is the dealer in gunpowder allowed to see how near his magazine may be located to a blacksmith's forge without being blown up. Nor is one using a steam engine to see how much steam he can possibly put on without bursting the boiler. No more are those in charge of small-pox patients allowed to experiment to see how little cleansing will answer; how much paper spit upon and bedaubed with small-pox virus, it will do to leave upon the walls of the rooms where the patients have been confined. The law will not tolerate such experiments. It demands the exercise of all possible care. In all cases of doubt the safest course should

---

[286] *Id.* at 121.

be pursued remembering that it is infinitely better to do too
much than run the risk of doing too little.[287]

Noting that the smallpox seemed to have been "unusually
prevalent," and that the safety of the city depended largely upon the
efforts of the city physician, the Court concluded that, despite the fact
that medical opinion was divided on the question, the city physician
was justified in advising the removal of wallpaper, and "the law
protected him in so doing." In effect, in reaching that conclusion, the
Court used the maxim, *salus populi suprema lex*, as a tie-breaker to
resolve the conflicting opinions of the medical community.

Punitive Damages Allowed

In *Pike v. Dilling* (1861),[288] Freeman Pike sued John Dilling for
damages for having assaulted and maimed him by biting off part of
his nose. At the trial of the case, the judge instructed the jury that if it
were to conclude that Dilling had committed the act wantonly, it could
award Pike punitive damages in addition to actual damages "as a
protection to the plaintiff, and as a salutary example to others, to deter
them from offending in like cases."[289] After deliberations, the jury
came back with a verdict in favor of the victim, Pike, in the amount of
$151.25. Dilling decided to appeal.

In his appeal, Dilling argued that the trial judge erred in
instructing the jury that it could award punitive damages. Dilling
took the position that punitive damages should never be allowed.
He challenged the whole idea of punitive damages. In support of
that position, Dilling contended that an award of actual damages

---

[287] *Id*. at 121-22. It is interesting to note that the Court, which here spoke so
earnestly about the "safety of the people" being the "supreme law," did not
extend that principle to cases involving employees who were injured as the
result of hazards of the workplace. See the chapter entitled "Employee Injuries."
Evidently, the Court regarded the workplace as a world that was separate unto
itself.

[288] 48 Me. 539 (1861).

[289] Punitive damages are also known as "exemplary damages" or "vindictive
damages."

provided an injured party adequate redress; that allowing punitive damages in civil actions, as a penalty in addition to fines that may be imposed in criminal cases, could result in an offender being twice punished for a single offense; and that allowing juries unlimited discretion to set the amount of punitive damages in civil actions would be inconsistent with the more limited authority of juries to set the amount of fines in criminal cases. How, Dilling's attorney asked, could it be considered just to allow a jury to assess, in addition to actual damages, "whatever pecuniary mulct the jury, in their uncontrolled caprice, may see fit to give"?

Dilling's arguments made a strong case against punitive damages, but the Court was not persuaded. It dismissed Dilling's appeal and upheld the trial judge's instructions to the jury. In so ruling, the Court explained that almost every state and federal court that had by then considered the issue had allowed punitive damages in cases of intentional infliction of personal injury in order to set a public example or to punish the assailant. In short, Dilling's appeal ran up against a substantial body of case law that directly contradicted the position he was advocating. And on a practical level, his appeal was less than compelling, given the nature of his offense and the modest sum of damages the jury assessed. Indeed, in rejecting Dilling's appeal, the Court itself indicated that it would not have been unhappy if the jury had awarded Pike a considerably larger amount of damages than it did.

As the Court probably saw it, an assailant who would go to the extreme of biting off part of someone's nose deserved to be taught a lesson that was strong enough to deter him from ever attacking the victim, or, for that matter, anyone else again. The public as well needed to know that the assailant's conduct was beyond unacceptable and would be dealt with harshly by the courts. In addition, the Court may well have felt that considering the particular circumstances of this case, the victim was entitled to exact his "pound of flesh" from his assailant in the form of punitive damages. As to the possibility that in any given case a jury might abuse its discretion by awarding an excessive amount of punitive damages, the Court probably felt that if that were to occur, the Court could correct the situation by vacating the verdict and ordering a new trial.

One member of the Court, Justice Richard D. Rice, filed a dissenting opinion in which he denounced the rule that allowed punitive damages as "unsound and pernicious in principle." But Rice failed to bring any of the other members of the Court over to his side. To them, the predicament of the assailant paled in significance when compared with the plight of the hapless victim. And to those members of the Court, Dilling's arguments opposing punitive damages were plainly outweighed by the necessity of using this case to send an unmistakably clear message that perpetrators of intentionally hurtful conduct should expect to find no safe haven in Maine courts.

Riotous Assault Condemned

The case of *State v. Yeaton* (1865)[290] arose out of a riotous assault that took place in 1864 at the district schoolhouse in Norway village. For some time, the schoolhouse had been used both as a school and as a lyceum for public debates and discussions. As the result of disturbances that had taken place at some of the lyceum meetings, the managers of the lyceum limited admission to lyceum meetings to scholars and ticket holders. The managers designated Joseph Packard and William Frost to act as doorkeepers—a job that would turn out to be a thankless task, at best. As the Court described the ensuing incident, six individuals, who were turned away at the door for not having tickets, "fell upon Packard and Frost and wounded both severely by heavy blows upon the head with slungshots and stones, fracturing the skull of the former."[291]

The assailants were charged and found guilty of unlawful assembly and riotous assault. On appeal, they contended that because they were inhabitants of the school district, the trial judge

---

[290] 53 Me. 125 (1865).

[291] A "slungshot" is defined in *Webster's New Collegiate Dictionary* as "a striking weapon consisting of a small mass of metal or stone fixed on a flexible handle or strap."

erred in refusing to instruct the jury that they had the legal right to enter the lyceum meeting and to use sufficient force to enter the schoolhouse for that purpose. The Court rejected those contentions as being utterly devoid of merit. As the Court explained, one may justify the use of such force as is necessary to "defend the possession of his house, lands or goods, or his person from threatened violence, but it does not follow that he may lead a riot to dispossess those who are peaceably, even if unlawfully, in possession of his tenements or goods under a claim of right." The Court then offered this succinct reminder of the importance of the rule of law:

> The substitution of law for brute force, in the maintenance of the rights of property, is one of the greatest triumphs of civilized society and good government.[292]

Underscoring that point, the Court concluded by leaving no doubt at all about what it thought of the arguments presented by the defendants' attorney in his misguided attempt to justify his clients' behavior:

> The positions assumed by the defendants' counsel in argument are not only plainly in contravention of the first principles of Christian morality, but utterly subversive of law, order and the peace of the community.[293]

It is not unusual for a lawyer to find that his advocacy has failed to carry the day, but it is difficult to imagine a more damning appraisal of counsel's advocacy than this memorable condemnation delivered by our Court in this case in the year 1865.

Assault Not Justified by Provocative Words

In his brilliant Civil War history, *April 1865*, Jay Winik relates that in the days immediately following the assassination of President Abraham Lincoln, "[a]cross the Union, those who professed the

---

[292] *Id.* at 128.

[293] *Id.*

slightest sympathy for the killing of Lincoln put their life in danger—literally."[294] One such incident took place in the town of Newport, Maine, on April 15, 1865, when news of Lincoln's assassination reached that locale. That incident eventually resulted in a decision of the Maine Court in the case of *Prentiss v. Shaw* (1869).[295] In that case, the plaintiff, George Prentiss, sued Elisha Shaw and three other men for damages on the ground that they had assaulted and wrongfully detained him. The defendants claimed that the provost marshal in Bangor had authorized them to arrest Prentiss on account of remarks he had made concerning Lincoln's assassination. The report of the case provides the relevant details, according to the evidence presented.

On the morning of April 15, 1865, George Prentiss was in a blacksmith shop in Newport having his horses shod. Addressing one Gilman, Prentiss said, "He that draweth the sword shall perish by the sword, and their joy shall be turned into mourning." Gilman, alluding to the assassination of Lincoln, replied, "I suppose there are some who are glad of it," to which Prentiss responded, "Yes; I am glad of it; and there are fifty more in town who would say so, if they dared to." Gilman then suggested that Prentiss take back those words, but Prentiss said he would not, whereupon Gilman told Prentiss that he should "report him." Gilman then went to Newport village, some three miles from the blacksmith shop, and told four men there what Prentiss had said about Lincoln's assassination.

About two hours later, those four men, who eventually became the defendants in Prentiss's lawsuit, went to the blacksmith shop, seized Prentiss, forcibly put him in a wagon, took him to Newport village, confined him in a hotel room there, and inflicted injuries upon him, the extent of which was in dispute. After several hours'

---

[294] Jay Winik, *April 1865: The Month That Saved America* (New York: Harper Collins, 2001), 428. As Winik there notes, one of those incidents involved the editor of a newspaper in Maryland who was killed while defending himself from an angry mob upset with his use of "disrespectful language" about Lincoln in his newspaper.

[295] 56 Me. 427 (1869).

confinement in that hotel room, the defendants took Prentiss to a public meeting at the Newport town-house. At that meeting, a moderator was chosen, and it was voted that Prentiss be allowed to be released upon his taking an oath to support the Constitution of the United States. After Prentiss took that oath, he was discharged from custody.[296]

At the conclusion of the trial of Prentiss's lawsuit against the defendants, the trial judge instructed the jury that the defendants had shown no justification for their actions and must be found guilty, so that the only question for the jury to decide was the amount of damages. The judge also instructed the jury that it could not consider the above-quoted provocative remarks that Prentiss had made about Lincoln's assassination in its deliberations regarding Prentiss's actual damages for his personal injuries and wrongful detention—that such damages should be allowed to the full amount proved, without diminution on account of any matters in provocation or extenuation. The judge, however, did allow the jury to consider those remarks in its deliberations regarding punitive damages and damages for intangible indignities suffered by Prentiss. The jury returned a verdict in favor of Prentiss, but only in the amount of $6.46. Disappointed with that award, Prentiss appealed.

On appeal, Prentiss maintained that the trial judge erred by allowing the jury to consider his provocative remarks in connection with any aspect of the jury's deliberations. But the Maine Court disagreed and affirmed the trial judge's instructions, finding them in accord with "common sense and the general principles of the law." Most significantly, however, the Court used this occasion to affirm the principle that words of provocation cannot justify a physical assault. Emphasizing that point, the Court declared that the law "sternly and unwaveringly" holds that words of provocation are "no excuse or justification."[297]

---

[296] In what seems a prime example of understatement, the report of the case, in its summary of the defendants' evidence, notes that "there was great excitement in the public mind upon the receipt of the news of the assassination." *Id.* at 429.

[297] *Id.* at 435.

It is interesting to note that, in one of those curious connections of history, this case—which stands for the proposition that acts of violence cannot be justified by words of provocation—had its origin in words spoken about the assassination of President Lincoln, a deed that was itself an act of violence that may have been at least partially precipitated by what John Wilkes Booth took to be words of provocation.[298]

Uncivil Behavior Discouraged

Two nineteenth century cases that concerned controversies between passengers and employees of common carriers afforded the Court convenient opportunities to teach the lesson that the law does not look favorably on uncivil behavior. In the first case, *Goddard v. Grand Trunk Railway* (1869),[299] Charles Goddard sued the defendant railroad corporation for damages after having been assaulted by a brakeman employed by the defendant while Goddard was traveling as a passenger on one of the defendant's trains. The incident began with the brakeman falsely accusing Goddard of trying to avoid paying for his trip. From there, the brakeman's behavior escalated to the point that he verbally assaulted, threatened, and insulted Goddard by, among other things, threatening to "split his head open and spill his brains right there on the spot." Complicating matters yet further for the defendant was the fact that at the time of the trial, Goddard happened to be a Justice of the Cumberland County Superior Court. The jury found the defendant liable for its brakeman's misconduct and awarded Goddard significant damages, including punitive damages. The defendant appealed.

---

[298] On April 11, 1865, Lincoln delivered what would be his last speech. Referring to the right of African Americans to vote, Lincoln said that he would "prefer that it were now conferred on the very intelligent, and on those who serve our cause as soldiers." One of his listeners, John Wilkes Booth, was heard to mutter, "That means nigger citizenship," and to declare, "That is the last speech he will ever make." Three days later, on the evening of April 14, Booth shot Lincoln at Ford's Theater. *See* Ronald C. White, Jr., *The Eloquent President: A Portrait of Lincoln Through His Words* (New York: Random House, 2005), 306.

[299] 57 Me. 202 (1869).

Two legal issues were presented by the defendant's appeal: first, whether a railroad corporation could be liable to a passenger for the willful misconduct of its employee; and second, if so, whether the corporation could be assessed punitive damages based on such misconduct. The Court answered both questions in the affirmative.

Regarding the issue of liability, the Court explained that a railroad corporation's liability to a passenger for the willful misconduct of its employee was based on its special duty as a common carrier to protect its passengers "from violence and insult, from whatever source arising." As for the issue of punitive damages, the Court disagreed completely with defendant's contention that it should not be liable for such damages because it had not directly or impliedly authorized its brakeman's willful misconduct. The Court found that contention preposterous. As the Court saw it, the willful misconduct of the brakeman was indistinguishable from the willful misconduct of the corporation itself, and it would be "sheer nonsense" to attempt to distinguish between the two. To the further dismay of the defendant railroad corporation, the Court added, "We confess that it seems to us that there is no class of cases where the doctrine of exemplary damages can be more beneficially applied than to railroad corporations in their capacity of common carriers of passengers." Stressing the importance of not allowing corporations to avoid punitive damages in cases where such damages were justified, the Court concluded:

> There is but one vulnerable point about these ideal existences, called corporations; and that is, the pocket of the monied power that is concealed behind them; and if that is reached they will wince. When it is thoroughly understood that it is not profitable to employ careless and indifferent agents, or reckless and insolent servants, better men will take their places, and not before.[300]

---

[300] *Id.* at 224. It is interesting to note that the Court did not apply that reasoning in cases involving workplace injuries. See the chapter entitled "Employee Injuries."

Twenty-six years after its decision in *Goddard*, the Maine Court in 1895 considered its second case involving an altercation between a passenger and an employee of a common carrier in *Robinson v. Rockland, Thomaston & Camden Street Railway* (1895).[301] That case concerned a passenger's claim that he had been wrongfully ejected from one of the defendant's streetcars. The passenger, Clarence Robinson, had been ejected for calling the conductor "a damned liar." Robinson claimed that he was justified in calling the conductor "a damned liar" because the conductor had falsely accused him of swearing. In his suit against the street railway company, the jury awarded Robinson damages. On appeal, however, that verdict was set aside by the Court in an opinion authored by Justice Charles W. Walton, the same Justice who had authored the Court's earlier opinion in the *Goddard* case.

In upholding the authority of the conductor to eject Robinson for his "damned liar" outburst, the Court noted that Robinson's ejection "vindicate[d] the authority of the law, which forbids the use of such language in a street car, or any other public place, where women and children have a right to be." The Court then emphatically rejected Robinson's attempt to justify that outburst. As the Court explained, even if the conductor had falsely accused Robinson of swearing, Robinson's calling the conductor "a damned liar" would not be justified:

> The fact, if it be a fact, that [Robinson] was innocent of the misconduct with which he was at first charged can be no

---

A lengthy dissenting opinion was filed in the *Goddard* case by Justice Rufus P. Tapley, who took issue with the Court's decision on damages. One sentence of that dissenting opinion is particularly memorable for its metaphorical rhetoric. Discussing what he considered to be the danger of a court's changing the law to conform to the court's view of correct public policy, Tapley proclaimed, "Perhaps there has been no one thing that has introduced into the law so much confusion and embarrassment as the engrafting policy of courts; adding here a little and there a little, till the original is covered with these judicial excrescences; and not unfrequently the jewel is lost in its surroundings of dross." *Goddard*, 57 Me. at 246.

[301] 87 Me. 387, 32 A. 994 (1895).

excuse for his subsequent offense. A thief can not excuse his crime by showing that before committing the theft in question he had been falsely accused of a similar offense. No more can a man excuse the use of indecent or profane language in a street railway car by proof that he was first falsely charged with the use of similar language. To be first falsely charged with an offense is not a license to become immediately guilty of a similar offense.[302]

The Court went on to clarify that its decision supporting the conductor in this case was "in harmony with" its earlier decision in favor of the passenger in the *Goddard* case: "Both decisions are in favor of morality and decency." It is also worthy of note that the Court's opinion in the *Robinson* case clearly shows that the Court believed that one of its responsibilities was to teach lessons in civility as occasions for its doing so arose. And the Court hoped that those lessons would reach a larger audience than the parties immediately concerned. As the Court stated:

> In [*Goddard*], the servants of railroads were taught to treat passengers with civility, and in this case, we hope to teach passengers to treat the servants of railroads with civility. To call a streetcar conductor, who, in a crowded car, half filled with ladies, is endeavoring to maintain order and suppress profanity, "a damned liar," is a poor foundation on which to rest a suit for punitive damages.[303]

Equal Protection Secured

The case of *Leavitt v. Dow* (1908)[304] arose out of an assault that took place on a sidewalk in the city of Westbrook, Maine in 1906. Because the assault was marked by an ethnic taunt directed at the victim, this case could be described as an early "civil-rights assault

---

[302] *Id.* at 393-94, 32 A. at 995.

[303] *Id.* at 394-95, 32 A. at 995.

[304] 105 Me. 50, 72 A. 735 (1908).

case." As summarized by the Court, the circumstances were essentially as follows.

On August 16, 1906, Hyman Leavitt was sitting on a box in front of the window at his dry goods store on Main Street in Westbrook when the defendant, Joseph Dow, came along. After making an insulting remark, Dow took off Leavitt's cap, caught hold of his vest, tearing off a button, and gave him two or three slaps on the head. Dow then left, but soon came back. Dow then took hold of Leavitt by his coat and started shaking him, stating, "Now you Jew, you can say to my face what you said behind my back." Dow then struck Leavitt in the face and pulled him off the box on which he had remained sitting. Leavitt then got hold of Dow around his body and pushed him over in front of an adjacent store, during which time Dow struck Leavitt, causing a black eye. As the result of his injuries, Leavitt incurred expenses of $30 and suffered continuing pain, which required the administration of morphine.

In Leavitt's suit against Dow, the jury found in favor of Leavitt, but awarded him only one cent in damages. Leavitt appealed on the ground that the damages awarded were "manifestly and grossly inadequate." In considering Leavitt's appeal, the Court carefully examined the record of the trial and concluded that "it is clearly shown by the whole evidence that two separate unprovoked assaults accompanied by grossly insulting language were publicly made by the defendant upon the plaintiff." In addition to actual damages for his physical injuries, the Court felt that Leavitt was entitled to "damages for injury to his feelings from the humiliation to which he was publicly subjected by the defendant." Noting that the damages awarded were "clearly inadequate," the Court concluded that there had been "an evident failure of justice to the plaintiff" and granted Leavitt a new trial. In taking that action, the Court explained that it was "convinced that the jury were influenced by prejudice or that their verdict was a compromise, which is essentially equivalent to a verdict for the defendant."

Beyond its obvious importance to Leavitt, the Court's decision in this case was extremely significant in a broader sense. In granting Leavitt a new trial, the Court made it clear that it would not allow the administration of justice to be contaminated by prejudice. In addition, by that ruling, the Court gave meaning and substance to the principle that the law aims to protect all citizens from violence, equally, and without discrimination.

Looking back at these various "public safety" cases, we can see that on a case-by-case basis the Court was gradually, but steadily, constructing a framework of legal principles and rules for society that would allow individual citizens to live their lives without undue fear for their personal safety. As we have seen, that framework included the principle, *salus populi suprema lex*; the principle that punitive damages may be allowed in cases of especially egregious behavior; the rule that physical violence cannot be used to dispossess those who are peaceably in possession of property under a claim of right; the rule that words of provocation cannot justify a physical assault; the rule that in appropriate cases, common carriers may be liable to their passengers for punitive damages; the rule that a false accusation cannot justify a breach of the peace; and the principle that the law aims to protect all citizens from violence, equally, and without discrimination. In establishing these rules, the Court was looking out for the safety and well-being of every member of the Maine community.

THE COURT AND THE
PUBLIC SCHOOLS

A lthough for the most part the daily educational activities of
schools were not the concern of the judiciary during Maine's
early years, several issues involving public schools found
their way into the courts in those times. Most of those cases involved
property and financial matters pertaining to the establishment and
management of local school districts.[305] Questions concerning the
legality of various votes and proceedings of school committees and
municipal officers were frequently at the center of those controversies. Occasionally, issues of broader interest came before the
Court. Two such issues were the legality of corporal punishment and
the legality of a school committee's Bible-reading policy.

Corporal Punishment

In the absence of any statute concerning the authority of
teachers to impose corporal punishment on unruly pupils, the Court
itself developed the governing rules. The Court first considered the
legality of corporal punishment in *Stevens v. Fassett* (1847).[306] In that
case, the Court approved jury instructions that upheld the authority
of a teacher to use such physical force as was necessary to remove a
student from a desk and seat that were reserved for the use of the

---

[305] These local school districts were at that time school districts *within*
municipalities, as contrasted with present-day school administrative districts
composed of two or more municipalities. School administrative districts have been
formed pursuant to the Sinclair Act, which was enacted by the Maine Legislature
in 1957. *See* An Act Relating to Educational Aid and Reorganization of School
Administrative Units, Me. P.L. 1957, ch. 364.

[306] 27 Me. 266 (1847).

teacher. In reaching that conclusion, the Court reasoned that since a teacher's use of corporal punishment was a permissible means of securing obedience to reasonable rules and commands, it followed that the teacher's use of force to secure possession of his desk and seat was also permissible.

Regarding corporal punishment, the Court suggested that the authority of teachers to impose that form of punishment derives from the authority of parents to "restrain and coerce obedience" in their children—that in sending their children to school, parents necessarily delegate to teachers that portion of their disciplinary authority as is needed in order to accomplish the purposes of education. Under that analysis, just as parents could "restrain and coerce obedience" in their children when their children were at home, teachers could discipline children while they were at school. As the Court put it,

> Although the town school is instituted by the authority of the statute, the children are to be considered as put in charge of the instructor for the same purpose, and he clothed with the same power, as when he is directly employed by the parents. The power of the parent to restrain and coerce obedience in children, cannot be doubted, and it has seldom or never been denied. The power delegated to the master, by the parent, must be accompanied for the time being, with the same right as incidental, or the object sought must fail of accomplishment.[307]

The Court also noted that the practice in the town schools in Maine had been in accordance with these legal principles "since the first settlement of the country" and that "resort has been had to personal chastisement, where milder means of restraint have been unavailing."[308] In addition, the Court clarified that Maine's student

---

[307] *Id.* at 280.

[308] "Personal chastisement" meant the same thing as corporal punishment. By whatever name, it was not a pleasant experience. In her interesting and extremely valuable *A History of Education in Maine*, Ava Chadbourne notes: "The punishments meted out in these early schools as well as the discipline was usually very severe." Among other examples, Chadbourne records that in one town, "the ferrule and the birch were often made use of and at times with great

expulsion statute, which had been enacted in 1825, did not have the effect of precluding teachers from imposing corporal punishment as a method of student discipline.[309]

Almost forty years later, in *Patterson v. Nutter* (1886),[310] the Court again addressed the topic of corporal punishment. In that case, a fifteen-year-old student who attended a town school in Dexter, Maine, sued his teacher for damages for assault and battery after the teacher used physical force to punish him.[311] The Court's decision does not discuss the facts of the case, but the trial judge's jury instructions shed some light on the circumstances involved.[312] As those instructions indicate, the teacher used physical force to punish the student for what the teacher thought was the student's resistance to authority and inattentiveness to doing classroom work. The student said that the reason he was not doing that work, which

---

severity, whenever the teacher thought it necessary." In another, "the lad who forgot to remove his hat when the master appeared was severely switched." Chadbourne also notes that corporal punishment in some schools continued well into the nineteenth century "with the old time severity"; that "[i]n Buxton, in 1830, flogging was resorted to, a stinging application of the birch, while in Bucksport, in 1860, pupils were often closeted in the cellar, to discipline them for misbehavior." Ava Harriet Chadbourne, *A History of Education in Maine: A Study of a Section of American Educational History* (Lancaster, Pa.: The Science Press Printing Co., 1936), 90-91, 237.

[309] That expulsion statute read as follows: "That the superintending school committees, in the several towns and plantations, are hereby authorized and empowered, for misconduct, to expel from any school, any obstinately disobedient and disorderly scholar, when after a proper investigation of his or her behaviour, they shall judge that the peace and usefulness of the school will thereby be promoted; and shall also have power to restore such scholar, on satisfactory evidence produced to them, of repentance and amendment." An Act in Addition to "An Act to provide for the Education of Youth," Me. P.L. 1825, ch. 311, § 2.

[310] 78 Me. 509, 7 A. 273 (1886).

[311] Because the student was a minor, the suit was instituted by his "next friend," meaning, in this case, his father.

[312] Some of the records of this case, including the trial judge's charge (instructions) to the jury, are on file at the Maine State Archives in Augusta, Maine. Much of the background information discussed in this chapter was derived from that resource.

consisted of writing down certain questions, was that he had lost his pencil.

The teacher and the student presented different versions of the facts. According to the jury instructions, the evidence presented by the teacher and his witnesses showed the following:

> [The teacher] found the boy was inclined to resist authority and he deemed it an occasion for punishment, and he went up to his seat, laid down the book which he had in his hand and cuffed the boy upon the cheek or ear and then struck him with his left hand and attempted to pull him out of his seat, but the boy resisted, clinging hold of the seat with both hands; that he then took hold of him with both hands and took him out into the aisle and afterwards ordered him to sit down and the boy refused at first, and he again put his hands upon his shoulders and he did sit down.

The student's version of these events, as summarized in the jury instructions, was that the teacher "came up the aisle and struck him first with clenched fist and then seized him by the shoulders and jerked him out into the aisle and across onto the bench on the other side, and then pushed him down so his back came against the back of the chair."

After hearing the case, the jury sided with the teacher. The student appealed. In support of the student's appeal, the student's attorney raised two points: he challenged the legality of corporal punishment generally, and he argued that the trial judge's instructions to the jury contained an erroneous definition of "excessive" punishment.

In urging the Court to reconsider the wisdom of allowing corporal punishment, the student's attorney described corporal punishment as "a relic of barbarism" and pointed out that it had been abolished in the army and navy and had been forbidden as a matter of policy by many school boards. Summarizing the position advanced by the student's attorney, the Court said: "He urges that the greater humanity and tenderness of this age should not tolerate it in any schools, and the courts of this day should not recognize it as a proper mode of school punishment." The Court, however, was not inclined in that direction. In the Court's view, the issue of whether the longstanding practice of corporal punishment of students should be prohibited was more properly the province of the Legislature and school committees than the Court. As the Court explained, "Whatever force this argument might have with legislatures or school boards, it should not move the court from the well established doctrine."

After explaining that the fate of corporal punishment was a matter for the Legislature or school committees to decide, the Court turned to the issue of what constitutes "excessive" corporal punishment. Recognizing the need for teachers to have a considerable amount of discretion in determining, on the spot, what constitutes a reasonable punishment, the Court concluded that a teacher should not be held liable for excessive punishment unless the punishment was "clearly excessive, and would be held so in the general judgment of reasonable men."[313] Ultimately, the Court granted the student a new trial because the trial judge had instructed the jury that corporal punishment would not be clearly excessive unless "all hands" would say it was so. As the Court saw it, that was going too far. As the Court noted, the trial judge's instructions "would permit a teacher to proceed in severity of punishment until it became so great as to excite the instant condemnation of all men, the stupid and ignorant as well as the rational and intelligent." The Court believed that its "reasonable man" standard gave teachers sufficient latitude under the circumstances.[314]

---

[313] *Patterson*, 78 Me. at 513 (quoting *Lander v. Seaver*, 32 Vt. 114, 124 (1859)).

[314] The archival records of this case indicate that following a second trial, the student received a jury verdict in his favor, but for only $1.00 in damages.

It is interesting to note that Justice Lucilius A. Emery, who wrote the Court's opinion in the *Patterson* case, had previously served as the trial judge in that same case. At the time when the *Patterson* case was litigated, the Justices of the Maine Court served as trial judges in addition to serving as Justices of the Maine Supreme Judicial Court in its capacity as a court of appeals. The archival records of the case contain a stenographer's transcription of the trial judge's instructions to the jury in the first trial of the case, entitled, "Judge Emery's charge to the Jury." Having found fault with Emery's jury instructions, the Justices, as a courtesy, may have afforded their colleague the opportunity to write the Court's

Although the Court in the *Patterson* case was not persuaded to reverse its support for the principle that corporal punishment is a permissible form of student discipline, it was moved to shore up the foundation on which the disciplinary authority of teachers was based. In place of the theory that teachers derive their disciplinary authority by delegation from parents—as the Court had previously suggested in *Stevens v. Fassett*—the Court in *Patterson* explained that, to fulfill their educational responsibilities, teachers are "necessarily invested" with disciplinary authority in order to carry out their important educational responsibilities. Quite likely, the Court was moved by the advocacy of the student's attorney to abandon the theory of parental delegation of disciplinary powers. One can almost hear the student's attorney asking, "Where in the record does it show that this young man's parents ever delegated authority to anyone to assault and injure him?"

The Court was quite sure of its footing when discussing the abstract subject of the rationale for the disciplinary authority of teachers, but when it came to the facts of the case, the Court seems to have been on much less comfortable ground. From reading the Court's opinion, one would hardly know that the case arose from a real-life scenario in which a child who went off to school one day was physically cuffed and struck by his teacher while the student was seated at his desk in his classroom. The Court's opinion scrupulously avoids mentioning the actual facts and reads like a treatise on an abstract issue of law. Evidently, the Court wanted to keep the messy

---

opinion, explaining the error in those instructions, instead of expressing their disagreement with him more directly. Or, alternatively, Emery was the first to realize that his jury instructions were too open-ended and asked his colleagues to allow him to write the Court's opinion correcting that error.

Although, by legislation enacted in 1852, Justices of the Supreme Judicial Court were prohibited from participating in decisions regarding their own rulings as trial judges (Me. P. L. 1852, ch. 246, § 11), that prohibition was repealed by the Legislature three years later (Me. P. L. 1855, ch. 174, §2), and the Legislature did not restore that prohibition until 1893 (Me. P.L. 1893, ch. 217, § 11), several years after *Patterson* was decided. *See generally* Herbert T. Silsby II, *History of the Maine Superior Court*, 14 Maine Bar Bulletin 109, 140 (1980).

details at a distance and certainly had no interest in mentioning them in its formal opinion. The Court used the term "corporal punishment" interchangeably with its more euphemistic synonym, "personal chastisement," but the Court's opinion provided no definition or examples that would illustrate what the Court really meant by those terms. Not until we read the trial court's jury instructions can we get a sense of the Court's understanding in that regard. In his explanation of the law to the jury, the trial judge stated:

> Again, gentlemen, a teacher has no right in inflicting punishment to employ such means of punishment as would naturally produce, or would be calculated to produce permanent injury. He has a right to inflict some bodily punishment, to produce severe pain, temporary pain; to produce, if you please, swellings. I have gone home many times myself with my hand swollen. The teacher had a right to inflict that punishment, to produce those swellings; but he has no right to inflict punishment which would produce permanent injury. He has no right to strike a scholar upon the head to produce a permanent injury; or to use a cord-wood stick upon a child or to throw him down against a desk, or anything of that kind.

On reading those instructions today, we find it shocking that a judge would speak of the "right" of a teacher to inflict bodily punishment on a student in order to produce "severe pain" and "swellings." The detached, clinical tone of the judge's description of that "right" is equally disturbing from the perspective of the present day. Today, such conduct would more likely be considered child abuse. Indeed, if a domestic animal were treated that way, it would be considered animal cruelty. And we wonder whether the student who was the plaintiff in the *Patterson* case might have suffered from a disability that today would make him eligible for special education services. Yet at the same time it is important to remember that the classroom circumstances involved in the town of Dexter in the 1800s, when the *Patterson* case was decided, were quite different from those one would expect to find in a Maine school today. In his instructions to the jury in *Patterson*, the trial judge described the large size of the plaintiff's class, and the corresponding need for his teacher to have "large power," as follows:

> You see by this necessity of the case a teacher with a large number of scholars, (in this case from fifty to eighty), all young and full of force and vigor, must be clothed with large power. He is to be judge, jury, legislature and sheriff, and in all within a certain measure his power is despotic. He cannot wait, he has to examine and then and there inflict punishment and govern the school according to his best judgment.

A class of that size may not in itself justify corporal punishment, but in such a setting it is certainly predictable, if not inevitable, that circumstances will arise that will severely test the outer limits of any teacher's ability to maintain classroom control. We should also remember that the classroom teacher in days gone by often had to fend for himself or herself without the benefit of on-site administrators and guidance counselors, to say nothing of such modern innovations as school resource officers.

The "relic of barbarism" argument that the student's attorney made to the Court in the *Patterson* case in 1886 ultimately prevailed in the Maine Legislature. In 1975, the Maine Legislature enacted a statute that in effect prohibited corporal punishment in the State of Maine.[315] As the result of that legislation, corporal punishment in Maine's public schools is now but a distant memory, and the Court's old corporal punishment decisions, discussed above, are now themselves relics of the past. That being said, however, it would be a

---

[315] The Maine Criminal Code, which was enacted by the Legislature in 1975 (Me. P.L. 1975, ch. 499), contains a provision that allows a teacher to use a reasonable degree of force against a student who creates a disturbance when and to the extent he or she reasonably believes it necessary to control the disturbing behavior or to remove the student from the scene of the disturbance. *See* 17-A M.R.S.A. §106(2) (2006). Significantly, the accompanying explanatory Comment for § 106 explains that this provision does not grant teachers authority to use force in order to punish students and that this provision therefore represents a change in Maine law.

serious mistake to discount the importance of maintaining order and discipline in our public schools. Corporal punishment, fortunately, is a thing of the past in Maine, but the need for order and discipline in our public schools, so that education can take place, is as important now as ever. Underscoring the necessity of an orderly educational environment in the public schools, our Court, in a decision issued almost a hundred years after its decision in the *Patterson* case, stated that a school board's "most basic obligation is to maintain order in the schools and to create a stable environment for the education of its students."[316]

With the passing of corporal punishment in Maine, the Court's opinion in *Patterson* no longer speaks with any authority on that topic. Nevertheless, that opinion continues to stand as a reminder of the importance, in a free society, of the role of public education in raising citizens who, in the words of the Court, are "moral" and "habituated to self-control." Drawing the connection between the disciplinary authority of teachers on one hand and the continuing viability of our "free political institutions" on the other, the Court set forth the following propositions:

> Free political institutions are possible only where the great body of the people are moral, intelligent, and habituated to self-control, and to obedience to lawful authority. The permanency of such institutions depends largely upon the efficient instruction and training of children in these virtues. It is to secure this permanency that the state provides schools and teachers. School teachers, therefore, have important duties and functions. Much depends upon their ability, skill and faithfulness. They must train, as well as instruct their pupils.... The acquiring of learning is not the only object of our public schools. To become good citizens, children must be taught self-restraint, obedience, and other civic virtues.

---

[316] *Solmitz v. Me. Sch. Admin. Dist. No. 59*, 495 A.2d 812, 818 (Me. 1985).

To accomplish these desirable ends, the master of a school is necessarily invested with much discretionary power.[317]

Entirely apart from anything having to do with corporal punishment, the continuing value of these propositions stands out clearly when we consider the state of our free society today. The free society called the United States can be seen as positioned between the two polar extremes of anarchy and totalitarianism. As our society evolves, it tends from time to time to move in the direction of one or the other of those extremes. Ideally, if it moves too far in one direction, countervailing societal forces return it to its optimal mid-point position. In instilling in citizens the virtues of morality and self-control, public education plays an important role in keeping us from sliding into a state of anarchy. Similarly, at the other end of the spectrum, in teaching citizens the importance of their rights and liberties, public education plays an important role in keeping us from sliding into a state of totalitarianism. Those dual roles of public education are essential to the maintenance of a free society. The propositions propounded by the Court in the *Patterson* case speak movingly to the "morality and self-control" aspect of public education. Understandably, because the issue in *Patterson* was student discipline, those propositions do not address the "rights and liberties" function of public education.

That "rights and liberties" function of public education is, however, addressed in Article VIII, Part First, Section 1 of Maine's Constitution, which provides for governmental support of public schools. The introductory clause of that section reads, "A general diffusion of the advantages of education being essential to the preservation of the rights and liberties of the people; to promote this important object, the Legislature are authorized," etc. The important role of public education in preserving those rights and liberties has perhaps never been better stated than by Maine's Governor Anson P.

---

[317] *Patterson*, 78 Me. at 511, 7 A. at 274.

Morrill, who, in an address he delivered to the Maine Legislature on January 6, 1855, stated:

> The main pillars of our free institutions rest upon the intelligence of the people. The only true ground of hope that this republic will survive the lapse of ages, and be perpetuated from generation to generation, following not in the downward course of those republics which have disappeared from the governments of the earth, is, that knowledge, in this country, is more universally diffused among the people, and that they know their political rights, and knowing, will insist on having those rights as intelligent freemen. Of what avail will it be, ere another century shall have elapsed, that we boast of a constitution surpassing in its provisions and principles, any other law written by man, if the people are not imbued with the spirit of liberty, and enjoy such means of education as shall qualify them to assert their political rights at the polls and in the halls of legislation?
>
> No subject can be urged upon your attention, more important to the vital interests of your constituents and country, than that of education. Educate the people and they become really, what without education they are but nominally, sovereign.[318]

These inspiring sentiments concerning the role of public education in inculcating a spirit of liberty—sentiments that echo the sense of the above-quoted language in Article VIII, Part First, Section 1 of Maine's Constitution—provide an essential counterpoint to the Court's propositions concerning the role of public education in inculcating the virtue of morality and a disposition of self-control, as stated in the *Patterson* case. It seems worthwhile to raise those sentiments and those propositions up from the darkness of history into the light, and dust them off for public viewing once again, for those sentiments and propositions, taken together, still have much of importance to tell us today.

---

[318] Anson P. Morrill, Address to the Senate and House of Representatives (January 6, 1855), set forth at 1855 Me. Laws 273, 276.

Bridget Donahoe and Bible Reading in the Public Schools

Before we take up the *Donahoe* case, it seems appropriate to mention a brief item of personal history. In 1975, I was counsel for the Ellsworth School Committee in a case that had been appealed to the Maine Supreme Judicial Court. As I stood before the Court to begin my explanation of why the lower court judgment should be affirmed, one of the Justices mentioned that this was an historic day for the Court, for reasons, he said, I surely knew. I replied that I regretted that I did not understand this historical reference. The Justice then patiently explained that the occasion was significant from an historic perspective because the last time the Ellsworth School Committee appeared before the Court was in 1854 in the case of *Donahoe v. Richards.* Immediately upon returning to my office, I looked up the Court's decision in that case and read it with interest. I only wish I had previously known of that case. Without doubt, it is one of the most famous decisions of our Court.

At issue in *Donahoe v. Richards*[319] was whether the Ellsworth School Committee acted lawfully in expelling Bridget Donahoe, a fifteen-year-old student, for refusing to read the Protestant (King James) version of the Bible at school. The School Committee had directed that the Protestant version should be used in all the public schools of Ellsworth and that all students should be required to read that version in school. Although Bridget was willing to read the Roman Catholic (Douay) version of the Bible, she refused to read the Protestant version because the church of which she was a member, the Roman Catholic Church, considered it a sin to do so. The Court decided the case in favor of the School Committee. In an opinion written by Justice John Appleton, the Court concluded that under Maine law the School Committee had the authority to expel Bridget and that her expulsion was not unconstitutional. In considering the legal issues presented by the *Donahoe* case, it is helpful first to note the political and social context out of which that case arose.

---

[319] 38 Me. 379 (1854).

The *Donahoe* case arose at a time of great controversy, nationally and in Maine, concerning the required reading of the Protestant version of the Bible in the public schools. The flames of this controversy were fanned by members of the nativist "Know-Nothing" party[320] and their supporters, who were becoming increasingly concerned that "outsiders" (immigrants) were importing Catholicism into "Protestant America." These Know-Nothings saw the Bible controversy as a good recruiting tool for their cause. They were also upset that a recent flood of immigrants into the labor market was putting downward pressure on prevailing wage rates. Spurred by these developments, a fever of anti-Catholicism ran rampant throughout parts of Maine, most notably in the city of Bath and the town of Ellsworth.

On July 6, 1854, the Old South Meetinghouse in Bath, which was being used for Catholic services, was burned to the ground. In Ellsworth, the Bible controversy was at the center of the violence that erupted in that locale. John Bapst, a Catholic priest who resided in Ellsworth in 1853-1854, was outspokenly opposed to the Ellsworth School Committee's Bible policy. In June, 1854, windows were broken at his rectory in Ellsworth, and an attempt was made to blow up his chapel school there. In July, 1854, a second attempt was made to destroy that building. Ellsworth has been described as being in a "state of anarchy" during the fall of that year, with gangs and mobs roaming the streets, "taunting Irish Catholics and daring anyone to stop them."[321]

---

[320] The party's name reflected its secrecy. If asked about the party's agenda or membership, the respondent was supposed to reply by disavowing any knowledge.

[321] James H. Mundy, *Hard Times, Hard Men: Maine and the Irish, 1830-1860* (Scarborough, Me.: Harp Publications, 1990), 158-59. Ultimately, Bapst was the victim of a violent physical assault. Late at night on Saturday, October 14, 1854, a mob of men broke into the house where he was staying in Ellsworth, robbed him, stripped him naked, tarred and feathered him, mounted him on a rail, and carried him to a shipyard where they abandoned him, exposed to the elements. Eventually, Bapst was appointed the first president of Boston College. For more about Bapst and his connection with the Bible controversy in Ellsworth, see *id.* at 156-59, and William Leo Lucey, S.J., *The Catholic Church in Maine* (Francestown, N.H.: Marshall Jones Company, 1957), 118-35. A contemporary account of the

In that highly charged atmosphere, the *Donahoe* case came before the Maine Court in the summer of 1854. The Ellsworth School Committee was represented by two preeminent attorneys, John A. Peters, who would later become the Chief Justice of the Maine Court, and Richard Henry Dana, Jr. of Boston, one of the nation's leading lawyers at that time.[322] The fact that the Ellsworth School Committee retained as nationally prominent an attorney as Dana shows how significant the Committee believed the case to be. Bridget Donahoe and her father were represented by the firm of Rowe & Bartlett of Bangor, which presented a persuasive case on their behalf. Justice Appleton, who wrote the opinion for the Court, and who would later become the Chief Justice of the Court, rounded out the impressive roster of legal talent that assembled when the case was argued before the Maine Court sitting in Bangor on July 22, 1854.[323]

October 14, 1854 assault is contained in the October 27, 1854 edition of *The Liberator*, quoting a contemporary report from the Bangor *Mercury*.

[322] This is the same Richard Henry Dana, Jr. who had previously authored *Two Years Before the Mast*, a classic account of his voyage around Cape Horn and his experiences in California. In 1854, Dana was a very busy attorney, having represented the fugitive slave, Anthony Burns, in his renowned, but ill-fated, attempt to gain his freedom through the courts in Boston in the months immediately preceding the submission of arguments to the Maine Court in the *Donahoe* case. In his *Journal*, Dana referred to the *Donahoe* case as "the Catholic case," and noted that the oral arguments before the Court in Bangor were well attended by "the principal men of Bangor & of women not a few. All speak of my argument in complimentary terms, & it seems to have hit the humor not only of the people, but of the Court." His description of his trip from Boston to Bangor is a reminder of the difficulty of travel in Maine at that time. Dana arrived in Portland at 4:00 a.m. on the morning of Thursday, July 20, 1854, after a nine-hour passage from Boston to Portland on the steamship *Atlantic*. From Portland, he proceeded "by cars" to Waterville, and from there to Bangor by stagecoach. It took ten hours to travel the last fifty miles, "a very hot & dusty day, and the ride disagreeable enough." He spent the next day at the Bangor House preparing his oral argument in support of the Ellsworth School Committee's Bible policy. Oral arguments were presented to the Maine Court by counsel for both parties on Saturday, July 22, 1854. *See The Journal of Richard Henry Dana Jr.*, ed. Robert F. Lucid, vol. 2 (Cambridge: Belknap Press of Harvard University Press, 1968), 648-50.

[323] The process by which the *Donahoe* case reached the Court was essentially as follows. In April, 1854, Laurence Donahoe and his daughter, Bridget (through

In a thorough and carefully crafted opinion for the Court, Justice Appleton first noted that by statute the Legislature had vested school committees with the authority to decide "what books shall be used in the respective schools." That statute, he pointed out, contained no limitation on the authority of a school committee to select books to be used in the schools. Nor did it contain any provision authorizing an appeal from a school committee's book selection decision to the courts. Therefore, Appleton concluded, if a school committee, acting within constitutional limits, selected a book that a citizen found objectionable, the remedy in our system of government was to be attained not through the courts, but through the ballot box, by the election of people to the school committee who share the citizen's views.[324]

---

her father) filed substantially identical suits against two members of the Ellsworth School Committee who had expelled Bridget from school on November 14, 1853. The defendants were a majority of the members of the School Committee. The plaintiffs claimed monetary damages from the defendants for the cost of having to provide for Bridget's private schooling. Instead of proceeding directly to a jury trial, the parties agreed to a procedure proposed by Justice Joshua W. Hathaway whereby, prior to any trial, a statement of the facts of the case, which the plaintiffs' attorney was prepared to prove, would first be referred to the full Court to decide "the question of law lying at the foundation of said suits," i.e., whether, under the Constitution of Maine, a student could be expelled from a public school for refusing to read the Protestant (King James) version of the Bible at school, as required by school committee policy. If that question were decided in favor of the plaintiffs, the case could then go forward for trial, but if that question were decided in favor of the defendants, that would be the end of the case. The full Court ultimately dismissed Laurence Donahoe's suit on the ground that under the common law at that time, a parent could recover damages for an injury to a child only in cases in which the parent had lost the services of the child or had incurred expenses in connection with such loss. *Donahoe v. Richards*, 38 Me. 376 (1854). The Court ultimately dismissed Bridget's suit on the ground that Bridget had been lawfully expelled. *Donahoe v. Richards*, 38 Me. 379 (1854). Accordingly, neither case ever went to trial. *See* Reporter's summary of procedure, *Donahoe*, 38 Me. at 376-77, and Justice Hathaway's order, outlining procedure, as noted above, in case file at Maine State Archives.

[324] *Donahoe*, 38 Me. at 394-97.

Turning to the constitutional issues,[325] Appleton noted that if the beliefs of any particular sect were to be taught in a public school it would "furnish a well grounded cause of complaint on the part of those, who entertained different or opposing religious sentiments." But here, Appleton said, "The Bible was used merely as a book in which instruction in reading was given," and therefore the selection of the Bible to teach reading was constitutionally permissible.[326]

Appleton then addressed Bridget's argument that the School Committee's policy violated the Religious Freedom and Religious Preference Clauses of Article I, Section 3 of Maine's Constitution, which, in relevant part, stated:

> All men have a natural and unalienable right to worship Almighty God according to the dictates of their own consciences, and no one shall be hurt, molested or restrained in his person, liberty or estate for worshipping God in the manner and season most agreeable to the dictates of his own conscience, nor for his religious professions or sentiments, provided he does not disturb the public peace, nor obstruct others in their religious worship;—and all persons demeaning themselves peaceably, as good members of the State, shall be equally under the protection of the laws, and no subordination nor preference of any one sect or denomination to another shall ever be established by law, nor shall any

---

[325] The constitutional issues considered in *Donahoe* concerned Maine's Constitution, not the U.S. Constitution. In *Donahoe*, the Maine Court had no occasion to consider the implications of the Religion Clauses, commonly known as the Establishment Clause and the Free Exercise Clause, of the First Amendment to the U.S. Constitution because that Amendment, by its terms, applies only to Congress ("Congress shall make no law respecting an establishment of religion, or prohibiting the free exercise thereof"). It was not until 1940 that the Supreme Court decided that, by virtue of the Fourteenth Amendment, the Religion Clauses of the First Amendment are also applicable to the states (and, consequently, to subdivisions of the states such as public schools). *Cantwell v. Connecticut*, 310 U.S. 296 (1940).

[326] *Donahoe*, 38 Me. at 398-99.

religious test be required as a qualification for any office or trust, under this State;....[327]

Appleton found no violation of the Religious Freedom Clause ("All men have a natural and unalienable right...their religious worship") because, as he interpreted that provision, its purpose was "to prevent pains and penalties, imprisonment or the deprivation of social or political rights, being imposed as a penalty for religious professions and opinions."[328] With reference to Bridget's contention that the school committee's policy constituted a "preference" in favor of Protestantism in violation of the Religious Preference Clause ("no subordination nor preference of any one sect or denomination to another shall ever be established by law"), Appleton narrowly interpreted that provision as applying only to statutes enacted by the Legislature, as distinguished, for example, from policies enacted by school committees.[329] In any event, as Appleton put it, "all that is shown by the selection of one version is simply a preference of one over the other, when there must from necessity be a difference of opinion."[330] Turning Bridget's argument against her, Appleton also noted that in his view, Bridget herself would be the beneficiary of a "preference"—the right to exempt herself from a "general regulation of the school"—if she were to prevail in this litigation.[331]

---

[327] In 1988, the first clause of this section was amended to make its terms gender neutral.

[328] *Id*. at 403.

[329] *Id*. Referring to that provision, Appleton there stated: "This relates to an Act of the Legislature, which shall establish the preference of one sect and the subordination of others. The selection of a school book is no preference within this clause."

[330] *Id*. at 401. The Court evidently shared the School Committee's preference for the Protestant (King James) version. As Appleton stated, referring to the School Committee's choice, "It is simply the adoption of a particular version of a work, which from the idiomatic English of the translation, and the sublime morality of its teachings, furnishes the best illustration which the language affords of pure English undefiled, and is best fitted to strengthen the morals and promote the virtues which adorn and dignify social life." *Id*. at 401-02.

[331] *Id*. at 406.

In response to Bridget's concern that her Church considered it a sin to read from the Protestant version of the Bible, Appleton replied that if courts were to allow exceptions from school rules on the basis of an individual's religious belief, that would amount to granting individuals the power to overrule the will of the majority. As Appleton explained:

> If one sect may object, the same right must be granted to others. This would give the authorities of any sect the right to annul any regulation of the constituted authorities of the State, as to the course of study and the books to be used. It is placing the legislation of the State, in the matter of education, at once and forever, in subordination to the decrees and the teachings of any and all sects, when their members conscientiously believe such teachings. It at once surrenders the power of the State to a government not emanating from the people, nor recognized by the constitution.[332]

Finding nothing in Maine's Constitution that prevented the School Committee from requiring the reading of the King James version of the Bible as a text for the teaching of reading, the Court dismissed Bridget's claims.

On its face, Appleton's opinion seems quite compelling. On closer examination, however, the reasoning of that opinion is questionable in several respects. To begin with, Appleton's assertion that the Bible was used merely as a reading book and not for religious instruction seems to be based on an artificial premise, namely, that a clear line of demarcation separates the act of reading from the reader's comprehension of the material that is read. Another difficulty with Appleton's assertion that the Bible was not being used for religious instruction is that, if that assertion were true, it would almost amount to ascribing sacrilegious intent to the School Committee. For would it not only be an artificial exercise, but a sacrilegious exercise as well, for a school committee to require that all students read the Bible at school, subject to the provisos that they

---

[332] *Id.* at 407.

read it only for the purpose of linguistics and moral instruction, and, most importantly, that they obtain no religious instruction from such reading?[333] Bridget's attorneys almost "dared" the School Committee to make that argument, presumably because it would make the School Committee's legal position look absurd and less than credible. As they stated:

> Our whole case proceeds upon the ground that the reading of the scriptures was required as a religious exercise. The Bible is the religious book of Christians. If the defendants admit they had no right to use it thus, but contend they had a right to use it for other than these primary purposes, or for the improvement of "style" or the cultivation of the fancy or imagination, then this fact should be set up, and shown in defence, and the jury should be allowed to pass upon the question for what purpose it was used.[334]

Next, Appleton's fear that allowing Bridget to read from the Douay version of the Bible would take the school system down a slippery slope—to the point that it would lose all authority over its curriculum—seems overstated and artificial. In the city of Bangor, about twenty-three miles from Ellsworth, the Bangor School Committee, at the time of the Bible controversy in Ellsworth, permitted Catholic students the option of reading the Douay version of the Bible. Yet it does not appear that the Bangor school system or its student body suffered as a result.[335] In addition, Appleton's slippery-

---

[333] In that regard, the Supreme Court of Illinois has observed, "The Bible is not read in the public schools as mere literature or mere history. It cannot be separated from its character as an inspired book of religion. It is not adapted for use as a text book for the teaching, alone, of reading, of history or of literature, without regard to its religious character. Such use would be inconsistent with its true character and the reverence in which the Scriptures are held and should be held." *People ex rel. Ring v. Bd. of Educ. of Dist. 24*, 245 Ill. 334, 348, 92 N.E. 251, 255 (1910).

[334] *Donahoe*, 38 Me. at 387-88.

[335] *See* Mundy, *Hard Times, Hard Men*, 158, 161 (noting that Bangor accepted the compromise of allowing Catholic children to read out of the Douay version); *see*

slope rationale overlooks the point that books such as the Bible, the Torah, the Koran, and other sacred texts of various religions are, on account of their uniquely religious nature, qualitatively different from other books that may contain religious and moral ideas. Accordingly, constitutional rules applicable to the former category of books need not necessarily apply to the latter.

Appleton's response to Bridget's argument that the School Committee's policy constituted an unconstitutional "preference" in favor of Protestantism seems particularly open to question. As noted above, Maine's Constitution, in relevant part, provides that "all persons demeaning themselves peaceably, as good members of the State, shall be equally under the protection of the laws, and no sub-ordination nor preference of any one sect or denomination to another shall ever be established by law." This provision leaves no doubt about its central meaning. With no less than triple emphasis ("equally under the protection of the laws," "no subordination," "nor preference"), this provision makes it unmistakably clear that government must maintain a stance of neutrality vis-a-vis religious sects and denominations. Indeed, it is difficult to imagine a more emphatic directive to that effect.

Under the School Committee's policy, the right of Catholic students to attend public schools in the town of Ellsworth was in effect conditioned on their submission to the requirement of reading the Protestant version of the Bible at school—even though their religion taught that it was a sin for them to do so.[336] The School

---

also Lucey, *The Catholic Church in Maine,* 124, 128 (noting that the issue had been peaceably settled in Bangor).

[336] From reading the official report of the case, one would not be aware of the overbearing nature of the conduct of the individual defendants in effectuating Bridget's expulsion. As recorded in Justice Hathaway's order referring the case to the full Court, those circumstances, which the plaintiffs' attorney offered to prove at trial, and which constituted the factual record in the case for purposes of deciding the legality of Bridget's expulsion, were as follows: "On said November 14th [1853], [the two defendants] as members of said [Ellsworth School] Committee and for the purpose of enforcing said directive of the Committee *visited Miss Richards' school, took down the names of Bridget and the other children who had thus refused, called them from their seats,* ordered them to leave the

Committee's Bible policy was really a "Protestant-Only Bible Policy." Plainly, was there not a preference here—a preference in favor of Protestantism, the majority religion in the Ellsworth community?

Appleton had considerable difficulty dealing with the preference issue. As noted above, at one point he attempted to avoid that issue altogether by accepting the School Committee's argument that the relevant constitutional provision, "no subordination nor preference of any one sect or denomination to another shall ever be established by law," was a limitation only on the authority of the Legislature and not the School Committee. But as Bridget's attorneys had persuasively argued, that would be to say that "the Legislature can confer upon the school committee a power to legislate which they cannot exercise themselves; that the protestants of the whole State cannot make a law to oppress their catholic fellow citizens, but they can confer power to do so upon the protestants of any village."[337]

At another point, Appleton tried to diminish the significance of the School Committee's preference in favor of the Protestant version of the Bible by describing the differences between that version and the Catholic version as "merely" a difference between two versions of the same book.[338] That, however, did not make the fact of the preference disappear. And the more Appleton tried to minimize the differences between the two versions, the more he left the Court exposed to the telling point made by Bridget's attorneys, who asked:

> But the [defense] counsel contends there is little difference in the two versions…. If the counsel is right as to the difference, why in the name of common sense and Christian charity, did not the Committee allow the child to use her own translation? The moral teaching of each is the same.[339]

---

school, and not to return to it until they would consent to read in said Protestant version, and thus expelled said Bridget from said school…." (emphasis added). The Court's paraphrase of the factual record, at 38 Me. 376-77, does not mention the italicized words.

[337] *Donahoe*, 38 Me. at 388.

[338] *Id.* at 400.

[339] *Id.* at 386.

Appleton was a jurist of such great intelligence and experience in the law that he must have been aware that his treatment of the preference issue was not the most compelling part of his written opinion. Accordingly, it appears that at one point he tried to get beyond that issue by changing the description of the legal issue presented by the case. Unable effectively to avoid the sticking-point that the School Committee's policy was a preference, Appleton shifted his focus and cast the issue before the Court as an attempt by an individual to claim exemption from a school regulation of general application on the basis of that individual's religious beliefs.[340] Appleton was on somewhat surer ground here, but the preference issue still could not be shunted aside. A "neutral" law or governmental policy of general application, such as an income tax statute, may trump a claim to an exemption from its requirements on the basis of one's religious beliefs. But the School Committee's "Protestant-Only Bible Policy" so directly favored Protestantism over Catholicism that it is difficult to see how it could be called "neutral." A school regulation that establishes a sectarian preference does not cease to be preferential simply by calling it a "general regulation of the school" from which a student claims to be "exempted." Moreover, Appleton's suggestion that Bridget was trying to exempt herself from a school regulation of general application overlooked the point that Bridget was not asking to be exempted from reading the Bible. All she was asking for was the right to read the Catholic version as an alternative to the Protestant version.

In considering whether the Maine Court "got it right" in *Donahoe*, it is instructive to compare that decision with decisions of other courts that saw the issues differently. Two such courts were the Supreme Court of Wisconsin and the Supreme Court of Illinois. In *State ex rel. Weiss v. District Board of School District 8 of Edgerton* (1890),[341] the Wisconsin Court decided that a school district's practice of allowing teachers to read the King James version of the Bible to students at school was forbidden by the Wisconsin Constitution,

---

[340] *Id.* at 406.

[341] 76 Wis. 177, 44 N.W. 967 (1890).

which prohibited "sectarian instruction" in the public schools, and by a Wisconsin statute that prohibited textbooks "which will have a tendency to inculcate sectarian ideas." In reaching that conclusion, the Wisconsin Court relied heavily on the historical background of the Wisconsin Constitution:

> The convention [that framed the Wisconsin constitution] assembled at a time when immigration had become very large and was constantly increasing. The immigrants came from nearly all the countries of Europe, but most largely from Germany and Ireland. As a class, they were industrious, intelligent, honest, and thrifty—just the material for the development of a new state. Besides, they brought with them, collectively, much wealth. They were also religious and sectarian. Among them were Catholics, Jews, and adherents of many Protestant sects. These immigrants were cordially welcomed, and it is manifest the convention framed the constitution with reference to attracting them to Wisconsin. Many, perhaps most, of these immigrants came from countries in which a state religion was maintained and enforced, while some of them were non-conformists and had suffered under the disabilities resulting from their rejection of the established religion. What more tempting inducement to cast their lot with us could have been held out to them than the assurance that, in addition to the guaranties of the right of conscience and of worship in their own way, the free district schools in which their children were to be, or might be, educated, were *absolute common ground*, where the pupils were equal, and where sectarian instruction, and with it sectarian intolerance, under which they had smarted in the old country, could never enter?[342]

In marked contrast with the Maine Court's decision in *Donahoe*, the Wisconsin Court had no difficulty seeing that in matters that directly involve religion, it is constitutionally imperative that the public schools be "absolute common ground" and that school committees not be allowed to prefer one sect over another. The

---

[342] *Id.* at 197-98, 44 N.W. at 974 (emphasis added).

Ellsworth School Committee's Bible policy would surely have failed to survive scrutiny under the Wisconsin Court's "absolute common ground" standard.

The constitutional significance of the preference issue in *Donohoe* may be brought into even clearer focus by considering the 1910 decision of the Illinois Supreme Court in *People ex rel. Ring v. Board of Education of District 24.*[343] The Illinois Court there decided that the practice of teachers reading either the Protestant or Catholic version of the Bible to students in the public schools of Illinois amounted to sectarian instruction and as such was prohibited by the Constitution of Illinois. As the Illinois Court succinctly stated:

> The reading of the Bible in school is instruction. Religious instruction is the object of such reading, but whether it is so or not, religious instruction is accomplished by it.[344]

The Illinois Court also emphatically rejected the notion, which had been accepted by the Maine Court in *Donahoe*, that the members of a school committee, having been elected by the majority vote of the community, are constitutionally empowered to require students to read the school committee's preferred version of the Bible in the public schools within their jurisdiction. In an eloquent reminder of the importance of protecting religious minorities from being dominated by religious majorities, the Illinois Court said:

> The importance of men's religious opinions and differences is for their own, and not for a court's, determination. With such differences, whether important or unimportant, courts or governments have no right to interfere. It is not a question to be determined by a court in a country of religious freedom what religion or what sect is right. That is not a judicial question. *All stand equal before the law,*—the Protestant, the Catholic, the Mohammedan, the Jew, the Mormon, the free-thinker, the atheist. Whatever may be the view of the majority of the people, the court has no right, and the majority has no

---

[343] 245 Ill. 334, 92 N.E. 251 (1910).

[344] *Id.* at 346, 92 N.E. at 254.

right, to force that view upon the minority, however small. It is precisely for the protection of the minority that constitutional limitations exist. Majorities need no such protection,—they can take care of themselves.[345]

In today's religiously diverse culture, of course, quite apart from constitutional considerations, any less even-handed vision for our public schools would be entirely unrealistic and unworkable from a practical point of view.[346]

The Maine Court's inability or unwillingness to see that the Ellsworth School Committee's Bible policy amounted to an unconstitutional governmental preference in favor of Protestantism seems today to be the most problematic feature of its decision in *Donahoe*. But considered in historical context, the Court's assessment of that policy is perhaps more understandable. The continuing, strong influence of the Protestant tradition in Maine in the mid-nineteenth century, despite the recent arrival of large numbers of immigrants from Ireland,[347] may to some extent explain why the Maine Court at that time was not more sensitive to the preference issue and other issues of religious conscience raised by Bridget Donahoe and her father.[348] Indeed, the societal shockwaves resulting from the arrival of those immigrants may have reinforced the Court's resolve to preserve the status quo. Perhaps it was the Maine Court's respect for the School Committee as a separate, elected branch of government that

---

[345] *Id.* (emphasis added).

[346] As the U.S. Supreme Court has observed: "Probably no deeper division of our people could proceed from any provocation than from finding it necessary to choose what doctrine and whose program public educational officials shall compel youth to unite in embracing." *W. Va. State Bd. of Educ. v. Barnette*, 319 U.S 624, 641 (1943).

[347] In the concluding paragraph of his opinion in *Donahoe*, Justice Appleton noted that "[l]arge masses of foreign population are among us, weak in the midst of our strength."

[348] The multicultural settlement of Wisconsin by immigrants from many different cultures and religions, as described by the Wisconsin Court in *Weiss*, certainly distinguishes the settlement of that state from the predominately Protestant heritage and early settlement of Maine.

caused the Court to be so deferential to the Committee's authority.[349] Most likely, all of these considerations were to some degree involved in the Maine Court's judgment. And, no doubt, the other members of the Maine Court were genuinely persuaded by the force of Justice Appleton's opinion.

In the end, we are left to speculate as to the underlying reason for the Maine Court's resistance to recognizing that a "Protestant-Only Bible Policy" constituted a governmental preference in favor of Protestantism. Some indication of what that underlying reason might have been is suggested by Appleton's awareness that if the Court were to accept Bridget's middle-ground position—permitting her to read one version of the Bible instead of another—it would follow that the Court would have to prohibit the reading of any version of the Bible in the public schools. As Appleton noted, if on the basis of conscientious religious belief Bridget were to be excused from having to read the Protestant version of the Bible at school, "it is obvious" that the Protestant version would have to be "entirely prohibited" for "it is not easy to perceive why she has not an equally valid ground of objection to hearing [the Protestant version] read"; and "as others may have their own consciences," it would follow, Appleton reasoned, that "no translation of the Bible" could be used as a reading text in the schools.[350] Thus, although Bridget herself was not asking that the School Committee be prohibited from requiring the reading of the Bible at school, that was the ultimate implication of her claim.

The members of the Maine Court who decided the *Donahoe* case were probably not prepared to take that far-reaching step. If the Court was not prepared to ban Bible reading completely, it surely had no interest in accepting a middle-ground position that would

---

[349] In the concluding paragraph of his opinion in *Donahoe*, Appleton urged the School Committee to discharge its duties with "magnanimous liberality and Christian kindness," yet he and his colleagues on the Court could not bring themselves to render a decision that, in effect, would require the School Committee to select some text other than the Bible for teaching reading or else permit Catholic students to read from the Douay version, as requested by Bridget and as was the practice in Bangor.

[350] *See Donahoe*, 38 Me. at 402.

inevitably lead to that result. It therefore appears that the Court's awareness of the far-reaching implications of Bridget's seemingly innocuous claim, coupled with the Court's reluctance directly to ban Bible reading in Maine's schools, may well have been the underlying reason for the Court's resistance to seeing that the School Committee's policy at issue in *Donahoe* constituted an unconstitutional preference in favor of Protestantism. Yet, as noted above, all of this is speculation.

In the final analysis, Appleton's famous opinion in *Donahoe* seems to have been based as much on what Oliver Wendell Holmes, Jr., called "the felt necessities of the time" as it was on articulated rationale. As Holmes has pointed out, "the felt necessities of the time" and other intangible factors have played an important role in the development of the law over the years:

> The life of the law has not been logic: it has been experience. The felt necessities of the time, the prevalent moral and political theories, intuitions of public policy, avowed or unconscious, even the prejudices which judges share with their fellow-men, have had a good deal more to do than the syllogism in determining the rules by which men should be governed.[351]

Ultimately, in 1963, in the case of *School District of Abington Township, Pa. v. Schempp*,[352] the U.S. Supreme Court decided that a public school's practice of having students read passages from the Bible at the beginning of each school day amounted to a religious exercise required by the State and, as such, violated the principle of neutrality that underlies the Establishment Clause of the First Amendment to the U.S. Constitution, even though students were not required to participate. In so ruling, the Court stressed the importance of the principle of governmental neutrality in matters concerning religion:

---

[351] Oliver Wendell Holmes, Jr., *The Common Law*, 1.

[352] 374 U.S. 203 (1963).

> The wholesome "neutrality" of which this Court's cases speak thus stems from a recognition of the teachings of history that powerful sects or groups might bring about a fusion of government and religious functions or a concert or dependency of one upon the other to the end that official support of the State or Federal Government would be placed behind the tenets of one or of all orthodoxies.[353]

At the same time, the Supreme Court made it clear that its decision did not preclude the study of the Bible for its literary and historical qualities, when presented objectively as a part of a secular program of education. The Court also clarified that its ruling did not affect the teaching of comparative religion or the history of religion.[354]

Although *Donahoe* was not explicitly overruled by the Supreme Court in *Schempp*, the Supreme Court's decision in *Schempp*, with its emphasis on governmental neutrality in matters of religion, clearly indicates that a public school's preferential Bible policy such as the "Protestant-Only Bible Policy" that was upheld by the Maine Court in *Donahoe* could not now pass muster under the Establishment Clause of the First Amendment. That final outcome of the *Donahoe* case is a useful, albeit humbling, reminder of the limits of one's ability to foresee the future and the ways in which one's judgment concerning matters of consequence will be judged in the years that lie ahead.

---

[353] *Id.* at 222.

[354] *Id.* at 225.

MAINE'S BLASPHEMY CASE

A lthough my original intent in this ramble through the early years of Maine law was to let the years 1820 and 1920 act as my temporal bookends, the Maine Court's 1921 decision in *State v. Mockus*[355] is so interesting from an historical point of view that the latter end of the shelf would seem incomplete without at least some mention of that case here. First, however, the defendant's previous involvement with the law of blasphemy in other states should be briefly noted.

Before being accused of having committed the crime of blasphemy in Maine, in 1919, Michael X. Mockus of Chicago, Illinois, had been charged with blasphemy in Connecticut and Illinois.[356] His first run-in with prosecutors resulted from statements he made in a series of lectures he gave in 1916 at the invitation of the Lithuanian Freethought Association of Waterbury, Connecticut. Mockus was convicted of blasphemy in the City Court of Waterbury and sentenced to ten days in jail. He appealed to the District Court of Waterbury, but the jury that heard his case there came back

---

[355] 120 Me. 84, 113 A. 39 (1921). The *Mockus* case is the only blasphemy case decided by the Maine Court.

[356] For information concerning Mockus's blasphemy cases in Connecticut and Illinois, as well as Maine, I am indebted to Leonard Levy's excellent book, *Blasphemy*. See Leonard W. Levy, *Blasphemy: Verbal Offense Against the Sacred, From Moses to Salman Rushdie* (New York: Alfred A. Knopf, 1993), 512-15. For information concerning Mockus's Maine case, I would also like to acknowledge the assistance of the Maine State Archives. For more information on Mockus's Connecticut case, see Theodore Schroeder, *Constitutional Free Speech Defined and Defended in an Unfinished Argument in a Case of Blasphemy* (New York: Free Speech League, 1919). Schroeder represented Mockus in that case, and his book contains the constitutional argument he made on Mockus's behalf. As Levy notes, Schroeder was a New York lawyer who founded the Free Speech League, which was a precursor of the American Civil Liberties Union.

deadlocked. Mockus's case was scheduled for retrial, but he failed to appear at his new trial date, as he had left the jurisdiction.

In 1917, Mockus surfaced in Waukegan, Illinois, where he was charged with disorderly conduct and blasphemy after delivering a lecture ridiculing Christianity. A jury acquitted him of the charge of disorderly conduct, and an Illinois county court judge dismissed the blasphemy charge on the grounds that Illinois did not have a blasphemy statute and that, regardless of how "reprehensible" Mockus's views were, in the absence of "acts of violence or other breach of peace," he could not be found guilty of a crime. This gust of fresh air in Mockus's sails, however, would prove to be short-lived, as he quickly moved on with his lectures and eventually ran headlong into an adverse ruling by the Maine Court.

On September 6, 8, and 10, 1919, Mockus gave a series of lectures in the town of Rumford, Maine, at the invitation of a society of Lithuanians in Rumford Falls. These lectures were delivered in the Lithuanian language to what the report of the case describes as a "large audience" and were accompanied by pictures of Biblical subjects projected upon a screen. Based on remarks made by Mockus as these pictures were displayed, the State charged him with the crime of blasphemy. Maine's blasphemy statute provided that "[w]hoever blasphemes the holy name of God by cursing, or contumeliously reproaching God, His creation, government, final judgment of the world, Jesus Christ, the Holy Ghost or the Holy Scriptures as contained in the canonical books of the Old or New Testament, or by exposing them to contempt and ridicule, shall be punished by imprisonment for not more than two years, or by fine not exceeding two hundred dollars."[357] Mockus's trial resulted in a jury verdict of guilty, and he was sentenced to a term of one to two

---

[357] Me. R.S. ch. 126, § 30 (1916). The Court explained that Maine adopted this statute from Massachusetts shortly after Maine became a separate state in 1820 and that the Massachusetts blasphemy statute derived from legislation originally enacted by the Colonial government of Massachusetts in 1646. Maine's blasphemy statute was eventually repealed by the Maine Legislature when it enacted the Maine Criminal Code in 1975. Me. P.L. 1975, ch. 499, § 5, effective May 1, 1976.

years in state prison.[358] Mockus appealed his conviction to the Maine Court.

Mockus contended that he had not committed blasphemy, and that in any event his conduct was constitutionally protected and Maine's blasphemy statute was unconstitutional.[359] The Court rejected all of those arguments. The Court disposed of Mockus's contention that his conduct did not constitute blasphemy by noting that there was ample evidence that some of the statements that Mockus had made exposed the Beings and Scriptures, mentioned in the statute, to contempt and ridicule. As reported by the Court, one example of those statements was as follows: "You see this fool (pointing to a picture of Jesus Christ upon the cross, with the private parts of his body covered with a cloth; which he had caused to be thrown upon a screen) and you believe in Him. The women were sorry for the holy thing and covered the holy thing, while the rest of the body was left uncovered." Evidently, the audience found this bizarre performance amusing, for as the Court stated, "The record discloses that as he spoke his auditors laughed and clapped their hands."

With reference to Mockus's contention that his conduct was constitutionally protected, the Court explained that the rights secured by the "religious freedom" and "freedom of speech" provisions of Maine's Constitution (Article I, Sections 3 and 4) are not unlimited. Under Section 3, the exercise of one's religious freedom is expressly limited by the proviso that one "not disturb the public peace, nor obstruct others in their religious worship." Similarly, under Section 4, one's freedom of speech is expressly conditioned on one's being "responsible for the abuse of this liberty." The Court then explained that Mockus's conduct was not constitutionally protected because in committing blasphemy one necessarily disturbs the public

---

[358] As Leonard Levy notes, Mockus did not serve time in Maine, but fled to Mexico instead. *See* Levy, *Blasphemy*, at 515.

[359] Mockus cast these arguments in terms of objections to the trial court's denial of his motion for a directed verdict and the trial court's refusal to give certain requested instructions to the jury.

peace and thus forfeits the protection of these constitutional provisions. That conclusion followed from two propositions asserted by the Court, namely, that "the religion of Christ is the prevailing religion of this Country and of this State" and that "stability of government in no small measure, depends upon the reverence and respect which a nation maintains toward its prevalent religion."[360]

To buttress those propositions, the Court quoted from the writings of Christopher G. Tiedeman, a then-influential legal scholar: "Public contumely and ridicule of a prevalent religion not only offend against the sensibilities of the believers, but likewise threaten the public peace and order by diminishing the power of moral precepts."[361] Under that analysis, blasphemy was presumed to constitute a disturbance of the peace regardless of whether or not an actual disturbance took place.

In rejecting Mockus's argument that Maine's blasphemy statute was unconstitutional, the Court relied upon and quoted at length from an opinion written by Massachusetts Chief Justice Shaw in the landmark Massachusetts blasphemy case, *Commonwealth v. Kneeland* (1838).[362] The Massachusetts Court there decided that the Massachusetts blasphemy statute did not violate the Massachusetts Constitution. Such was Shaw's stature as a jurist, even well into the

---

[360] *Mockus*, 120 Me. at 93, 113 A. at 42.

[361] Christopher G. Tiedeman, *A Treatise on State and Federal Control of Persons and Property in the United States* (St. Louis: F.H. Thomas Law Book Co., 1900), § 65.

[362] *Commonwealth v. Kneeland*, 37 Mass. (20 Pick.) 206 (1838). In that case, a majority of the Massachusetts Court affirmed the conviction of Abner Kneeland, whose "crime" consisted of "wilfully" denying the existence of God. In a dissenting opinion in that case, Justice Marcus Morton explained that because "[e]very person has a constitutional right to discuss the subject of a God, and to affirm or deny his existence," he could not agree that "a man may be punished for *wilfully* doing what he has a legal right to do." Shaw's opinion in *Kneeland* has been described as "one of the worst opinions ever written by Chief Justice Shaw." Leonard W. Levy, *The Law of the Commonwealth and Chief Justice Shaw* (Cambridge: Harvard University Press, 1957), 43. In contrast, the Maine Court in *Mockus* said that "the reasoning of the court in the Kneeland case is so satisfactory that we crave indulgence while we quote somewhat at length from the words of the learned Chief Justice Shaw." *Mockus*, 120 Me. at 96, 113 A. at 44.

twentieth century, that the Maine Court evidently felt it could do no better than to rely on the authority of Shaw's reputation. Unfortunately, Shaw's opinion shed little light on the issues in the *Mockus* case, other than to clarify that Shaw believed that the word "wilfully," as used in the Massachusetts statute defining the crime of blasphemy ("That if any person shall wilfully blaspheme the holy name of God," etc.), meant "not merely 'voluntarily,' but with a bad purpose...[having] an intended design to calumniate and disparage the Supreme Being, and to destroy the veneration due to him." Conversely, as Shaw saw it, the Massachusetts blasphemy statute did not prohibit the "fullest inquiry, and the freest discussion, for all honest and fair purposes, one of which is, the discovery of truth."[363]

In considering Mockus's appeal, the Maine Court could have looked to the dissenting opinion of Justice Marcus Morton, one of Shaw's colleagues on the Massachusetts Court, in the *Kneeland* case. In contrast with Shaw, who justified the Massachusetts blasphemy statute on the ground that it was "intended to restrain and punish acts which have a tendency to disturb the public peace," Morton at one point in his opinion suggested that to pass constitutional muster, the statute must be construed as prohibiting only speech that "wantonly or maliciously assails the rights and privileges of others, or disturbs the public peace." Explaining that, as he saw it, government lacks authority to punish blasphemy in the absence of actual injury to a human being or civil society, Morton declared:

> I cannot think that any state of mind or temper in reference to God or religion, goes to make up this legal offence. Anger towards God, indignity to him, to our Saviour, or the Holy Ghost, a disposition to scoff at religion, do not seem to me to be the subjects of human punishment. These sins may be committed when no one is present, and be known to God alone; and cannot be reached by a human tribunal. But if made known, they would not be the subject of punishment, because they inflicted no injury upon any human being, and so did not

---

[363] *Mockus*, 120 Me. at 96, 113 A. at 44 (quoting Shaw's opinion in *Kneeland*, 37 Mass. at 220).

violate the rights of society. It is only the injury to civil society which can give civil government jurisdiction of them.[364]

The Maine Court, however, apparently found Morton's reasoning unpersuasive. With no mention of Morton at all, it rejected Mockus's appeal, relying instead on the preeminence of Shaw to guide the way.

In deciding *Mockus*, the Court did not reach the question of whether Maine's blasphemy statute violated the Religion and Speech Clauses of the First Amendment to the U.S. Constitution because, as the Court explained, the First Amendment, as then interpreted by the Supreme Court, did not operate as a limitation on the powers of state legislatures. A few years after the Maine Court's decision in *Mockus*, the Supreme Court decided that, by virtue of the Fourteenth Amendment, the First Amendment's limitations on the powers of Congress also applied to the states.[365] As of 1921, however, when *Mockus* was decided, that doctrine had not yet been developed.

On first reading the Maine Court's decision in *Mockus*, I found it curious that, in upholding the constitutionality of Maine's blasphemy statute, the Court never mentioned the Religious Preference Clause in Article I, Section 3 of Maine's Constitution, which provides that "no subordination nor preference of any one sect or denomination to another shall ever be established by law." From the perspective of the present day, Maine's old blasphemy statute, which, in effect, granted Christianity a special, protected status under the law, a status not granted to other religions, plainly violated that constitutional provision. Wasn't that just as clear to the Maine Court when it decided *Mockus* in 1921? Evidently not. In looking at issues of Church and State, the Court at that time used a different lens than courts would

---

[364] *Kneeland*, 37 Mass. at 242.

[365] In *Gitlow v. People of New York*, 268 U.S. 652 (1925), the Supreme Court decided that the Freedom of Speech provision of the First Amendment was incorporated in the Fourteenth Amendment's Due Process Clause and as such was applicable to the states. Similarly, in *Cantwell v. Connecticut*, 310 U.S. 296 (1940), the Supreme Court decided that the "Religion Clauses" (the Establishment Clause and the Free Exercise Clause) of the First Amendment were also applicable to the states.

generally use today. The Court that decided the *Mockus* case did not consider the blasphemy statute to be a legislatively prescribed preference in favor of Christianity. On the contrary, the Court looked at that statute as a legislatively prescribed way of preserving the stability of the State itself—by protecting Maine's "prevalent religion" from disrespect and in that way securing the foundation on which, in the Court's view, the stability of the State "in no small measure" ultimately depended. Disavowing any intention to claim superiority for any religion, the Court stated this concept in these terms:

> It is farthest from our thought to claim superiority for any religious sect, society or denomination, or even to admit that there exists any distinct, avowed connection between Church and State in these United States or in any individual State, but as distinguished from the religions of Confucius, Gautama, Mohammed, or even Abram, it may be truly said that, by reason of the number, influence and station of its devotes within our territorial boundaries, the religion of Christ is the prevailing religion of this Country and of this State. With equal truth it may be said that, from the dawn of civilization, the religion of a country is a most important factor in determining its form of government, and that stability of government in no small measure, depends upon the reverence and respect which a nation maintains toward its prevalent religion.[366]

With the Legislature's repeal of Maine's blasphemy statute in 1975, the Court's decision in *Mockus* no longer had any practical significance as far as blasphemy was concerned. Indeed, over the years since *Mockus* was decided, First Amendment jurisprudence has changed so substantially that *Mockus* is no longer an authoritative judicial precedent at all. First, as noted above, the U.S. Supreme Court has since decided that, through the Fourteenth Amendment, the prohibitions of the First Amendment apply not only to Congress, but to the states as well. Second, our Court has clarified that under the First Amendment and the Maine Constitution, language that is

---

[366] *Mockus*, 120 Me. at 93, 113 A. at 42.

"merely distasteful" cannot be punished. In *State v. John W.* (1980), our Court declared that "[o]ur fundamental interest in free speech 'demands the existence of a compelling governmental interest to justify legislative restrictions upon it.'"[367] As the Court there explained, "When dealing with fighting words there is a legitimate governmental interest in preventing words 'which by their very utterance inflict injury or tend to incite an immediate breach of the peace,' but language which is merely distasteful cannot be punished."[368] Consistent with that analysis, the Court expressly declared that its 1921 decision in *Mockus* "can no longer be considered valid."[369] And with that, *Mockus* was relegated to the dustbin of legal history, where it rests serenely, a reminder of times past.

Although no longer authoritative, the Court's decision in *Mockus* is still worth contemplating because it illustrates how easily a court can drift into believing that, in the interest of fostering civility, it is doing the right thing by prohibiting speech that is offensive to a majority of the community. Recalling the eventual demise of our Court's decision in *Mockus* would be a helpful antidote to any tendency to drift in that direction, as would consideration of judicial decisions that convincingly elucidate the central purpose of our Bill of Rights. Justice Robert H. Jackson's opinion in the U.S. Supreme

---

[367] *State v. John W.*, 418 A.2d 1097, 1101 (Me. 1980) (quoting *Opinion of the Justices*, 306 A.2d 18, 21 (Me. 1973)). In *John W.*, the Court held that on the facts of that case the defendant's abusive language to the police was constitutionally protected.

[368] *Id.* at 1102.

[369] *Id.* at 1102 n.3. In so ruling, the Maine Court also cited the U.S. Supreme Court's decision in *Joseph Burstyn, Inc. v. Wilson*, 343 U.S. 495 (1952) (holding that under the First and Fourteenth Amendments a state may not ban a film on the basis of a censor's conclusion that it is "sacrilegious") and the decision of the Maryland Court of Special Appeals in *State of Maryland v. West*, 9 Md. App. 270, 263 A.2d 602 (1970) (striking down Maryland's blasphemy statute as a violation of the Establishment and Free Exercise Clauses of the First Amendment). In the former case, *Joseph Burstyn, Inc.*, the Supreme Court stated: "It is not the business of government in our nation to suppress real or imagined attacks upon a particular religious doctrine, whether they appear in publications, speeches, or motion pictures." *Burstyn*, 343 U.S. at 505.

Court's 1943 Pledge of Allegiance case remains a classic in that genre. As Justice Jackson there explained:

> The very purpose of a Bill of Rights was to withdraw certain subjects from the vicissitudes of political controversy, to place them beyond the reach of majorities and officials and to establish them as legal principles to be applied by the courts. One's right to life, liberty, and property, to free speech, a free press, freedom of worship and assembly, and other fundamental rights may not be submitted to vote; they depend on the outcome of no elections....
>
> ....
>
> If there is any fixed star in our constitutional constellation, it is that no official, high or petty, can prescribe what shall be orthodox in politics, nationalism, religion, or other matters of opinion or force citizens to confess by word or act their faith therein. If there are any circumstances which permit an exception, they do not now occur to us.[370]

The Court's decision in *Mockus* is also important from an historical point of view because that decision marks a significant turning point in Maine's legal history. The legal framework and the vision of society on which the Court's decision was predicated were soon to become little more than memories from the past. *Mockus* was decided in 1921—a time when, in justifying Maine's blasphemy statute, the Court, as we have seen, could assert as a "truth" that "stability of government in no small measure, depends upon the reverence and respect which a nation maintains toward its prevalent religion."[371] That time was also of an era when it was generally accepted that one of the important functions of government was to

---

[370] *W. Va. Bd. of Educ. v. Barnette*, 319 U.S. 624, 638-642 (1943) (holding that the West Virginia Board of Education's policy requiring public school students to salute the flag of the United States and recite the Pledge of Allegiance violated the First Amendment to the U.S. Constitution).

[371] *Mockus*, 120 Me. at 93, 113 A. at 42.

promote civility and discourage offensive behavior.[372] Those "truths," once prominent features of our legal landscape, have been so eroded by cultural and legal developments over time that they no longer serve as the sure jurisprudential footings they did in days gone by.

Among the more significant cultural developments that played a role in that process has been the increasing diversification of our society. We have become a much more ethnically and religiously diverse people than we were in 1921 when *Mockus* was decided. Legal developments that have contributed to that process include judicial rulings that have expansively interpreted the right of free speech and required that government maintain a stance of neutrality where religion is concerned. These cultural and legal developments, in combination, have taken us into a new world of freedom, a more pluralistic world, a world far removed from the more stable and uniform world that served as the backdrop to the drama played out in Michael Mockus's blasphemy case in 1921.[373]

The implications of these changes are profound. Indeed, it remains to be seen whether this new world of freedom and multiculturalism contains enough cohesive social and moral fiber to prevent it from disintegrating into a mere collection of disparate elements. In view of the significant role that judicial rulings played in bringing the post-*Mockus* era into being, it can be expected that decisions of our courts will continue to play an important role in determining the nature of our society in the years ahead.

---

[372] See, for example, our Court's decision in *Robinson v. Rockland, Thomaston & Camden St. Ry.*, 87 Me 387, 32 A. 994 (1895), discussed above under the heading "Uncivil Behavior Discouraged," in the chapter entitled "Ensuring Public Safety."

[373] From the perspective of the present day, the vision of society underlying the Court's decision in *Mockus* seems remarkably quaint and old-fashioned. One is reminded of dated pictures from yesteryear, such as the old school-house in John Greenleaf Whittier's poem, "In School-Days": "Still sits the school-house by the road / A ragged beggar sleeping / Around it still the sumachs grow / And blackberry-vines are creeping." Times have changed.

THE CIVIL WAR

In addition to managing its customary docket of civil and criminal cases, our Court in the third quarter of the nineteenth century found itself called upon to decide legal issues of extraordinary significance concerning developments leading up to the Civil War and the ability of the North ultimately to prevail in that war. Recognizing the importance of those issues, the Court gave them the conscientious attention they deserved. In doing so, our Court left us valuable reminders of the importance of the principle of equality of rights under the law and the importance of not allowing the "rebellion" to succeed.

The importance of the principle of equality of rights under the law was most powerfully articulated by two members of the Maine Court, Justices John Appleton and Woodbury Davis, in opinions they wrote that criticized the U.S. Supreme Court's infamous decision in *Scott v. Sandford* (1857) (the "*Dred Scott* case").[374] Our Court's view of the urgency of defeating the South was demonstrated by the Court's emphatic rejection of the notion that taxpayers could be required to pay commutation fees to enable residents of draft age to buy their way out of military service. To those topics we now turn.[375]

---

[374] 60 U.S. 393 (1857).

[375] Other significant issues relating to the Civil War that were addressed by the Maine Court included the question of the constitutionality of Maine's "personal liberty laws," which were enacted by the Maine Legislature in response to the Fugitive Slave Act of 1850, and the question of whether the owners of a Maine-built ship (the "Golden Rocket") could recover under an insurance policy after that vessel had been raided, looted, and burned at sea by the Navy of the Confederate States. As to the "liberty laws," see *Opinion of the Justices*, 46 Me. 561 (1861). For a discussion of that subject, see Jerry R. Desmond, "The Attempt to Repeal Maine's Personal Liberty Laws," 37 *Maine History* 194 (1998). Regarding

Responding to the Dred Scott Case

It has been aptly remarked that "a judge is like an oyster, anchored solidly to one spot and confined in his diet to such foods as the currents of causes bring within his reach."[376] In contrast with the legislative and executive branches of government, the judicial branch generally lacks the power to reach out on its own and render decisions and judgments on issues it may consider important. Rather, like the oyster on the ocean floor, courts must wait passively for cases to be brought before them by litigants or other petitioners. In that sense, the nature of the cases a court decides is largely a matter of accident and happenstance. Occasionally, among the relatively routine cases on a court's docket, a case will appear that involves issues of transcendent significance. Just such a case came before the Court in 1857 when the Maine Senate sought the Maine Court's opinion regarding the voting rights of African Americans in light of the U.S. Supreme Court's decision earlier that year in the *Dred Scott* case. It is interesting to note that these circumstances, this accident of history, presented the Maine Court a unique opportunity to address important constitutional principles that otherwise might not have commanded its attention for years to come.

The *Dred Scott* case concerned the attempt by a slave, Dred Scott, to establish his freedom through the courts by virtue of the fact that, after having resided in a slave state (Missouri), he had for several years resided in a free state (Illinois) and a free territory (Wisconsin), where he had been taken by his owner. Having lost his case in the Supreme Court of Missouri and the federal circuit court in St. Louis, Scott finally appealed that federal court decision to the U.S. Supreme Court. By a 7-2 majority, the Supreme Court ruled against

---

the ship owners' claim under their insurance policy, see *Dole v. Merchants' Mutual Marine Ins. Co.*, 51 Me. 465 (1863).

[376] *See* Frank M. Coffin, Chief Judge, U.S. Court of Appeals, First Circuit, "Justice and Workability: Un Essai," 5 *Suffolk Law Review* 567, 567 (1971) (referring to remarks made by First Circuit Chief Judge Calvert Magruder).

Scott.[377] Several separate opinions were filed, but the opinion of Chief
Justice Roger B. Taney is generally considered to be the ruling of the
Court. In his "opinion of the Court," Taney rejected Scott's suit on the
ground that because Scott was a black person and a descendant of
slaves, he was not a citizen of the United States, even if he were free;
and because he was not a citizen of the United States, he could not
bring suit in federal court.[378]

Although the U.S. Constitution contained no provision denying
black persons citizenship, Taney declared that, as a matter of federal
constitutional law, black persons who were slaves or descendants of
slaves could not be considered citizens of the United States, even if
freed from slavery. Taney based that sweeping conclusion on his
belief that such persons were not regarded as citizens of the United
States when the Constitution was adopted. As Taney put this:

> [Such persons] are not included, and were not intended to be
> included, under the word "citizens" in the Constitution, and
> can therefore claim none of the rights and privileges which

---

[377] Justices John McLean of Ohio and Benjamin R. Curtis of Massachusetts filed
dissenting opinions.

[378] More specifically, Taney decided that Scott was not a "citizen" within the
meaning of that term in the "diversity of citizenship" provision of Article III,
Section 2 of the U.S. Constitution, which extends federal court jurisdiction to
controversies between "citizens" of different states.

Beyond that point, Taney also decided that Scott was still a slave, despite
his having resided in a free territory and a free state. In coming to that
conclusion, Taney decided that Congress lacked power under the Constitution to
prohibit slavery in the federal territories as it had done in the Missouri
Compromise of 1820 and that Scott's status upon returning to Missouri was an
issue of Missouri law that had previously been decided adversely to him by the
Missouri Supreme Court. For a thorough analysis of the Supreme Court's
decision, see Don E. Fehrenbacher, *The Dred Scott Case: Its Significance in American
Law and Politics* (New York: Oxford University Press, 1978). The Supreme Court's
Dred Scott decision, far from resolving the national debate concerning slavery,
simply made the Civil War all the more inevitable. *See, e.g.,* John H. Franklin &
Alfred A. Moss Jr., *From Slavery to Freedom, A History of African Americans,* 8th ed.
(New York: Alfred A. Knopf, 2000), 216 ("With the highest court in the land
openly preaching the proslavery doctrine, there was little hope that anything
short of a most drastic political or social revolution would bring an end to
slavery.").

that instrument provides for and secures to citizens of the United States. On the contrary, they were at that time considered as a subordinate and inferior class of beings who had been subjugated by the dominant race, and, whether emancipated or not, yet remained subject to their authority, and had no rights or privileges but such as those who held the power and the Government might choose to grant them.

 ....

 In the opinion of the court, the legislation and histories of the times, and the language used in the Declaration of Independence, show that neither the class of persons who had been imported as slaves nor their descendants, whether they had become free or not, were then acknowledged as a part of the people, nor intended to be included in the general words used in that memorable instrument.[379]

It did not take long for the Maine Legislature to express its condemnation of the U.S. Supreme Court's decision. Taney announced that decision on March 6, 1857. On April 15 of that year, the Maine Legislature passed a resolution that emphatically denounced that decision as being wholly contrary to principles of freedom and justice.[380] The *Dred Scott* decision, the Legislature stated, "is conclusive proof of the determination of the slaveholding states to subvert all the principles upon which the American Union was formed, and degrade it into an engine for the extension and perpetuation of the barbarous and detestable system of chattel slavery." The Legislature further resolved that the Court's decision "is not binding, in law or conscience, upon the government or citizens of the United States, and that it is of an import so alarming and dangerous, as to demand the instant and emphatic reprobation of the country."

---

[379] *Scott*, 60 U.S. at 404-07.

[380] *See* Resolves in relation to the decision of the supreme court [lower case in original] of the United States, in the case of Dred Scott, Me. Resolves 1857, ch. 112. Among additional resolves included in that legislative denunciation of the *Dred Scott* decision, was this emphatic resolve regarding slavery: "That Maine will not allow slavery within its borders, in any form or under any pretence, for any time, however short, let the consequences be what they may."

Indeed, the Legislature found Taney's opinion so offensive that it went so far as to resolve that the Supreme Court be "so reconstituted as to relieve it from the domination of a sectional faction, and make it a tribunal whose decisions shall be in harmony with the constitution of the United States and the spirit of our institutions, and at whose hands all classes of persons in the United States, without regard to race or locality, shall receive even and exact justice."

In the meantime, less than three weeks after the Supreme Court's decision was announced, the Maine Senate, on March 26, 1857, sought an advisory opinion from the Maine Court regarding the implications of *Dred Scott* on the right of "free colored persons, of African descent" to vote in Maine, in light of the fact that, as regards the election of the Governor, Senators, and Representatives, Maine's Constitution limits the right to vote to persons who, among other criteria, are "citizen[s] of the United States."[381]

In responding to the Maine Senate's request for the Court's advisory opinion, all of the members of the Maine Court, except one, Justice Joshua W. Hathaway, concluded that the voting rights of black persons were secured by Maine's Constitution and that those rights were not adversely affected by the Supreme Court's *Dred Scott* decision.[382] Before reaching the opinions of the justices who affirmed the voting rights of blacks in Maine, we might briefly note Hathaway's opinion here.

The lone dissenter, Justice Hathaway, stressed the importance of a uniform definition of national citizenship that would not vary from state to state. Hathaway was of the view that the definition of United States citizenship was governed by the Supreme Court's *Dred Scott* decision and that consequently Maine's free black residents who were descendants of slaves could not vote in Maine.[383] Hathaway, however, found no support for that view from his colleagues on the Court. And with the passage of time, his opinion has fared no better. Considered from the perspective of the present day, Hathaway's

---

[381] Me. Const. Art. II, § 1.

[382] *See Opinion of the Justices*, 44 Me. 505 (1857).

[383] *See id.* at 516-21.

willingness to disenfranchise Maine's free black residents who were descendants of slaves (which in practical effect would be to establish a race-based caste system for Maine) stands out from the pages of Maine's legal history as a radical misjudgment that betrays the ideals of liberty and equality in a democratic society.[384]

The other members of the Maine Court submitted three separate opinions. One of those opinions, the opinion of a five-member majority of the Court, was signed by Chief Justice John S. Tenney and Justices Richard D. Rice, Jonas Cutting, Seth May, and Daniel Goodenow. Justices John Appleton and Woodbury Davis each submitted written opinions of their own.

The opinion submitted by the majority of the Maine Court began by noting that the U.S. Supreme Court's decision in *Dred Scott* was not pertinent to the issue at hand because, in contrast with *Dred Scott*, which concerned the issue of whether black persons were citizens of the United States within the meaning of the United States Constitution, the question presented by the Maine Senate's request for an advisory opinion concerned the different issue of whether black persons were citizens of the United States within the meaning of the Maine Constitution. Brushing aside the Supreme Court's *Dred Scott* decision as having no effect on the question before them, these justices said that they expressed "no opinion" on the "correctness" of that decision.[385]

Turning to the question of the meaning of Maine's Constitution, this group of justices pointed out that in the debates that took place at the constitutional convention that resulted in the wording of

---

[384] Hathaway's willingness to sacrifice the voting rights of Maine's free black residents on the basis of the exclusionary uniform rule of national citizenship prescribed in Taney's opinion in *Dred Scott* seems all the more misguided, considering that in that opinion, Taney himself distinguished the situation in Maine from that of the rest of the country, noting that "in no part of the country except Maine did the African race, in point of fact, participate equally with the whites in the exercise of civil and political rights." *See Dred Scott*, 60 U.S. at 416 (referencing James Kent, *Commentaries on American Law*, 6th ed., 1848, vol. 2, at 258 n. b).

[385] *See Opinion of the Justices*, 44 Me. at 508.

Maine's Constitution, a delegate had proposed that "negroes" be
excluded from the description of persons eligible to vote, but that the
convention had rejected that proposal after John Holmes, chairman
of the committee appointed to frame a constitution for Maine,
expressed his position on that matter, as follows:

> But I know of no difference between the rights of the negro
> and the white man; God Almighty has made none—our
> declaration of rights has made none. That declares that 'all
> men' (without regard to colors) 'are born equally free and
> independent.'[386]

These justices also noted that from the time of the adoption of the
Massachusetts Constitution in 1780, "free men of African descent"
had "enjoyed the rights of the elective franchise in that state," and
that from the time of the adoption of the Maine Constitution in 1820,
"it is believed there has been no instance in the state in which the
right to vote has been denied to any person resident within the state,
on account of his color." Against that background, the justices constituting a majority of the Maine Court concluded that, notwithstanding
the Supreme Court's decision in *Dred Scott*, the voting rights of black
persons were guaranteed by Maine's Constitution.[387]

Justices Appleton and Davis agreed with that interpretation of
Maine's Constitution, but were not content to let the matter rest
there. They believed that the Supreme Court's *Dred Scott* decision
was utterly wrong. They also believed that it was their responsibility
to explain why it was wrong. Appleton opened his opinion with the
resounding declaration that Maine's Constitution is founded on the
fundamental principle of equality of rights under the law:

> The constitution of Maine recognizes as its fundamental idea,
> the great principle upon which all popular governments
> rest—*the equality of all before the law*. It confers citizenship and

---

[386] See discussion of the proceedings of Maine's constitutional convention, *id.* at
515 (opinion of Tenney, C.J. et al.) and *id.* at 574 (opinion of Appleton, J.).

[387] *See id.* at 514-16.

entire equality of civil and political rights upon all its native born population.[388]

After a comprehensive review of historical events that took place before and after the adoption of the Constitution of the United States, Appleton concluded there was nothing in the U.S. Constitution that could be read as defining citizenship in terms of color or race:

> The conclusion to which I have arrived, after a careful consideration of the question, and a full examination of the authorities bearing thereupon, is, that there is no prohibition in the constitution of the United States, express or implied, to free men of African descent becoming citizens of a state, and as such, by virtue of their state citizenship, becoming citizens of the United States. I can find no justification for any such interpolation in the clause in the constitution conferring general citizenship upon the citizens of *each* state as that it shall read "the citizens of *each* state (the *free native colored citizens of each state excepted*,) shall be entitled to all privileges and immunities of citizens in the several states." The framers of the constitution made no such article. The people adopted no such article. Interpolation is no judicial duty.[389]

Appalled by the injustice of Taney's opinion in *Dred Scott*, which in effect relegated slaves and even free descendants of slaves to an inferior, hopeless, non-citizen class, Appleton stated:

> [N]o more melancholy illustration can be furnished of, no more terrible denunciation can be uttered against a system, than that its results are such that even freedom will not elevate the subject, nor free and liberal institutions humanize the dominant race; that the former dare not claim their legal rights and the latter will not respect them.[390]

---

[388] *Id.* at 522.

[389] *Id.* at 556-57.

[390] *Id.* at 563.

Mindful of the fact that as a state court judge he was in the unusual position of criticizing a decision of the highest court in the land, Appleton pointed out that "whatever may be the authoritative force of a decision of the Supreme Court of the United States, there can be no doubt that its statements, as to the past history of the country, are binding neither on the historian nor the jurist."[391] If Taney correctly understood history, he would, Appleton suggested, have realized that at the time when the Constitution was adopted, free black persons were recognized as citizens in several states and that they had served as soldiers in the Revolutionary War. Appleton, in a final point that settled the matter, then asserted that if Taney had gotten his history right, his legal conclusions would have been the exact opposite of what they were:

> If these [historical facts] be so, and that they are so cannot be denied or even doubted, and if they had been known to the learned Chief Justice, his conclusions would have been different, for he says, "every person and every class and description of persons, who *were at the time of the adoption of the constitution recognized as citizens of the several states, became also citizens of this new political body*." His published opinion, therefore, rests upon a remarkable and most unfortunate misapprehension of facts, and his real opinion upon the actual facts must be considered as in entire and cordial concurrence with that of his learned dissenting associates.[392]

Before leaving Appleton's opinion, it would be a shame not to mention some of the aphorisms that ornament that opinion. Appleton had an exceptional ability to express important principles of law in a concise and memorable manner. For example:

> All members of a civil society, bound by its laws, liable to its penalties, are entitled to its aid in the enforcement of right, and for protection against wrong.[393]

---

[391] *Id.* at 561.

[392] *Id.* at 573.

[393] *Id.* at 522.

[T]he law favors life and liberty...[394]

[T]he equality of all before the law is the elementary principle of our institutions....[395]

[T]he people of this state, in convention assembled, formed a constitution upon principles of the purest democracy, making no distinctions and giving no preferences, but resting upon the great *idea of equality before the law*.[396]

Like the opinion submitted by Justice Appleton, the separate opinion submitted by Justice Davis was also sharply critical of the Supreme Court's *Dred Scott* decision. Because Davis believed that the Supreme Court's decision did not control the meaning of "citizen of the United States" in Maine's Constitution, he concluded that *Dred Scott* "should therefore receive that consideration, and that only, to which its intrinsic merits entitle it." As Davis saw it, that decision had no merits, intrinsic or otherwise. In his view, all free persons who were born in the United States were citizens of the United States and of the states in which they resided.

Getting directly to the heart of his disagreement with the Supreme Court's decision, Davis pointed out that Taney's opinion presumed that the members of one race have the right to deny citizenship to the members of another. But, Davis replied, such a right "does not exist under any free government":

If it be said that history shows that at the time when the federal constitution was adopted, the white population of the country did not intend to admit colored persons of African descent to the privileges of citizenship, while the assertion is denied, it is also replied that we have no right to inquire what one class of persons intended, in derogation of the rights of

---

[394] *Id.* at 561.

[395] *Id.*

[396] *Id.* at 574.

any other class. It would be just as legitimate to inquire whether the African race intended to admit the whites to the privileges of citizenship. They all resided together, participants of that freedom which was the fruit of their common struggles and sacrifices. Whatever their disparity in numbers, or condition, neither had the right to eject the other from the common purchase, or make them aliens from the commonwealth. Such a right does not exist under any free government; certainly not under a government whose corner stone was laid upon the principle "that all governments derive their just powers from the consent of the governed."[397]

Davis then went on to explain that Taney's opinion and the assertions on which it was based were completely at odds with the ideals of the founding fathers. In words that reflect the depth of his disappointment with Taney's opinion, Davis stated:

It seems to me that such assertions and such doctrines need only to be stated, in order to be rejected. They are so clearly in conflict with the whole tone and spirit, both of the writings and the deeds of the great men of the revolution, that it is difficult to conceive how they can be credited by any intelligent, unprejudiced mind. The worst enemy of our institutions could hardly say anything better adapted to blacken the character of our ancestors, and cast reproach upon their memories.[398]

Invoking the great principles of equality and liberty enshrined in the Declaration of Independence, Davis concluded with three paragraphs that deserve a place of honor in the history of Maine law. So stirring are these words that any attempt at paraphrase would fall woefully short. With excerpts from Taney's opinion referred to in quotation marks, Davis wrote:

---

[397] *Id.* at 586.

[398] *Id.* at 593-94.

If the Declaration of Independence "was not intended to include the enslaved African," but was a mere compact of their oppressors for their own advantage, while "the unhappy black race were never thought of or spoken of, except as property, and when the claims of the owner or the profit of the trader were supposed to need protection," then a decent respect for the opinions of mankind should have kept its authors silent. Such compacts had long been common enough, in limited monarchies, in aristocracies; even among brigands and pirates. Freedom of privileged classes, and equality among themselves, while trampling on the rights of others, was no new thing. The world did not need to be informed of it. As the manifesto of such a doctrine, the Declaration of Independence would not have merited the respect of mankind; it would not have justified a revolution; it would have given Washington and his compatriots no glory to fight for it, and their toil, and sacrifice, and blood, were offered in vain.

But it was not so. The Declaration of Independence was a heroic utterance of great truths, for all men; so understood by the world, so intended by its authors. They freely devoted fortune, honor, life, to sustain it. And they often avowed their purpose, as soon as the government should be established, to extend its blessings to the slaves. No man ever condemned slavery in stronger terms than Jefferson, Washington, and those who with them stood foremost in the revolutionary struggle. A resolution solemnly denying its right was unanimously passed by the congress of 1775. The hope and the prophecy of general emancipation were the common theme of correspondence and public debate.

With this avowed purpose in view, the federal constitution was formed, and adopted by the people of the several states. It was designedly so made as to need no amendment when slavery should be abolished. Its privileges were granted to all, without distinction of race or color. Free colored persons have always been recognized as citizens under it, and

they are entitled to the same privileges and immunities which
the constitution guarantees to other citizens.[399]

For Davis, the "great truths" proclaimed in the Declaration of
Independence—that all men are created equal in their having been
endowed with unalienable rights that no government can take from
them—constituted the foundation upon which our nation and
Constitution were built. In that view, the Constitution could not be
properly understood without taking those truths into account.

It is remarkable that John Appleton and Woodbury Davis,
associate justices of a state court, had the courage and fortitude to
write opinions that were so critical of a decision rendered by the
highest court in the land. But what duty required seems not to have
been in doubt for them. The stakes were high, involving as they did
nothing less than the question whether U.S. citizenship would
depend on one's ancestry or the color of one's skin. The injustice of
the *Dred Scott* decision was clear. If a majority of the Maine Court
was not disposed to enter the fray and take on the highest court in
the land, Davis and Appleton decided that they themselves would do
so. They seized the opportunity presented, and by the opinions they
wrote, gave new life to the principles of the Declaration of Independence. To fully appreciate the significance of their achievement, we
need only imagine the gaping hole that would exist in the history of
Maine law if the injustice of Taney's decision had been allowed to go
unchallenged by any member of Maine's highest court.

Appleton and Davis, of course, proved to be on the right side of
history. Ultimately, following the Civil War, their views regarding
the Supreme Court's decision in *Dred Scott* became the established
law of the land, with the adoption in 1868 of the Fourteenth
Amendment to the U.S. Constitution. The first sentence of the first
section of that Amendment, known as the Citizenship Clause,
declares, "All persons born or naturalized in the United States, and
subject to the jurisdiction thereof, are citizens of the United States

---

[399] *Id.* at 594-95.

and of the State wherein they reside."[400] As U.S. Supreme Court
Justice (later Chief Justice) William H. Rehnquist has explained, the
"paramount reason" for that clause was "to amend the Constitution
so as to overrule explicitly the *Dred Scott* decision."[401]

As we conclude our discussion of our Court's response to the
Dred Scott case, it is interesting to note that the views expressed by
Justice Davis concerning the continuing vitality, relevance, and
importance of the Declaration of Independence were shared by
Abraham Lincoln. In the summer of 1857, at the same time that Davis
and his colleagues on the Maine Court were getting back to the
Maine Senate with their opinions concerning the Supreme Court's
decision in *Dred Scott*, Lincoln delivered a speech in which he
expressed his disagreement with that decision.[402] In that speech,
Lincoln explained that as he read the Declaration of Independence,
the authors of that document "defined with tolerable distinctness, in
what respects they did consider all men created equal—equal in
'certain inalienable rights, among which are life, liberty, and the
pursuit of happiness.'" Like Maine's Justice Davis, Lincoln stressed
the enduring importance of the Declaration for all time. The authors
of the Declaration, Lincoln explained,

---

[400] The first section of the Fourteenth Amendment reads in full as follows: "All
persons born or naturalized in the United States, and subject to the jurisdiction
thereof, are citizens of the United States and of the State wherein they reside. No
State shall make or enforce any law which shall abridge the privileges or
immunities of citizens of the United States; nor shall any State deprive any
person of life, liberty, or property, without due process of law; nor deny to any
person within its jurisdiction the equal protection of the laws."

[401] *Sugarman v. Dougall*, 413 U.S. 634, 652 (1973) (Rehnquist, J., dissenting). Yet
despite the ratification of the Fourteenth Amendment, the principle of equality
embodied in that Amendment was far from being immediately realized on the
national level. Following the U.S. Supreme Court's decision in *Plessy v. Ferguson*,
163 U.S. 537 (1896), which approved the "separate but equal" doctrine, fifty-eight
years passed before the Supreme Court rejected that doctrine by its landmark
decision in *Brown v. Board of Education*, 347 U.S. 483 (1954).

[402] *See* Speech on the Dred Scott Decision at Springfield, Illinois (June 26, 1857),
Abraham Lincoln: Speeches and Writings, vol. 1, *1832-1858*, ed. Don E. Fehrenbacher
(New York: The Library of America, 1989), 390.

meant to set up a standard maxim for free society, which
should be familiar to all, and revered by all; constantly looked
to, constantly labored for, and even though never perfectly
attained, constantly approximated, and thereby constantly
spreading and deepening its influence, and augmenting the
happiness and value of life to all people of all colors every-
where. The assertion that "all men are created equal" was of
no practical use in effecting our separation from Great Britain;
and it was placed in the Declaration, not for that, but for
future use. Its authors meant it to be, thank God, it is now
proving itself, a stumbling block to those who in after times
might seek to turn a free people back into the hateful paths of
despotism. They knew the proneness of prosperity to breed
tyrants, and they meant when such should re-appear in this
fair land and commence their vocation they should find left
for them at least one hard nut to crack.[403]

Two years later, in a letter he wrote in 1859, Lincoln made the
same point, again invoking his "stumbling block" metaphor. With
reference to Jefferson's role in drafting the Declaration, Lincoln
penned these lines, which have lost none of their verve over the
years:

All honor to Jefferson—to the man who, in the concrete
pressure of a struggle for national independence by a single
people, had the coolness, forecast, and capacity to introduce
into a merely revolutionary document, an abstract truth,
applicable to all men and all times, and so to embalm it there,
that to-day, and in all coming days, it shall be a rebuke and a
stumbling-block to the very harbingers of re-appearing
tyranny and oppression.[404]

---

[403] Speech on the Dred Scott Decision, *Speeches and Writings*, vol. 1, 398-99.

[404] Lincoln to Henry L. Pierce, & others, April 6, 1859, *Speeches and Writings*, vol.
2, *1859-1865*, 19.

Rejecting the Use of Tax Dollars to Facilitate Draft Avoidance

As the result of expiration of enlistments and a decline in volunteering, the Union Army in 1863 faced the prospect of impending troop shortages. To meet the Army's manpower needs, Congress, in March of that year, enacted a federal conscription statute that authorized a federal draft. Under that statute, commonly known as the Conscription Act, a draftee could avoid military service by procuring a substitute or by paying a commutation fee of $300, a price that then amounted to almost a year's wages for an unskilled laborer.[405] In response to that federal statute, some Maine municipalities voted to use tax dollars to enable draftees to procure substitutes or pay commutations and thereby avoid military service. The legality of those practices was challenged in several cases that came before the Maine Court during and after the war.

The Maine Court first addressed those issues in an advisory opinion it submitted in response to a request by Governor Abner Coburn in June of 1863.[406] Noting that various Maine towns were voting to raise money by taxation to pay commutations for their residents who might be drafted, Governor Coburn requested the Court's opinion on the legality of that practice. In reply, the Court explained that under Maine law, towns were not allowed to make such payments.

The Court began its opinion by affirming the authority of Congress to enact the Conscription Act. Emphasizing the extensive powers of Congress under the perilous circumstances facing the nation, the Court stated:

---

[405] *See* James M. McPherson, *Battle Cry of Freedom: The Civil War Era* (New York: Oxford University Press, 1988), 601-02. Criticism of the commutation provision, which in effect allowed those who could afford it to buy their way out of the draft, resulted in its repeal in 1864. *See id.* at 601 n. 21. In his concurring opinion in *Thompson v. Inhabitants of Pittston*, 59 Me. 545 (1871), Justice Jonathan G. Dickerson noted that the effect of that draft-avoidance provision upon the soldiers in the field and the recruiting service was "so disastrous" that Congress was soon impelled to repeal that "odious" feature of the Act.

[406] *Opinion of the Justices*, 52 Me. 595 (1863).

By the express terms of the constitution, Congress has power "to declare war," "to raise and support armies," "to provide and maintain a navy," "to make rules for the government and regulations of the land and naval forces," "to provide for calling forth the militia *to execute the laws of the Union, suppress insurrection* and repel invasion," "to provide for organizing, arming and disciplining the militia, and for governing such part of them as may be employed in the service of the United States," and "to make all laws which shall be necessary and proper for carrying into execution the foregoing powers," &c. The power of Congress in the premises is supreme. In a great national emergency, when the national unity and republican institutions are in peril, whether from foreign foes, or, worse still, from domestic enemies treasonably endeavoring to over-throw the Union and subvert our institutions, it has the right to command all the resources of the nation, and the lives of its citizens, to prevent by any and all proper means that fearful anarchy, which would be so imminent, if its dissolution should become an accomplished fact.[407]

The Court then explained that the purposes for which muni-cipalities were permitted to raise funds by taxation were established and limited by a statute that had been enacted by the Maine Legislature. That statute authorized municipalities to raise funds by taxation for various specified municipal purposes (schools, road repair, etc.) and "other necessary town charges." The payment of commutations was not one of the specified purposes permitted by that statute. Nor, as the Court saw it, did the payment of commu-tations come within the phrase, "other necessary town charges." Explaining that this latter phrase was not an unlimited grant of power to municipalities, the Court unanimously concluded that Maine municipalities had no statutory authority to raise money by taxation for the purpose of paying commutation fees for their resi-dents who might be drafted.

---

[407] *Id.* at 596.

The Court could have concluded its opinion on that note, but it felt the need to express its opposition to the concept of commutation payments, generally. Such payments, the Court said, enabled citizens "to escape the performance of services which every citizen should cheerfully render, as due to a government upon the prosperity and perpetuity of which the future hopes of humanity must rest." The Court also expressed grave concern for the implications that would ensue if towns were allowed to pay commutation fees for their draftees. Noting that the Conscription Act "is an Act to raise soldiers, not to raise money," the Court stated:

> Its primary and especial purpose is to suppress insurrection by means of an armed force to be raised in pursuance of its provisions. If one town may assess taxes to pay the commutation money of those who may be drafted, so may all, and the Government would thus be left without a soldier for its protection, and the nation surrendered into the power of those who are warring for its destruction; the wealth and taxable property of the community would be diverted from the defence of government, and the resources of the State would be turned to its destruction, by thus depriving it of the means necessary for its preservation.[408]

The Court's advisory opinion cast a dark cloud over the practice of the payment of commutations by towns.

Although the Court had expressed contempt for that practice, those payments at least had the equitable effect of offsetting the injustice inherent in the commutation provision of the Conscription Act. By raising funds to pay commutations for their draftees, towns could give draftees who could not afford to pay commutations the same "opportunity" to avoid military service that was available under the Conscription Act to draftees who could afford to make such payments.

Under these circumstances and in response to the Court's 1863 advisory opinion—which was based primarily on the absence of

---

[408] *Id.* at 599.

statutory authority for towns to make commutation payments—the
Maine Legislature eventually tried to construct a satisfactory
statutory underpinning for that practice. To that end, the Legislature
in 1869 enacted a statute that expressly validated all past acts and
doings of towns in connection with their having made, or having
agreed to make, commutation payments.[409] But even this validating
statute would prove to be insufficient to permit towns to make
commutation payments.

In *Thompson v. Inhabitants of Pittston* (1871),[410] the Maine Court
decided that the Legislature's attempt to validate the payment of
commutations by towns was "devoid of legal and binding force"
because towns were constitutionally prohibited from making commutation payments in the first place. The Court explained that a
town's payment of a draftee's commutation fee would be "a clear
violation of the constitutional guaranties of private property"
because it would burden the town's taxpayers with paying what the
Court described as a "purely private benefit, without the possibility
of any corresponding public advantage." Based on that reasoning,
the Court rejected the plaintiff's claim that the town of Pittston owed
him $300 in accordance with the town's vote to reimburse its draftees
who paid commutation fees. With its ruling in this case, the Court
made it clear that Maine's Constitution stood in the way of any
legislative attempt to validate the payment of commutations by
Maine's towns and other municipalities.[411]

In addition, the Court in *Thompson* made it clear that it had no
reservations concerning the constitutionality of the draft. Reiterating
sentiments it had expressed in its 1863 advisory opinion to Governor
Coburn, the Court stated:

---

[409] An act to render valid certain doings of towns in voting commutations, Me.
P.L. 1869, ch. 55.

[410] 59 Me. 545 (1871).

[411] In contrast, the Maine Court upheld the validity of a Maine statute (Me. P.L.
1864, ch. 226) that validated the acts and doings of towns in paying or agreeing
to pay bounties to drafted men, volunteers, and substitutes who actually
performed military service. *See Barbour v. Inhabitants of Camden*, 51 Me. 608
(1865).

In the emergency then existing, the country, the public, the government which represented both, had a right to the services of as many able-bodied men, within certain ages, as were necessary to protect us all against the machinations of treason,—had the right to draft from the whole number of those fit for military duty, so many as were required for that purpose.[412]

In a concurring opinion in that case, Justice Dickerson expressed his scorn for the whole idea of commutation payments. The difference between the draftee who rendered military service and the draftee who paid a commutation was, he wrote, "the difference between the man who performed his duty to his country, in the hour of her greatest peril, and the man who paid a fine for not doing such duty." Dickerson's disdain for the plaintiff, who had paid a commutation to avoid military service, could not have been more telling:

[That payment] was not paid to promote the public advantage or welfare, but to purchase his own exemption from the performance of a personal duty, to enable him to enjoy his ease and pleasure, advance his private interests, and escape the privations, sufferings and perils of war.[413]

As these cases show, the Maine Court was resolute in its support of the Union war effort. It backed the draft. And it forbade the practice of towns' paying commutations to enable draftees to avoid military service—even though to do so, the Court ultimately had to invalidate a statute that had been enacted by the Legislature for the very purpose of validating such payments. As the Court explained in its advisory opinion of 1863, using tax dollars to subsidize commutations would only make it more difficult for the North to raise the troops it needed to win the war. With the Union in extreme peril, the Court plainly had no interest in doing anything that would undermine the Union war effort in the slightest degree.

---

[412] *Thompson*, 59 Me. at 549.

[413] *Id*. at 554 (Dickerson, J., concurring).

Similarly, after the war, with its 1871 decision in the *Thompson* case, the Court continued to disallow municipal commutation payments that had been authorized by towns years earlier. In so doing, the Court kept faith with those who served their country in its time of greatest need.

MAINE'S RIVERS

Considering the importance of rivers in Maine's economic development, we should not find it surprising that during the early years of Maine law, numerous disputes involving conflicting claims to the use of Maine's rivers found their way onto the docket of the Maine Court for final adjudication. Those cases concerned a wide variety of valuable uses of rivers, including, as we shall see, their use for floating logs from the forest to saw mills, for generating power to operate mills, and for harvesting ice for refrigeration. For Maine's developing economy, much was at stake here. Rivers, it is well to recall, were then the state's major arteries of commerce. Cutting their way through what was largely a vast, undeveloped wilderness, Maine's rivers provided access to the wealth of the state's timberlands, opened the state for development, and served as a source of power for Maine's manufacturing industries. The fact that today the major population centers of Maine are situated either on the coast or on the banks of rivers attests to the enormous and lasting significance of Maine's rivers, not only for commerce, but for the entire social and political fabric of the state as well.

In the absence of legislatively prescribed rules for resolving conflicting claims to the use of Maine's rivers, the Court, in accordance with the tradition of the common law, assumed responsibility for developing those rules.

Rivers as Public Highways

Recognizing the importance of rivers to the development of Maine, our Court at an early date established the basic rule that "[a]ll streams in this State of sufficient capacity, in their natural condition, to float boats, rafts or logs, are deemed public highways, and as such,

[are] subject to the use of the public."[414] Under this rule, the right of the public to use Maine's rivers and streams was not limited to those waterways that were navigable in the sense of being deep and wide enough to afford passage for ships and other vessels. The rule established by the Court was considerably broader than that. If, for instance, a river or stream was capable of being used for floating logs from the forest to mills downstream, log drivers could use it for that purpose, and landowners along the way could not prohibit that use, even though the river or stream was not really navigable in the ordinary sense of the word. In the eyes of the law, such rivers and streams were deemed "public" waterways.

Moreover, as the Court insightfully explained in the leading case of *Brown v. Chadbourne* (1849),[415] the question of whether a river or stream was a public waterway did not depend on the length of time it had been used by the public:

> If a stream could be subject to public servitude, by long use only, many large rivers in newly settled States, and some in the interior of this State, would be altogether under the control and dominion of the owners of their beds, and the community would be deprived of the use of those rivers, which nature has plainly declared to be public highways.[416]

Nor did it matter that a waterway was capable of floating timber only during certain times of the year when the volume of water was sufficient for that purpose. As the Court noted in *Brown v. Chadbourne*, considering the geography of Maine, a rule that limited the definition of public rivers to rivers that were "floatable" in all seasons of the year would be devastating for Maine's lumber industry.

---

[414] *Veazie v. Dwinel*, 50 Me. 479, 484 (1862) (citing *Brown v. Chadbourne*, 31 Me. 9 (1849), and other early Maine cases).

[415] 31 Me. 9 (1849) (upholding verdict in favor of log owner in suit against landowner whose dam obstructed passage of logs on Little River, flowing from "Boyden's lake" to tide water).

[416] *Brown v. Chadbourne*, 31 Me. at 21.

Rejecting the argument that the trial court should have instructed the jury in accordance with such a rule, the Court stated:

> Most of the great rivers of the State, in some portions of their passage, are so much impeded by rocks, falls and other obstructions, that logs cannot be floated in them, any great distance, at what might be called an ordinary state of water. It is only in the spring and fall, and occasionally at other times, when their channels are filled with water, that they are capable of floating timber to market. They generally remain in this condition, a sufficient length of time to answer the purposes of a common highway, and their fitness and character as such cannot be destroyed, because they cannot be used in their ordinary state.
>
> A test so rigid and severe as that [which would limit the definition of public rivers to rivers that were floatable in all seasons of the year] would annihilate the public character of all our fresh rivers, for many miles in their course, from their sources towards the ocean. The timber floated upon our waters to market is of great value, and neither the law nor public policy requires the adoption of a rule, which would so greatly limit their use, for that purpose.
>
> The right to the use of the stream in question, must prevail, whenever it may be exercised, at any state of the water.[417]

Consistent with these sentiments, the Court in later cases frequently noted the importance of its "floatable streams" doctrine for Maine's lumber industry and for the State's overall economy and welfare in general. For example, in *Veazie v. Dwinel* (1862),[418] the Court made that point in these terms:

> [T]he right of the public to the use of our *floatable* streams has ever been guarded with jealous care by our Courts. They are

---

[417] *Id.* at 23.

[418] 50 Me. 479, 487 (1862).

the great highways over which vast amounts of the property of our citizens are transported to market, and without which much of the wealth of the State would be locked up in inaccessible forests.

In *Davis v. Winslow* (1863),[419] the Court put it this way:

As human society advanced from its primeval state, navigable rivers and public streams came to be the arteries of commerce, permeating parts otherwise inaccessible, developing occult mineral resources, and bearing upon their bosom immense wealth to the more genial abodes of man. The history of our legislation, no less than the decisions of our courts, attest the solicitude of the community to make these great highways, both the means of developing the resources of the country, and of transporting their products to more remote regions.

And, as another example, in *Woodman v. Pitman* (1887),[420] the Court had this to say:

The court of no state has probably ventured so far as this court has, in maintaining that small streams have floatable properties belonging to the public use. Our climate and forests, together with the interests and wants of the community, make the doctrine here reasonable—a reasonable interpretation of the law.

From reading these several quotations, one might conclude that the Court's public rivers doctrine was an abstract theory of law that had little to do with the realities and practicalities of ordinary life. But that was definitely not the case. As the early case of *Knox v. Chaloner* (1856)[421] illustrates, that doctrine had real teeth to it, and any dam owner who disregarded the doctrine, did so at his peril.

---

[419] 51 Me. 264, 289-90 (1863).

[420] 79 Me. 456, 460, 10 A. 321, 323 (1887).

[421] 42 Me. 150 (1856).

The case of *Knox v. Chaloner* concerned a dam that had been built across "Chase's stream" in Washington County. The plaintiff, William Knox, claimed that the dam, which had been maintained by the defendant, Benjamin Chaloner, obstructed the passage of Knox's logs on that stream. As the result of that obstruction, Knox had to drive his logs from the stream into Chaloner's mill pond and then haul them past the dam and falls to the stream below, from whence they were run into the East Machias River. Relying on the precedent of *Brown v. Chadbourne*, Knox sued Chaloner for damages. Chaloner countered with the argument that Chase's stream was not a public stream because in its natural state it was not capable of floating logs at the site of the dam. He also contended that the Legislature had authorized the construction of the dam in question as a way of creating water power for the operation of his mill. In addition, Chaloner argued that in any event Knox's claim was barred by the passage of time inasmuch as no similar complaint had been made during the seventy-two years that the dam had existed. The jury, however, sided with Knox and awarded him monetary damages. Chaloner appealed.

On appeal, the Court found Chaloner's arguments to be completely without merit and affirmed the jury's verdict in favor of Knox. The Court first noted that the jury had properly found that the stream was a "public river," which the Court defined as a river or stream that in its natural state was "capable of floating boats or logs." In providing that definition, the Court cited its earlier decision in *Brown v. Chadbourne*, and pointed out that the same rule applied in the Province of New Brunswick and in Lower Canada (modern-day Québec). Evidently, the Court felt it was important to consider the law of those neighboring Canadian jurisdictions because of the common interest Maine shares with them in rules concerning rivers that both define and cross their borders.

As for Chaloner's contention that the Legislature had authorized the construction of the dam in question, the Court replied that the statutory right to build mills and mill-dams "must be deemed as in subjection to the paramount right of passage of the public in all cases where the streams in their natural state were capable of floating boats or logs." The Court also rejected Chaloner's passage-of-time argument, explaining that a dam that obstructed the right of the public to float boats or logs in a floatable stream was a public nuisance and that a nuisance of that sort could never be legitimized by the passage of time. In short, the Court's decision in *Knox* was a resounding affirmation of its public rivers doctrine.

Some fifty years later, in *Smart v. Aroostook Lumber Co.* (1907),[422] our Court extended the reach of that doctrine by clarifying that if a river or stream was capable of floating boats or logs, and thereby qualified as a "public highway," the public's right to use that waterway for transportation was not limited to log driving and other commercial activities. In accordance with that clarification, the Court decided that the plaintiff and other owners of summer cottages along the Presque Isle Stream had the right to use that waterway at the location in question for transporting themselves and their possessions to and from their cottages and that the defendant lumber company had unreasonably obstructed that use by not providing an open passageway for boats and canoes to get through its logs stored in that stream. The Court also noted that "sportsmen were accustomed to pass up and down the stream" and remarked that their use of the stream, like that of the summer cottage residents, was also "legitimate." Predicting that recreational uses of rivers might in time eclipse commercial uses, the Court stated:

> The existing conditions which create the purposes of the public use of the Presque Isle Stream are subject to change, and the driving and temporary storing of logs now of principal importance, may become secondary in importance to the travel of summer residents and the transportation of merchandise for their accommodation. In this State, recreation is assuming features and incidents as valuable to the public as trade and manufacturing.[423]

The Court's prediction that the use of rivers for log driving might become less important in the future proved to be accurate.

---

[422] 103 Me. 37, 68 A. 527 (1907).

[423] *Id.* at 48, 68 A. at 532.

Indeed, in 1971, the Legislature, for environmental reasons, enacted legislation that prohibited the use of Maine's inland waters for log driving after October 1, 1976.[424] As the result of that legislation, log driving on Maine's rivers and streams is now but a memory from the past. The demise of that tradition, however, did not affect the continuing viability of the Court's public rivers doctrine because, as the Court explained in the *Smart* case, discussed above, the right of public use protected by that doctrine was not limited to log driving or other commercial activities.

Looking back over the entire history of the public rivers doctrine in Maine—from its log-driving roots in the earliest days of Maine law; through its clarification to encompass recreational uses many years later in *Smart v. Aroostook Lumber Co.*; to the point where today, many more years later, it has now outlived the demise of the log driving tradition that gave it birth—we see how the common law was able to evolve, one case at a time, to meet the changing needs of the community over a considerable span of time.

Although now somewhat tarnished by pollution that has accompanied development along many of Maine's waterways, our Court's vision that the floatable rivers and streams of our State are public highways that "afford an equal right to each citizen to their reasonable use,"[425] continues to serve as a reminder that all citizens of Maine have a common interest in the waterways of our State—that Maine's rivers truly belong to all the people of Maine. Seen in that light, the great rivers of Maine stand out, like Mt. Katahdin, as natural symbols of our commonality, in much the same way our nation's great monuments do.

Resolving Conflicting Uses of Rivers: A Rule of Reason

The principle that the public had the right to use Maine's rivers and streams that were sufficiently floatable to qualify as "public

---

[424] An Act Phasing out Log Driving in the Inland Waters of the State, Me. P.L 1971, ch. 355.

[425] *Smart*, 103 Me. at 47, 68 A. at 531.

highways" became the basis for the Court's adjudication of disputes involving competing and conflicting uses of those waterways. That principle meant that, absent legislative authorization,[426] no party was entitled to the exclusive right to use such a river or stream. In litigated cases, that principle naturally evolved into a rule of reason, whereby one party's right of use was not allowed unreasonably to interfere with another's, as the case of *Davis v. Winslow* (1863)[427] demonstrates.

In *Davis v. Winslow*, the plaintiffs, who owned sawmills in the town of Bethel, Maine, claimed that the defendants, by erecting a boom across the Androscoggin River at Milan, New Hampshire, had unreasonably obstructed the passage of the plaintiffs' logs on their way to the plaintiffs' mills downstream in Bethel. The plaintiffs sued the defendants for damages, alleging that by the time their logs had been released from the defendants' boom, the water level had gone down to the point that the river was no longer floatable. The defendants, on the other hand, maintained that they had the right to erect the boom in order to collect their own logs for their own saw-mill operations at Berlin Falls, New Hampshire. The defendants argued that their detention of the plaintiffs' logs was not unrea-sonable because the plaintiffs' logs were mixed in with their own and that the defendants were impeded in the task of separating out the plaintiffs' logs because of the great number of logs that had accumu-lated and because of the dangerously high level of water in the river at that particular time.[428] The jury found in favor of the plaintiffs, and

---

[426] *See Mullen v. Penobscot Log-Driving Co.*, 90 Me. 555, 567, 38 A. 557, 560 (1897) (upholding the right of the Legislature to grant a corporation a monopoly in log driving between certain points on the Penobscot River) ("The state represents all public rights and privileges in our fresh water rivers and streams, and may dispose of the same as it sees fit."). The extent to which that broad authority of the Legislature might today be considered limited by constitutional consider-ations or "public trust" theories is beyond the scope of our discussion here.

[427] 51 Me. 264 (1863).

[428] Some idea of the magnitude of that task is shown by the trial judge's jury instructions, which noted that the accumulation of logs "formed a solid jam, extending, as variously estimated by the witnesses, from three-fourths of a mile to a mile and a half up the river." *Id.* at 268.

the defendants appealed to the Maine Court, which, in the end, affirmed the jury's verdict.

Addressing the issues presented, the Court explained that although, as a general rule, each party using a river has an equal right to reasonable use, the determination as to what constitutes "reasonable use" in any particular case depends upon the specific circumstances of that case:

> [N]o positive rule of law can be laid down to define and regulate such use, with entire precision, so various are the subjects and occasions for it, and so diversified the relations of parties therein interested.[429]

The Court then listed some of the many factors that might appropriately be taken into account in determining the issue of reasonable use in any given case:

> In determining the question of reasonable use, regard must be had to the subject matter of the use, the occasion and manner of its application, its object, extent, necessity, and duration, and the established usage of the country. The size of the stream, also, the fall of water, its volume, velocity and prospective rise or fall, are important elements to be taken into the account. The same promptness and efficiency would not be expected of the owner of logs thrown promiscuously into the stream, in respect to their management, as would be required of a shipmaster in navigating his ship.[430]

Under the circumstances, it seems that the Court did all it could reasonably have been expected to do by establishing a general rule of reason to govern river-usage disputes such as this. In instructing a jury, a court could list the factors the jury could consider in coming to its verdict. It would be unrealistic, however, to expect a court to define the governing rule—that each user has an equal right to reasonable use—with greater specificity. The weight to be given to

---

[429] *Id.* at 297.
[430] *Id.*

factors such as the "subject matter," "object," and "necessity" of two or more competing uses is simply incapable of objective measurement from either a quantitative or qualitative point of view. While a state administrative agency, operating under statutory guidelines, might conceivably be able to establish criteria for evaluating the weight to be given to such factors, courts are not institutionally suited to perform such assignments.

The Court's use of a standard as indefinite as "reasonableness" in resolving disputes between conflicting uses of rivers might be seen as a shortcoming of the judicial process, particularly in view of the considerable importance of the issues sometimes at stake. But, as the Court correctly noted, the particular circumstances of such disputes are so "various" and "diversified" that a governing standard cannot be laid down with "entire precision." For the same reason, general standards of conduct are employed in many areas of the law. The law of negligence, for example, is based on standards of conduct as general as "due care" and "reasonable prudence," and lawsuits are resolved by applying those general standards to the circumstances of the case at hand.

In another case involving conflicting uses of a river, *Pearson v. Rolfe* (1884),[431] the Court again had occasion to comment on the indefinite nature of its rule of reasonable use. In *Pearson*, log owners and mill owners squared off against each other in a dispute concerning their respective rights "in the use of the water at certain falls in the Penobscot river at West Great Works, in the town of Oldtown." Although the parties submitted their dispute directly to the Maine Court, the Court declined their invitation to decide the matter. In an opinion written by Chief Justice John A. Peters, the Court reminded the parties of the rule of reasonable use, stating that "'the rights of each must be so exercised as not unnecessarily or unreasonably to interfere with or obstruct the rights of the other. And such is the law.'"[432] That said, Peters stated that the Court would refer the case for trial by jury if the parties could not settle the matter themselves. He cautioned the

---

[431] 76 Me. 380 (1884).

[432] *Id.* at 391 (quoting *Veazie v. Dwinel*, 50 Me. 479 (1862)).

parties that, considering the indefinite nature of the rule of reasonable use, they would be well advised to settle the case. As Peters put it:

> The parties would act wisely to indulge a spirit of mutual forbearance and concession in these matters. In no other way are the embarrassments and difficulties, usually incident to such contentions, avoidable. *The rule that governs some of their rights is a general and necessarily an indefinite one.* Emergencies may often arise when the different interests will clash. Discreet words and acts are a better resort, in the first instance, than law-suits.[433]

While we are considering the indefinite nature of the common law rule of reasonable use, it seems worth noting that the respective merits of the common law and statutory law have been debated at length throughout the years.[434] The common law has sometimes been criticized on the ground that the generality of some of its rules allows judges too much discretion in interpreting those rules and thus makes it difficult to predict the outcome of litigation. On the other hand, proponents of the common law tradition hail the general nature of the principles of the common law as a mark of its superiority. As Justice Jonathan G. Dickerson explained in *Davis v. Winslow*, the Androscoggin River "log-boom case" discussed above:

> While, however, the general principles of the common law remain fixed, their adaptation to the vicissitudes of human affairs renders them sufficiently comprehensive to meet new

---

[433] *Id.* at 392 (emphasis added).

[434] During the nineteenth century, there was a strong movement to codify the common law, the most notable illustration of which was the work of David Dudley Field, brother of U.S. Supreme Court Justice Stephen J. Field, in endeavoring to codify the common law of the State of New York. In the twentieth century, various uniform codes, adopted by the states, converted large areas of the common law into statutes in the interest of national uniformity, certainty, and predictability. Likewise, the American Law Institute's "Restatements of the Law," ongoing projects that began early in the twentieth century and continue to the present day, attempt for the same reasons to clarify the current state of the common law throughout the country on a wide range of topics.

institutions and states of society, and new systems of intercommunication between man and man, as they unfold themselves in the progress of civilization.[435]

The Court's decision in *Pearson* suggests an additional consideration in any debate concerning the respective merits of the common law and statutory law: Does the general nature of common-law principles encourage the settlement of disputes that would otherwise consume limited judicial time and resources, as suggested by the Court in that case? Or, conversely, does that feature of the common law encourage litigation, on the theory that the more general the rules, the more litigation becomes a gamble on which a prospective litigant might be willing to take a chance? Although the debate as to the respective merits of the common law tradition and statutory law will probably never be fully resolved (and here it should be noted that statutory law has its own share of indefinite rules and standards of conduct), the Court's insight in *Pearson*—that the degree of specificity with which legal rules are framed has a bearing on the dispute resolution process—is a valuable contribution to that discussion.

Frozen Rivers: Rights of Passage

In two nineteenth-century cases that involved the loss of horses that fell through the ice, the Court developed rules of the common law concerning conflicting uses of Maine's frozen winter waterways. These cases might just as well have been noted in the chapter entitled "Maine Law's Debt to Animals," but they are mentioned here instead because of their significance in the development of Maine law relating to rivers.

The first of these cases, *French v. Camp*,[436] was decided by the Court in 1841. While lawfully traveling with his horse on the ice-covered Penobscot River, Mr. French lost his horse when it fell

---

[435] *Davis*, 51 Me. at 289.

[436] 18 Me. 433 (1841).

through a hole in the ice that had been cut by the defendants. French maintained that the defendants were liable for his loss. The defendants claimed that they had the right to cut a hole in the ice for the purpose of watering their horses and cattle. The jury sided with French and awarded him damages. On appeal by the defendants, the Court affirmed that verdict. The specific location of the watering hole cut by the defendants ultimately determined the outcome of the case.

In upholding the plaintiff's verdict, the Court first explained that the waters of the Penobscot River constituted a public highway, in both their liquid and frozen states: "[W]hen [those waters were] congealed, the citizens have still a right to traverse their surface at pleasure." More specifically, the Court noted that the right of public passage over the ice on the river pertained both to ways for crossing at ferry locations and to "well marked and beaten ways" that have been used by the public for traveling in winter. Assuming that the defendants had as good a right as French to the use of the river, the Court held that the defendants were nevertheless required to exercise their right so as not to injure the rights of another. The act of the defendants, in cutting a hole in the center of a "road" upon the ice, or so near to it as to entrap a traveler, was, the Court concluded, "a direct violation of that great principle of social duty, by which each one is required so to use his own rights, as not to injure the rights of others."

Forty-six years later, in the case of *Woodman v. Pitman* (1887),[437] the Court again addressed the question of rights of passage over the ice on the Penobscot River. By then, the frozen rivers of Maine were providing, in abundance, the raw material for the extremely prosperous national and international ice-harvesting business. Mr. Woodman and the defendants each operated ice fields on the river. One winter day, Woodman lost his two-horse team when it fell through a hole that had been cut by the defendants in one of their ice fields. Evidently, that loss occurred while the driver of Woodman's team was taking a shortcut across the defendants' ice fields to one of Woodman's ice fields.

---

[437] 79 Me. 456, 10 A. 321 (1887).

Woodman sued the defendants for having caused the loss of his horses and won a jury verdict in his favor. On appeal by the defendants, however, the Court set that verdict aside on the ground that Woodman's loss had been caused by the recklessness of his own driver and because the rights of the defendants had not been properly considered in the trial court. The case could have been decided solely on the ground of the recklessness of Woodman's driver, without having to delve into the uncharted territory of ice-harvesting law. But the Court chose to enter that territory, nevertheless.

The Court began its opinion by pointing out that the case presented novel issues of law because the recent increase in the commercial importance of ice-harvesting was itself a new development in Maine. That circumstance provided a perfect opportunity for the Court to explain the duty of a court in adjudicating novel issues of law:

> The inexhaustible and ever-changing complications in human affairs are constantly presenting new questions and new conditions which the law must provide for as they arise; and the law has expansive and adaptive force enough to respond to the demands thus made of it; not by subverting, but by forming new combinations and making new applications out of, its already established principles,—the result produced being only "the new corn that cometh out of the fields."[438]

In weighing the significance of the relative rights of the parties, the Court explained that the interests of the public had to be taken into account. Weighing the importance of Woodman's claimed right to travel on the ice against the importance of the defendants' right to operate its commercial ice field, the Court had no difficulty concluding that the latter outweighed the former in terms of its importance to the public. Indeed, as the Court saw it, the importance of the ice-harvesting industry to the public was "incomparably greater" than Woodman's claimed right of traveling on the ice. This

---

[438] *Id.* at 458, 10 A. at 322.

was particularly so, the Court explained, because roadways along the banks of the Penobscot River had, for some time, made it unnecessary to travel by ice at the site of the accident.

Some important insight into the mind of the Court at this stage of its history (1887) is revealed by the importance the Court ascribed to the ice-harvesting business and to the commercial development of the State in general. As the following excerpt from the Court's decision in this case shows, the Court gave great weight in its deliberations to the importance of commercial development. Significantly, the Court also explained how, as it saw it, private enterprise inures to the benefit of the public at large. Describing the numerous, diverse benefits of the ice-harvesting industry that flourished in Maine at the time, the Court stated:

> [T]he business of gathering ice for merchantable purposes has assumed extraordinary importance on our rivers. Large amounts of capital are invested; thousands of men and of teams are employed at a season of the year when other employment cannot be obtained by them; the outlay is mostly in bills for labor, widely circulated; a crop of immense value is annually produced from an exhaustless soil without sowing; the shipping business is materially aided by it; the wealth of the state is greatly increased by it; *it is eminently a business of the people.* It would seem unreasonably to embarrass such an important enterprise by according to the traveling public a paramount right of passage, when such right, even to its possessor, is scarcely good for anything.[439]

In today's world, the interests of management and labor, employer and employee, producer and consumer, are often seen as separate and more or less adversarial in nature. The Court in 1887, however, may not have had such a polarized view of society. In lending its support to the owners and financiers of commercial enterprises, the Court apparently believed that it was simultaneously supporting the interests of labor, those "thousands of men and...

---

[439] *Id.* at 461, 10 A. at 324 (emphasis added).

teams... employed at a season of the year when other employment cannot be obtained by them." From our present-day perspective, one might be inclined to describe Maine's prosperous ice-harvesting business as having been "eminently a business of Wall Street," but to our Court in 1887, that enterprise was, in its words, "eminently a business of the people."

Although the business of ice harvesting in Maine has now all but completely disappeared, along with the tradition of log driving on Maine's rivers and streams, those activities in their heyday generated what for us today is a treasure trove of judicial literature in the form of opinions of the Maine Court that illustrate and explain the methods and merits of the common law in developing and adapting legal principles to meet the changing circumstances of the times.

Norway Liberal Institute, Norway, Maine,
site of assault in *State v. Yeaton* (1865).

Courtesy of Norway Historical Society, Norway, Maine.

Log drive on Androscoggin River where the river flows between Hanover
(on the north) and Bethel (on the south), ca. 1900, downriver from
site of controversy in *Davis v. Winslow* (1863).

Courtesy of The Bethel Historical Society, Bethel, Maine.

Androscoggin River with logs en route to mills, downriver from Bethel,
at Rumford Falls, Rumford, Maine, ca. 1900.

Collections of Maine Historical Society (Image no. 20438).

Log jam at Rumford Falls, 1873.

Courtesy of The Bethel Historical Society, Bethel, Maine.

Consolidated Ice Co. ice-harvesting operations, Kennebec River
near Bowdoinham, Maine, ca. 1895.

Collections of Maine Historical Society (Image no. 1203).

The early Maine Court's jurisprudence concerning various uses of rivers stands as a model of the common law's ability to adapt to meet the changing needs and circumstances of the times.

Main Street, Westbrook, Maine, ca. 1905, site of assault in *Leavitt v. Dow* (1908).

Courtesy of Westbrook Historical Society, Westbrook, Maine.

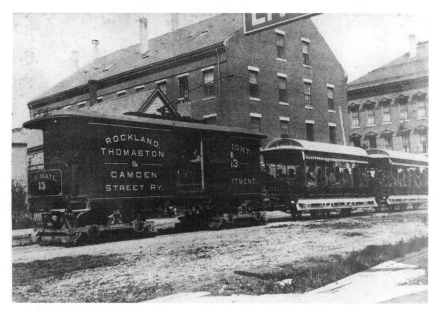

Rockland, Thomaston & Camden Street Railway passenger cars and mail car
at Main and Park Streets, Rockland, Maine, ca. 1898, vicinity of incident
in *Robinson v. Rockland, Thomaston & Camden Street Railway* (1895).

Courtesy of Rockland Historical Society, Rockland, Maine.

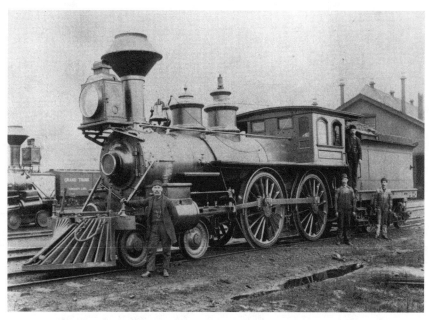

Grand Trunk locomotive, ca. 1875.

Collections of Maine Historical Society (Image no. 5788).

Bangor and Aroostook Engine 183, ca. 1920.

Collections of Oakfield Historical Society, Oakfield, Maine,
Courtesy of Maine Historical Society (Image no. 14758).

Bangor and Aroostook Engine 86, ca. 1920.

Collections of Oakfield Historical Society, Oakfield, Maine,
Courtesy of Maine Historical Society (Image no. 14763).

Railroads were a powerful force for economic progress in Maine's early years and had a major impact on the development of early Maine law.

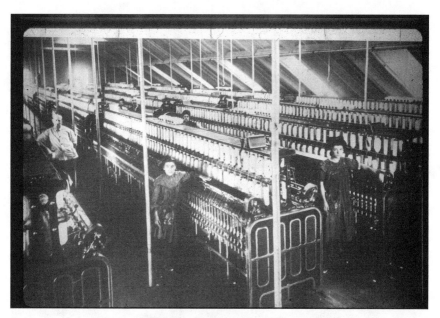

Textile mill workers, ca. 1900.

Courtesy of Lewiston Public Library, Lewiston, Maine, Gridley Barrows Collection.

Mill workers, ca. 1900.

Courtesy of Lewiston Public Library, Lewiston, Maine, Gridley Barrows Collection.

Workplace injury claims were a frequent subject of litigation in Maine's early years.

Prentiss Mellen, Chief Justice, Supreme Judicial Court of Maine, 1820–1834.
Detail from portrait by Joseph B. Kahill.
Courtroom, Maine Supreme Judicial Court, Portland, Maine.

John Appleton, Associate Justice and Chief Justice,
Supreme Judicial Court of Maine, 1852–1862, 1862–1883.

Jonathan G. Dickerson, Associate Justice,
Supreme Judicial Court of Maine, 1862–1878.

*Maine Legal Photograph Collection of
The Nathan & Henry B. Cleaves Law Library, Portland, Maine.*

John A. Peters

JUSTICE AND CHIEF JUSTICE OF MAINE 1873-1883 1883-1900

John A. Peters, Associate Justice and Chief Justice,
Supreme Judicial Court of Maine, 1873–1883, 1883–1900.

Supreme Judicial Court of Maine, May 11, 1859–May 7, 1862.
Seated, left to right: Edward Kent, Seth May, John S. Tenney (C.J.), Jonas Cutting.
Standing, left to right: Daniel Goodenow, Richard D. Rice, Woodbury Davis, John Appleton.

Supreme Judicial Court of Maine, April 12, 1894–May 14, 1897.
Seated, left to right: Enoch Foster, Charles W. Walton, John A. Peters (C.J.),
Lucilius A. Emery, Thomas H. Haskell.
Standing, left to right: Andrew P. Wiswell, William Penn Whitehouse, Sewall C. Strout.

Supreme Judicial Court of Maine, Portland Term, 1902.
Left to right: Albert M. Spear, Frederick A. Powers, Sewall C. Strout,
Andrew P. Wiswell (C.J.), Albert R. Savage, Henry C. Peabody.
Front left: Benjamin C. Stone, Clerk.
Not present: Lucilius A. Emery, William Penn Whitehouse.

Supreme Judicial Court of Maine, June 24, 1919.
Left to right: Luere B. Deasy, John A. Morrill, Warren C. Philbrook, Albert M. Spear,
Leslie C. Cornish (C.J.), George M. Hanson, Charles J. Dunn, Scott Wilson.

Supreme Judicial Court of Maine, 1921.
Left to right: Warren C. Philbrook, Scott Wilson, Albert M. Spear, Charles J. Dunn,
Leslie C. Cornish (C.J.), John A. Morrill, George M. Hanson, Luere B. Deasy.

Joseph Story

Joseph Story, Associate Justice, Supreme Court of the United States, 1812–1845.

From the Historical Collection of Herman H. Diers,
Collection of the Supreme Court of the United States.

RESOLVING DISPUTES BETWEEN NEIGHBORS

I n the early years of Maine law, before the arrival of zoning ordinances in the twentieth century, the owner of real estate was generally free to use his land as he wished, provided he did not cause harm to his neighbors. This general rule was a bedrock principle of the common law. As the Maine Court in 1847 stated, "Nothing in the law can be more certain, than one's right to occupy and use his own land, as he pleases, if he does not thereby injure others."[440] That principle is expressed by the ancient legal maxim, *sic utere tuo ut alienum non laedas*, meaning "Use your own so as not to injure another's property." That maxim, the Court explained, "expresses not only the law, but the elements of good neighborhood and mutual right."[441] In a case decided in 1866, the Court described that maxim as "the legal application of the gospel rule of doing unto others as we would that they should do unto us."[442]

As population density and industrialization increased in Maine over the years, the *sic utere tuo* maxim would eventually be supplemented by comprehensive land use statutes and zoning ordinances. But during the early years of Maine law, that maxim and the neighborly principles it represents provided the substance of the common law of "nuisance," which was applied by the courts in resolving land use disputes.[443] Two early Maine cases show how our Court dealt with such matters.

---

[440] *Pierre v. Fernald*, 26 Me. 436, 440 (1847).

[441] *Wilkins v. Monson Consol. Slate Co.*, 96 Me. 385, 386, 52 A. 755, 756 (1902).

[442] *Barnes v. Hathorn*, 54 Me. 124, 125 (1866).

[443] An early and rudimentary precursor to modern zoning laws, one of Maine's earliest statutes provided that the selectmen of a town, together with two justices

Mr. Haines's Bowling Alley

State v. Haines (1849)[444] concerned a bowling alley located in the town of Winthrop, Maine. At issue there was whether the defendant, Dudley Haines, by operating a bowling alley, was guilty of maintaining a "common nuisance." A common nuisance has been defined as "a species of catch-all criminal offense, consisting of an interference with the rights of the community at large."[445] A Maine statute provided that if a person was found guilty of erecting, causing, or continuing a common nuisance, the court might impose a $100 fine and order the nuisance discontinued or abated. The jury found Haines guilty. On appeal, the Court sustained that verdict.

Among other arguments, Haines contended that the allegations in the indictment were insufficient to charge him with maintaining a common nuisance. The Court disagreed. The indictment consisted of two counts. The first count alleged that the bowling alley was a common nuisance but did not set forth any particular examples of how it disturbed the public. The Court nevertheless found the allegations of that count sufficient because, as the Court explained, it considered a bowling alley to be a common nuisance per se. The second count alleged that the bowling alley was a common nuisance because its operation had occasioned "great noises" at night, to the discomfort of the community. Citing an English precedent, the Court found that count sufficient, stating that "the mere fact of occasioning such noises in the night time, to the disturbance of the neighborhood, has been decided to be a nuisance."

The Court's decision on the first count, declaring a bowling alley a nuisance per se, is particularly interesting from an historical perspective because it illustrates the broad scope of judicial power

---

of the peace, could establish certain places in a town to be used for "killing creatures for meat, distilling of spirits, trying of tallow or oil, currying of leather, and making earthern ware." An Act for the Prevention and Removal of Nuisances, Me. P.L. 1821, ch. 24.

[444] 30 Me. 65 (1849).

[445] Prosser & Keeton on The Law of Torts, ed. W. Page Keeton, 5th ed. (St. Paul: West Publishing Co., 1984), 618.

exercised by the Court in the early years of Maine law. In his opinion for the Court concerning that count, Chief Justice Ether Shepley began by explaining that the question presented was "whether the keeping of a bowling alley for gain and common use, as an inducement for persons to play on it in the day and night time, is a common nuisance." Addressing that question, Shepley noted that William Blackstone, in his *Commentaries on the laws of England* (1765-69), had defined a nuisance to be "any thing, that worketh hurt, inconvenience, or damage." In England, Shepley observed, the common law divided nuisances into two categories: activities that were nuisances *per se* and activities that were nuisances because of their particular location or effect on neighboring property.[446] Nuisances *per se* included "stages for rope-dancing, for mountebanks, gaming houses and bawdy-houses." The other category of nuisances included "the trades of the soap-boiler, tallow-chandler, brewer and tanner."

In concluding that a bowling alley was a common nuisance *per se*, Shepley expressed his concern about the harmful impact he believed bowling alleys inevitably had on the morals and well-being of the community:

> The "hurt" or injury to the community, which has occasioned bowling alleys kept for gain and common use to be regarded as common nuisances, arises from their tendency to withdraw the young and inconsiderate from any useful employment of their time, and to subject them to various temptations. From their affording to the idle and dissolute encouragement to continue in their destructive courses. Clerks, apprentices and others are induced, not only to appropriate to them hours, which should be employed to increase their knowledge and reform their hearts, but too often to violate higher moral duties to obtain means to pay for the indulgence. Other bad habits are in such places often introduced or confirmed. The

---

[446] As to the latter category, what we might call "situational" nuisances, the U.S. Supreme Court has remarked that "[a] nuisance may be merely a right thing in the wrong place,—like a pig in the parlor instead of the barnyard." *Village of Euclid v. Ambler Realty Co.*, 272 U.S. 365, 388 (1926).

moral sense, the correct principles, the temperate, regular and industrious habits, which are the basis of a prosperous and happy community, are frequently impaired or destroyed. Bowling alleys without doubt may be resorted to by many persons without such injurious results. The inquiry is not what may be done at such places without injury to persons of fixed habits and principles, but what has been in the experience of man, their general tendency and result.[447]

By declaring that bowling alleys were unlawful nuisances on the basis of their "general tendency" to be injurious to the community, regardless of the circumstances of each particular case, the Court in effect assumed the role and extensive powers of a legislative body that enacts laws it considers to be in the public interest.[448] As ensuing events would show, however, a court that exercises that kind of authority may well find that the legislature, in its law-making capacity, has the final word. In 1855, six years after the Court handed down its decision in *Haines*, the Maine Legislature in effect overruled Shepley's categorical *per se* approach to bowling alleys by enacting legislation authorizing municipalities to license the operation of bowling alleys, provided those operations did not disturb the peace and quiet of any neighborhood or family.[449]

Here we might pause to note that in developing the common law in Maine's early years of statehood, the Maine Court was not timid about pronouncing moral judgments in the course of deciding

---

[447] *Haines*, 30 Me. at 75-76.

[448] In a case decided in 1978, the Maine Court described its ruling in *Haines* as follows: "Because in the mid-1800's, as *State v. Haines* decided, a bowling alley was deemed *per se* a common nuisance, the keeping of a bowling alley was *per se* unlawful; the activity itself was evil, as exerting 'immoral' influences." *Roy v. Inhabitants of Augusta*, 387 A.2d. 237, 239 (Me. 1978). Noting the change in public perception of bowling alleys that had taken place over the years since 1849 when *Haines* was decided, the Court in *Roy* remarked that "[i]n modern times...bowling and playing billiards weigh much differently in our scale of values; they are acceptable, and indeed respectable, as beneficial recreational pursuits."

[449] An act for the regulation of bowling alleys, Me. P.L. 1855, ch. 167.

appeals, as its decision in *Haines* indicates. Indeed, the content and tone of that decision suggest that the Court believed that in expressing its moral judgment on the issue at hand, it was performing a vital teaching function for the benefit of the community at large and that in doing so it was fulfilling one of its highest duties as the Supreme Judicial Court of Maine.

The Maine Court was not alone in using its written opinions as opportunities to reinforce moral values during those early years. For example, in 1823, U.S. Supreme Court Justice Joseph Story, in a decision he wrote in his capacity as a circuit court justice in Maine, lashed out at the chicanery of ship owners who provisioned their ships with an inadequate supply of medicines needed for the treatment of crew members who might become sick during a voyage.[450] Those ship owners evidently believed that a statute relieved them from liability for medical care expenses incurred by members of the crew if their ships were provided with "a chest of medicines," regardless of the sufficiency of those medicines. Story denounced that practice in words that were designed to sting:

> In the course of the investigation of this suit, it has come to the knowledge of the court, that there is a most criminal neglect and indifference on this subject, that cannot but excite the most painful surprise and mortification. When we find, that some merchants in this neighborhood, instead of directing a medicine chest to be furnished and replenished with an adequate stock of all the necessary medicines, drive a hard bargain for a supply of the most ordinary kinds, and of those least adapted to the voyage, at a very trifling fixed price; and when even such medicines are insufficient in quantity, it cannot but create a feeling little short of indignation, that there should exist among a moral people, such an insensibility to human suffering, and such a carelessness of human life. This information, which for the first time has been brought to the notice of the court, is most unwelcome, and calls upon it, as an imperious duty, to pronounce the most pointed

---

[450] *Harden v. Gordon*, 11 F. Cas. 480 (C.C.D. Me. 1823) (No. 6,047).

reprobation of the practice. If owners will persist in this practice, they shall not, so far as this court is concerned, derive any benefit from such a violation of duty.[451]

On another occasion, twenty-two years later, Story used a decision he wrote while on circuit in Maine to condemn the deplorable state of the morals of the marketplace.[452] Story left no doubt about his feelings regarding misrepresentations made by vendors in purchase and sale transactions:

> It appears to me, that it is high time, that the principles of courts of equity upon the subject of sales and purchases should be better understood, and more rigidly enforced in the community. It is equally promotive of sound morals, fair dealing and public justice and policy, that every vendor should distinctly comprehend, not only that good faith should reign over all his conduct in relation to the sale, but that there should be the most scrupulous good faith, an exalted honesty, or, as it is often felicitously expressed, *uberrima fides*, in every representation made by him as an inducement to the sale. He should, literally, in his representation, tell the truth, the whole truth, and nothing but the truth. If his representation is false in any one substantial circumstance going to the inducement or essence of the bargain, and the vendee is thereby misled, the sale is voidable; and it is usually immaterial, whether the representation be willfully and designedly false, or ignorantly or negligently untrue. The vendor acts at his peril, and is bound by every syllable he utters, or proclaims, or knowingly impresses upon the vendee, as a lure or decisive motive for the bargain. And I cannot but believe, if this doctrine of law

---

[451] *Id.* at 487.

[452] *Doggett v. Emerson*, 7 F. Cas. 804 (C.C.D. Me. 1845) (No. 3,960) (deciding that a contract for the sale of timberlands should be set aside on the basis of gross mistake and gross misrepresentation). Story began his opinion with this observation: "This is one of that unfortunate class of cases, which grew out of the marvelous spirit of speculation in timber lands, which a few years ago pervaded the whole state of Maine, and spread such wide ruin and disaster in many directions, and produced a most sad spectacle of delusion and moral infirmity."

had been steadfastly kept in view, and fairly upheld by public opinion, the various speculations, which have been so sad a reproach to our country, would have been greatly averted, if not entirely suppressed, by its salutary operation.[453]

As a member of the U.S. Supreme Court, Story was the virtual embodiment of "the Law" while he was sitting as a circuit court justice in Maine. In view of his commanding status, Story was uniquely situated to condemn unethical conduct that came to his attention in the course of his official duties.

For a number of reasons, courts today, in deciding ordinary civil actions, might be much less likely to so openly express the moral values that underlie their decisions: it might be considered arrogant for any single court or judge to do so because there are so many more courts and judges today than there were in Story's day; it might be considered no part of a judge's business to do so where standards of personal conduct in a given case have already been established by a legislative body; it might be considered both presumptuous and risky to do so, considering that in our diverse culture today, consensus concerning moral values is a more elusive goal than it was in years gone by. Yet, that being said, it would be a loss for society at large if courts were ever to abdicate wholly their role as expositors of the moral values on which justice depends. We may be a more diverse society than we once were, but the administration of law and our existence as a civilized community continue to depend on commonly supported moral precepts, among the most basic of which are the importance of truth and the wrong of deceit. As Justice Story's opinions discussed above show, courts are at least as well suited as any other governmental institution to speak to those particular principles, as appropriate occasions for doing so arise.

---

[453] *Id.* at 816.

Mary Hathorn's Tomb

In *Barnes v. Hathorn* (1866),[454] the Court again considered the issue of what constitutes an unlawful nuisance. This time the question was whether a tomb located on the property of the defendant, Mary Hathorn, was an unlawful nuisance because of the proximity of the tomb to the home of the plaintiff, William Barnes. Barnes brought suit against Hathorn for damages, claiming that the recent interment of a body in the tomb decreased the market value of his premises. The tomb in question was described by the Court as made of brick, with ventilators at each end, the whole covered by a whitewashed, wooden-frame building. The Court pointed out that although Hathorn's property consisted of 130 acres of land, the tomb was situated on her property only forty-four feet from Barnes's dwelling. As Justice Edward Kent, who authored the Court's opinion, observed:

> It was only some fifteen paces from the windows of his dining and sitting room. It was certainly not a very cheering or exhilarating prospect which met the plaintiff's vision, whenever he looked abroad.[455]

With one Justice dissenting, the Court concluded that Barnes had presented enough evidence that the tomb was a nuisance to warrant submitting the case to the jury. The Court was persuaded that based on health concerns caused by noxious odors that had emitted from the tomb in the past, when the tomb contained up to nine dead bodies, Barnes could reasonably have been concerned that the renewed use of the tomb for the interment of bodies could be injurious to his physical and mental health, even though there had been no noxious emissions for several years.

In a dissenting opinion, Justice Jonathan G. Dickerson criticized the majority opinion for disregarding the legal maxim, *de minimis non curat lex*, meaning "The law takes no notice of trifles." Dickerson was

---

[454] 54 Me. 124 (1866).

[455] *Id.* at 129.

concerned that unless that maxim was honored by the Court, the definition of what constitutes an unlawful nuisance might be stretched to the point that it would seriously impede the expansion of industrial enterprise in Maine. For as he noted, almost any industrial expansion could arguably be considered harmful in some way or other. Referring to the maxim *sic utere tuo ut alienum non laedas* (use your own so as not to injure another's property), Dickerson stated:

> This rule however, must have a reasonable construction, or it would become oppressive in many instances, and defeat the benevolent purpose it was designed to subserve.... It is plain that the literal enforcement of this maxim would embarrass the industry of the country, and materially retard the rapid development of the national resources, while, at the same time, it would diminish the sum of individual and social comfort and well-being.
>
> ...The annoyance, inconvenience or discomfort complained of must be a subsisting and substantial grievance, materially affecting the ordinary physical comfort of human existence, as understood by the American people in their present state of enlightenment, and not according to the crude and fanciful notions of a semi-barbarous, or less enlightened age.[456]

In what appears to be a response to Dickerson's concerns, Kent clarified that the majority of the Court did not intend to define "unlawful nuisance" so broadly that it would unreasonably interfere with property rights. As Kent stated:

> There may be many acts which, to the eyes of others, appear to be unneighborly and even unkind, and entirely unnecessary to the full enjoyment of the property—vexatious and irritating, and the source of constant mental annoyance, and

---

[456] *Id.* at 130-31. Although Dickerson was the only dissenter in *Barnes v. Hathorn*, the concerns he there expressed were subsequently acted on by the whole Court in *Monk v. Packard*, 71 Me. 309 (1880). In holding that a cemetery was not a nuisance *per se*, the Court there stated, "The law protects against real wrong and injury combined, but not against either or both when merely fanciful."

yet they may be but the legal exercise of the right of dominion, and therefore cannot be deemed nuisances.[457]

At the same time, however, Justice Kent explained that the "right of dominion" is not unlimited: "Every man gives up something of this absolute right of dominion and use of his own, to be regulated or restrained by law, so that others may not be hurt or hindered unreasonably in the use and enjoyment of their property."

In time, a jurisprudence based on these ancient, competing maxims—*sic utere tuo ut alienum non laedas* and *de minimis non curat lex*—would to a considerable extent be replaced by land use legislation and zoning regulations that defined the permissible uses of land in various zoning districts, such as residential, commercial, industrial, and so on. In the formative years of Maine law, however, these maxims of the common law, despite their lack of specificity, were the only legal tools at hand for resolving all kinds of land use disputes.[458] That these simple maxims capably did that job throughout that time is all the more remarkable considering that those years witnessed industrial expansion in Maine on a scale never before seen. The enduring usefulness of these old maxims as judicial tools is further evidenced by the fact that to the present day they continue to play an important role in the ongoing development of the law of nuisances and in determining the constitutionality and scope of land use legislation. As the U.S. Supreme Court stated in *Village of Euclid v. Ambler*

---

[457] *Barnes*, 54 Me. at 126.

[458] In addition to the "bowling alley" and "tomb" cases discussed above, see, for example, the Court's decisions balancing the interests of the parties in *Norcross v. Thoms*, 51 Me. 503 (1863) ("The business of a blacksmith, though honorable, necessary and useful, should be carried on so as not to injure others. The close proximity—twelve feet distant—of defendant's blacksmith shop to the plaintiff's hotel could scarcely be occupied as such without causing serious annoyance, and inconvenience to the plaintiff's guests, and consequent loss to himself."); and *Wilkins v. Monson Consol. Slate Co.*, 96 Me. 385, 52 A. 755 (1902) ("With suitable precautions, blasting can be done in the quarry, without throwing rocks upon plaintiff's premises.").

Realty Co. (1926),[459] its landmark ruling upholding the constitutionality of a zoning ordinance:

> The ordinance now under review, and all similar laws and regulations, must find their justification in some aspect of the police power, asserted for the public welfare. The line which in this field separates the legitimate from the illegitimate assumption of power is not capable of precise delimitation. It varies with circumstances and conditions. A regulatory zoning ordinance, which would be clearly valid as applied to the great cities, might be clearly invalid as applied to rural communities. In solving doubts, the maxim *sic utere tuo ut alienum non laedas*, which lies at the foundation of so much of the common law of nuisances, ordinarily will furnish a fairly helpful clew. And the law of nuisances, likewise, may be consulted, not for the purpose of controlling, but for the helpful aid of its analogies in the process of ascertaining the scope of, the power.[460]

---

[459] 272 U.S. 365 (1926).

[460] *Id.* at 387-88.

GOVERNMENTAL POWER AND PRIVATE PROPERTY

S ome of the most controversial issues of constitutional law concern the extent of the power of the State to take private property by eminent domain,[461] to tax private property, to spend public funds, and to regulate and restrict the use of private property. What makes these issues particularly controversial is the fundamental importance of the competing interests at stake on both sides of the question. On the one hand, we have the State, exercising its sovereign powers in the public interest, while on the other, we have the property owner, relying on the constitutionally protected right of ownership of private property.

During its first hundred years, the Maine Court decided numerous cases involving these issues. The resolution of cases concerning eminent domain and the power of the State to tax and spend hinged largely on the definition of the terms, "public use" and "public purpose." For example, was property being taken for a "public use"? Were tax dollars being spent for a "public purpose"? The resolution of cases concerning the regulation and restriction of the use of private property involved the concept that came to be known as the "police power"—the power of government to regulate the use of private property for the common good and general welfare.

To understand these matters in historical context, it is necessary to travel back to the earliest days of Maine law. Two provisions of

---

[461] "Eminent domain" can be generally defined as the inherent power of the State to take private property for public use. The Maine Court has described the power of eminent domain as follows: "The power of eminent domain is not created by constitution or statute. It is an inherent attribute of sovereignty; it existed in the sovereign long before the adoption of any constitution." *Kennebec Water Dist. v. City of Waterville*, 96 Me. 234, 242, 52 A. 774, 777 (1902).

Maine's Constitution, as originally adopted in 1820, directly concern the right of private property.[462] The most basic of those provisions is found in the first section of the first article (the Declaration of Rights) in Maine's Constitution, which secures to all people the "natural, inherent and unalienable right" of "acquiring, possessing and protecting property." That section reads:

> All people are born equally free and independent, and have certain natural, inherent and unalienable rights, among which are those of enjoying and defending life and liberty, acquiring, possessing and protecting property, and of pursuing and obtaining safety and happiness. [463]

The second provision in Maine's Constitution that directly pertains to the right of private property is the twenty-first section of the Declaration of Rights. That section, which recognizes the right of private property and imposes limits on the authority of the State to take private property by eminent domain, states:

> Private property shall not be taken for public uses without just compensation; nor unless the public exigencies require it.[464]

---

[462] A third provision that directly concerns the right of private property became part of Maine's Constitution by an amendment in 1963, well after the early years of Maine law with which we are concerned here. That amendment, which added Section 6-A to the first article (the Declaration of Rights) of Maine's Constitution, reads as follows: "No person shall be deprived of life, liberty or property without due process of law, nor be denied the equal protection of the laws, nor be denied the enjoyment of that person's civil rights or be discriminated against in the exercise thereof." It should also be noted that Article I, Section 6 of Maine's Constitution, which sets out the rights of persons accused in criminal prosecutions, includes this provision concerning property: "The accused shall not be compelled to furnish or give evidence against himself or herself, nor be deprived of life, liberty, property or privileges, but by judgment of that person's peers or the law of the land." For a most helpful and lucid discussion of these and other provisions of Maine's Constitution, see Marshall J. Tinkle, *The Maine State Constitution: A Reference Guide* (Westport, Conn.: Greenwood Press, 1992).

[463] Me. Const. Art. I, § 1. Until 1988, this provision of Maine's Constitution began, "All men are born equally free," etc. In that year, the Maine Constitution was amended to make its provisions gender neutral.

[464] Me. Const. Art. I, § 21.

In the landmark case of *Proprietors of the Kennebec Purchase v. Laboree* (1823),[465] Chief Justice Prentiss Mellen explained that these constitutional provisions, which protect private property and limit the power of the State in taking private property for "public uses," necessarily imply that the government may not take the private property of one person and give it to another for "private uses" under any circumstances. As Mellen put this:

> But the *private* property of one man cannot be taken for the *private uses* of *another* in any case. It cannot by a *mere act of the legislature* be taken from *one man*, and vested in *another* directly....[466]

The principle that the government may not take the property of one person for the private use of another is a cornerstone of our nation's constitutional jurisprudence that was well established by the time Maine became a state in 1820. In 1798, in the case of *Calder v. Bull*,[467] U.S. Supreme Court Justice Samuel Chase described a law that "takes property from A. and gives it to B." as an example of legislation that would violate "certain vital principles in our free Republican governments." It would, he said, be "against all reason and justice" for the people to entrust such a power to a legislature. And, he added, to suggest that a legislature possessed such a power "would, in my opinion, be a political heresy, altogether inadmissible in our free republican governments."[468]

---

[465] 2 Me. 275 (1823). This case was discussed above in the chapter entitled "Foundational Constitutional Principles."

[466] *Id.* at 290-91.

[467] 3 U.S. (3 Dall.) 386 (1798).

[468] *Id.* at 388-89. *See also* Laurence H. Tribe, *American Constitutional Law*, 2d ed. (Mineola, N.Y.: Foundation Press, 1988), 588 ("As early as 1798, Justice Chase, in his memorable dictum in *Calder v. Bull*, had expressed constitutional law's undisputed condemnation of any law attempting to 'take property from A. and give it to B.' General principles of law, enforceable in a proper forum, had settled that no form of legislative authority could be employed to serve private ends: taking, taxing, and regulation were all inherently linked to the public good and depended for their legitimacy upon the preservation of that link.") and U.S.

While we are considering the constitutional basis of the right of private property in Maine, we might also note that at an early date in Maine's legal history, the Maine Court had occasion to express its views on the importance of that right and the importance of vigilance in protecting that right. In *Comins v. Bradbury* (1833),[469] the Court decided that in exercising the power of eminent domain, the State must make or provide for compensation when property is taken and not leave the landowner to petition the Legislature for compensation. Concerning the constitutional right of private property, the Court stated:

> [T]he history and experience of mankind prove that it is essential to individual and to public prosperity, that every man should be secure in the enjoyment of the fruits of his own industry. The force of this principle cannot in any degree be impaired, without relaxing the springs of exertion and enterprize. When the right of property is assailed by private injustice, fraud or oppression, the laws of all civilized governments furnish adequate remedies. But there have been periods when, and there are now portions of the world where, the insecurity of property has been occasioned, and does arise, principally from the injustice of the government.[470]

Against that background, we turn now to the Maine Court's jurisprudence regarding the extent of the State's power over private property during the formative years of Maine law.

The Power of Eminent Domain—Defining "Public Use"

As we have seen, under the terms of Maine's Constitution, the State, on paying "just compensation," has the power to take private

---

Supreme Court Justice Joseph Story in *Wilkinson v. Leland*, 27 U.S. 627, 658 (1829) ("We know of no case, in which a legislative act to transfer the property of A. to B. without his consent, has ever been held a constitutional exercise of legislative power in any state in the union.").

[469] 10 Me. 447 (1833).

[470] *Id.* at 449.

property for "public uses" when "public exigencies require it." In cases where the taking of property by eminent domain was challenged, the early Maine Court decided that as a general rule it would not second-guess the Legislature on the issue of the "exigency" (or necessity) for the taking. But the Court consistently reserved for itself the final say on the question of whether the "public use" requirement had been met. As the Court explained, "The legislature ...cannot make a private use public by calling it so."[471]

The Court was very clear on the point that while the taking of property for public uses was permitted by Maine's Constitution, the taking of property for private uses was not. Indeed, perhaps nowhere has the principle that the government may not take the property of one person for the private use of another been more strongly stated than by the Maine Court in its decision in *Bangor & Piscataquis Railroad Co. v. McComb* (1872):

> This exercise of the right of eminent domain is, in its nature, in derogation of the great and fundamental principle of all constitutional governments, which secures to every individual the right to acquire, possess, and defend property. As between individuals, no necessity, however great, no exigency, however imminent, no improvement, however valuable, no refusal, however unneighborly, no obstinacy, however unreasonable, no offers of compensation, however extravagant, can compel or require any man to part with an inch of his estate. The constitution protects him and his possessions, when held on, even to the extent of churlish obstinacy.[472]

As the two cases discussed below illustrate, however, the line separating the taking of property for a public use (a lawful taking) from the taking of property for a private use (an unlawful taking) was not always clear. Since both of these cases, *Ulmer v. Lime Rock Railroad Co.* (1904) and *Brown v. Gerald* (1905), involved the exercise of

---

[471] *Brown v. Gerald*, 100 Me. 351, 360, 61 A. 785, 789 (1905).

[472] 60 Me. 290, 295 (1872).

the power of eminent domain by private corporations, as distinguished from the Legislature, it should be noted that the Court had previously decided that the Legislature could delegate the power of eminent domain to private corporations for certain public uses.[473]

In *Ulmer v. Lime Rock Railroad Co.* (1904),[474] Fred and Mary Ulmer attempted to prevent the Lime Rock Railroad Company from taking a right of way over their land for the construction of a branch line leading from one of the railroad's main lines to a lime quarry owned by the Rockland-Rockport Lime Company. They argued that the easement in question was not being taken for a public use, but was solely for the private use and benefit of the railroad company and the lime company. The Court, however, disagreed.

In ruling in favor of the railroad company, the Court first noted that the Legislature had properly invested the railroad company with the power of eminent domain. Referring to railroad companies generally, the Court explained:

> These great thoroughfares of public travel could not be constructed if the acquisition of their necessary rights of way depended upon the whim, caprice or unreasonable demands of the owners of all lands over which it is necessary for them to be constructed. For this reason public railroad corporations are very properly endowed by the legislature of all states with the power to exercise the right of eminent domain. It is plain that such transportation lines from place to place, whether in the same or in different towns, are as much a public enterprise

---

[473] *See Riche v. Bar Harbor Water Co.*, 75 Me. 91, 96 (1883) ("There is nothing better settled than the power of the legislature to exercise the right of eminent domain, for purposes of public utility. This may be done through the agency of private corporations, although for private profit when the public is thereby to be benefitted. It is upon this principle that private corporations have been authorized to take private property, for the purpose of making public highways, railroads, canals, erecting wharves and basins, establishing ferries, &c."). *See also Hayford v. Mun. Officers of Bangor*, 102 Me. 340, 66 A. 731 (1907) (affirming Legislature's delegation of the power of eminent domain to municipal officers of the city of Bangor in connection with the taking of land for a public library building).

[474] 98 Me. 579, 57 A. 1001 (1904).

and use as are public roads constructed for the same purpose.[475]

The Court then found that the taking of the easement in question was permissible because the branch line for which the easement was sought connected with one of the railroad's main lines, and the branch line, like the main line, would be open for use by the public as a matter of right, even though it appeared that for the time being the railroad company and the lime company were the only parties that would have occasion to use the branch line. As the Court put it:

> If the branch track is to be built solely and exclusively for the benefit and accommodation of the railroad company and of the owner of the private business enterprise, it may well be said that it would serve no public purpose and would be of no public use, although the existence of such a track might be of great but indirect benefit to the community by enabling the private enterprise to be carried on, and in thereby giving employment to labor. But the mere fact that the primary purpose of such a branch is to accommodate a particular private business enterprise is by no means a controlling test. The character of the use, whether public or private, is determined by the extent of the right by the public to its use, and not by the extent to which that right is or may be exercised.[476]

One year later, in *Brown v. Gerald* (1905),[477] the Court again took up the question of whether the taking of property primarily for the benefit of a private business could qualify as a taking for a "public use." In that case, Joseph Brown sought an injunction to restrain the defendants from laying out a line of poles and wires across his farm in the town of Benton. The defendants were a power company and its president. The power company had been granted a charter from

---

[475] *Id.* at 585-86, 57 A. at 1003.

[476] *Id.* at 586, 57 A. at 1003.

[477] 100 Me. 351, 61 A. 785 (1905).

the Legislature to manufacture and sell electricity. To that end, it had built a dam, was installing a power plant, and had almost completed installing a line of poles and wires some six miles long in the town of Benton. That line was being built by the power company to provide electricity to a privately owned manufacturing facility pursuant to an agreement to provide that facility with the power company's entire electrical output for a period of ten years.

The power company maintained that the operation of the manufacturing facility was a benefit to the public that justified the power company's taking an easement across Brown's land for the purpose of transmitting electrical power to that facility. In this case, however, the Court sided with the landowner.

The Court readily acknowledged that any instrumentality that tended to promote manufacturing was of "great public benefit,"[478] but the Court pointed out that "public use," not "public benefit," was the test for determining the legality of a taking of property by eminent domain. Most significantly, the Court explained that if courts were to fail to distinguish between those two concepts, there would be practically no limit to the power of eminent domain:

> Taking the decided cases generally, we think that the weight of authority does not sustain the doctrine that a public use such as justifies the taking of private property against the will of the owner, may rest merely upon public benefit, or public interest, or great public utility.... Something more than mere public benefit must flow from the contemplated use. Public benefit or interest are not synonymous with public use. Neither mere public convenience nor mere public welfare will justify the exercise of the right of eminent domain. If the doctrine of public utility were adopted in its fullest extent, there would practically be no limit upon the exercise of this power.[479]

---

[478] As the Court stated: "It is beyond question that any instrumentality which tends to promote the manufacturing industries of a state, to furnish labor for its mechanics, to create the need of markets for its products, and to develop and utilize its natural advantages, is of great public benefit." *Id.* at 361, 61 A. at 789.

[479] *Id.* at 370, 61 A. at 793 (citations omitted).

The development of power for manufacturing purposes, the Court went on to say, "may be incidentally a public benefit. But it is nevertheless, in its legal aspect, merely an aid to private enterprise." Taking property for such a purpose, the Court observed, "would be taking the property of one private person for the use of another private person, and this has been denominated 'not legislation, but robbery.'"[480]

In deciding that the transmission of electrical power for manufacturing purposes was not a public use, the Court distinguished the circumstances of the case at hand from the distribution of electricity for public lighting, which in its view would have been a public use. The Court noted that a corporation engaged in the creation and distribution of power for manufacturing was a private enterprise in aid of private enterprise, and pointed out that in contrast with railroads, for example, such corporations were not then subject to government regulation as public enterprises. The Court also considered it significant that the power company was not required, as a matter of law, to serve the public: "The case at bar lacks one of the essential conditions of a public service by a quasi public corporation, namely, the right of the public, or so much of it as has occasion, to be served as a matter of right, and not of grace."[481] Finally, the defendants' additional argument that their electricity might be used for the lighting of homes in the future was deemed too speculative to carry any weight.

In drawing a line beyond which the government may not go in authorizing the taking of property by eminent domain, the Court in *Brown v. Gerald* protected the rights of landowners from a jurisprudence that would have placed their property at considerable risk.[482] Over the century since 1905 when *Brown* was decided,

---

[480] *Id.* at 371, 61 A. at 794.

[481] *Id.* at 376, 61 A. at 796.

[482] As the Court stated in ruling in favor of the plaintiff in *Brown v. Gerald*: "But mere convenience and advantage in private business must yield to the property rights of citizens sacredly guarded by the constitution. We cannot find any

however, courts have not always been so respectful of those rights. In some cases, courts have vastly expanded the power of eminent domain by finding the constitutional standard of "public use" satisfied by a use that provides a "public benefit."

That development is reflected by the recent 5-4 decision of the U.S. Supreme Court in *Kelo v. City of New London* (2005),[483] upholding the constitutionality of the taking of property for an economic development project in New London, Connecticut. In her dissenting opinion in that case, Justice Sandra Day O'Connor noted that the majority opinion could not be squared with the "public use" criterion of the U.S. Constitution that limits the power of government to take property by eminent domain:

> Today the Court abandons this long-held, basic limitation on government power. Under the banner of economic development, all private property is now vulnerable to being taken and transferred to another private owner, so long as it might be upgraded—*i.e.*, given to an owner who will use it in a way that the legislature deems more beneficial to the public—in the process. To reason, as the Court does, that the incidental public benefits resulting from the subsequent ordinary use of private property render economic development takings "for public use" is to wash out any distinction between private and public use of property—and thereby effectively to delete the words "for public use" from the Takings Clause of the Fifth Amendment.[484]
>
> ....
>
> In moving away from our decisions sanctioning the condemnation of harmful property use, the Court today significantly expands the meaning of public use. It holds that the sovereign may take private property currently put to

---

ground for sustaining the defendant's contention, except that of 'public benefit,' or general utility, and we think that is not sufficient." *Id.* at 374, 61 A. 795.

[483] 545 U.S. 469 (2005).

[484] *Id.* at 494. The Takings Clause of the Fifth Amendment to the U.S. Constitution provides: "[N]or shall private property be taken for public use, without just compensation."

ordinary private use, and give it over for new, ordinary private use, so long as the new use is predicted to generate some secondary benefit for the public—such as increased tax revenue, more jobs, maybe even aesthetic pleasure. But nearly any lawful use of real private property can be said to generate some incidental benefit to the public. Thus, if predicted (or even guaranteed) positive side-effects are enough to render transfer from one private party to another constitutional, then the words "for public use" do not realistically exclude *any* takings, and thus do not exert any constraint on the eminent domain power.[485]

Consistent with that view, Justice Clarence Thomas, also dissenting, said: "Today's decision is simply the latest in a string of our cases construing the Public Use Clause to be a virtual nullity, without the slightest nod to its original meaning."[486]

In contrast with the Supreme Court's recent decision in *Kelo*, the Maine Court's 1905 decision in *Brown v. Gerald* emphatically rejected the notion that a taking of property for a "public benefit" could be considered to be a taking for a "public use." There, as we have seen, the Maine Court noted that the failure to distinguish between those two terms would result in a situation in which "there would practically be no limit upon the exercise of this power [of eminent domain]." Remarkably, the U.S. Supreme Court, ignoring that sound counsel, has now allowed that very situation to come to pass.[487]

---

[485] *Id.* at 501.

[486] *Id.* at 506.

[487] As the Supreme Court pointed out in *Kelo*, its decision in that case, while authoritative with respect to the Takings Clause of the Fifth Amendment to the U.S. Constitution, does not preclude the states from interpreting "public use" requirements of state law in a manner that would give the property owner more protection than the property owner now has under the Fifth Amendment. For an insightful discussion of the *Kelo* case, see Orlando E. Delogu, "*Kelo v. City of New London* —Wrongly Decided and a Missed Opportunity for Principled Line Drawing with Respect to Eminent Domain Takings," 58 *Maine Law Review* 17 (2006).

Governmental Power to Tax and Spend — Defining "Public Purpose"

We now move along from the topic of eminent domain to the related topic of the power of government to tax the property of its citizens. As we have seen, the U.S. Supreme Court's recent expansive interpretation of the power of eminent domain under the U.S. Constitution in *Kelo* has significantly diminished the property rights of individual citizens. In recent years, a similar transformation of the law has taken place in Maine with respect to the power of taxation as the result of the Maine Court's decision in *Common Cause v. Maine* (1983).[488] As we shall see, the Court's decision in *Common Cause* reflects a jurisprudence that contrasts sharply with the Court's earnest solicitude for property rights in the early years of Maine law.

From the beginning, the Maine Court has made it clear that taxes may be imposed only for governmental (or public) purposes. In *Allen v. Inhabitants of Jay* (1872),[489] Chief Justice Appleton, writing for the Court, underscored the fundamental nature of that proposition:

> If there is any proposition about which there is an entire and uniform weight of judicial authority, it is that taxes are to be imposed for the use of the people of the State in the varied and manifold purposes of government, and not for private objects or the special benefit of individuals. Taxation originates from, and is imposed by and for the State.[490]

The issue involved in *Allen* was whether under Maine's Constitution the Legislature had the power to enact a statute authorizing the town of Jay to lend money to the owners of a sawmill and box factory as an inducement to them to move that business from the town of

---

[488] 455 A.2d 1 (Me. 1983).

[489] 60 Me. 124 (1872).

[490] *Id.* at 128. It should be noted that the Maine Court considered public support of the poor to be a public purpose of government for which money may be raised by taxation. *See, e.g., Brewer Brick Co. v. Inhabitants of Brewer*, 62 Me. 62, 73 (1873) (taxes may be imposed "for the poor, lest they may suffer from want").

Livermore Falls to the town of Jay. Appleton framed the legal issue as follows:

> The question proposed is whether the legislature can authorize towns to raise money by taxation, for the purpose of loaning the money so raised to such borrowers as may promise to engage in manufacturing or any other business the town may prefer, for their private gain and emolument. Is the raising of money to loan to such persons as the town may determine upon as borrowers, a legal exercise of the power of taxation? [491]

In an opinion remarkable for its force and passion, Appleton emphatically answered that question in the negative. "It is," he stated, "beyond the legislative power, by force of an enactment to make that public which is essentially private."[492] In reply to the suggestion that the loan by the town was justified because the public would benefit from the transaction, Appleton asked, "Is it any more for the public use than any other industry, the benefit of which incidentally results to the public, but which is carried on for private gain?"[493] With similar rhetorical flourish, Appleton asked, "But can any one conceive a more arbitrary exercise of the powers of government than the enforced collection of money from one man to loan the same to another?"[494]

In concluding that the statute authorizing the loan in question was unconstitutional, the Appleton Court relied to a significant extent on the property rights provision in the Declaration of Rights in Maine's Constitution, which, as noted above, reads as follows:

> All people are born equally free and independent, and have certain natural, inherent and unalienable rights, among which are those of enjoying and defending life and liberty, acquiring,

---

[491] *Allen*, 60 Me. at 127.

[492] *Id.* at 136.

[493] *Id.* at 135.

[494] *Id.* at 138.

possessing and protecting property, and of pursuing and obtaining safety and happiness.[495]

The importance of these rights in the mind of the framers of Maine's Constitution is shown by the fact that these rights were set forth in the first section of the first article of that document. In effect, it might be said that with this provision, the framers of Maine's Constitution wrote into it the "unalienable rights" of "Life, Liberty and the pursuit of Happiness" set forth in the Declaration of Independence and thereby "constitutionalized" those rights.[496] Explaining how the property rights provision of this section of Maine's Constitution related to the issue at hand, Appleton stated:

> By the constitution of this State, 'certain natural inherent and unalienable rights' are guaranteed to the citizens of this State, 'among which are those of...acquiring, possessing, and protecting property, and of pursuing and obtaining safety and happiness.' What motive is there for the acquisition of property, if the tenure of the acquisition is the will of others? How can our property be protected, if the legislature can enable a majority to transfer by gift or loan, to certain favored and selected individuals through the medium of direct taxation, such portions of one's estate as they may deem expedient. Men only earn when they are protected in the acquisition, possession, and enjoyment of their property. The barbarous nations of Asia have neither industry nor capital, the result of saving, for the reason that property is without protection. Where is the protection of property if one's money or his goods can be wrested from him and loaned to others? Where is the difference between the coerced contribution of the tax-gatherer to be loaned to individuals for their benefit, and those of the conqueror from the inhabitants of the

---

[495] Me. Const. Art. I, § 1.

[496] In contrast, the U.S. Constitution contains no similar "unalienable rights" provision.

conquered territory?... All security of private rights,[497] all protection of private property is at an end, when one is compelled to raise money to loan at the will of others, or to pay his contributory share of loans of money or bonds made to others for their own use and benefit, when the power is given to a majority to lend or give away the property of an unwilling minority.[498]

In addition to the property rights section of Maine's Constitution, the Court also relied on the eminent domain provision of Maine's Constitution, which, as we have seen, allows private property to be taken for "public uses," but not "private uses." As the Court stated:

> The line of demarcation between the case when property is taken for public, and when taken for private purposes, may not always be easily determined. But in the case before us, the removal by the owners of their mill, and the business connected with it, from one town to another, cannot, under the most liberal construction, be deemed other than a private matter. It may be a loss to one town and a gain to another, but the removal is for the private gain of the persons moving. It is in no respect other than the moving of one business man with his implements of business from one place to another.

> Neither can it be deemed a public use to raise money from all the inhabitants of a town to be given, or to be loaned to one of its number, to be used by him for his individual gain.[499]

---

[497] The early Maine Court evidently saw the right of private property as being essential for the protection of all other rights. In his *Commentaries on the Constitution of the United States*, U.S. Supreme Court Justice Joseph Story expressed the same idea this way: "[I]n a free government, almost all other rights would become utterly worthless, if the government possessed an uncontrollable power over the private fortune of every citizen." 2 Joseph Story, *Commentaries on the Constitution of the United States* (3d ed. 1858), 596.

[498] *Allen*, 60 Me. at 133-34.

[499] *Id.* at 140-41.

As he concluded his opinion, which surely ranks as one of the most famous and most powerful opinions in the history of the Court, Appleton closed with a resounding reminder of the importance of the right of private property and the gravity of the constitutional issue at stake:

> The constitution of the State is its paramount and binding law. The acquisition, possession, and protection of property are among the chief ends of government. To take directly or indirectly the property of individuals to loan to others for purposes of private gain and speculation against the consent of those whose money is thus loaned, would be to withdraw it from the protection of the constitution and submit it to the will of an irresponsible majority. It would be the robbery and spoilation of those whose estates, in whole or in part are thus confiscated. No surer or more effectual method could be devised to deter from accumulation—to diminish capital, to render property insecure, and thus to paralyze industry.[500]

One year later, the Maine Court addressed the similar question of whether, under Maine's Constitution, the Legislature had the power to authorize towns to grant property tax exemptions for certain manufacturing facilities. In *Brewer Brick Co. v. Inhabitants of Brewer* (1873),[501] the Court, again in an opinion authored by Chief Justice Appleton, ruled that a statute authorizing such a tax exemption was unconstitutional. As Appleton explained, such an exemption in effect amounted to a compulsory gift from the town's taxpayers to the business that would be exempted from taxation. Consistent with its earlier decision in *Allen*, the Court reaffirmed the point that a governmental subsidy to a private enterprise cannot be justified by any public benefits that might result from such a subsidy. "The inhabitants of a town," Appleton declared, "cannot legally be taxed to raise money to give or to loan to individuals or corporations for private purposes on account of any supposed incidental

---

[500] *Id.* at 142.

[501] 62 Me. 62 (1873).

advantages which may possibly accrue therefrom."[502] In the Court's view, that principle was a necessary limitation on the power of taxation: absent that limitation, virtually any governmental tax exemption or subsidy to an individual or a corporation might be said to be justified on the basis that it would ultimately redound to the benefit of the public in one way or another.[503]

In sum, by its decisions in *Allen* and *Brewer Brick*, the Appleton Court constructed a sturdy wall to protect the constitutionally guaranteed property rights of the people of Maine. That wall had three major components. First, the Court made it clear that taxes may be imposed only for public purposes. Second, in the event there might be any question concerning that rule, the Court clarified that taxes may not be imposed for the benefit of selected individuals or corporations. And third, to make certain that this wall would be insurmountable, the Court specified that taxes may not be imposed to raise money to give or loan to individuals or corporations for private purposes on account of any supposed incidental public advantages that might possibly accrue therefrom.

In *Laughlin v. City of Portland* (1914),[504] the Court reaffirmed those principles. That case concerned the constitutionality of a Maine

---

[502] *Id.* at 72.

[503] *Allen* and *Brewer Brick* were two of a trilogy of pronouncements by the Maine Court in the 1870s concerning the constitutionality of governmental subsidies to private businesses. In addition to *Allen* and *Brewer Brick*, see *Opinion of the Justices*, 58 Me. 590 (1871), where the members of the Court gave their advisory opinions to the Maine House of Representatives on the question of whether the Legislature had the authority to enact a statute authorizing towns to give or lend money to individuals or corporations to locate and carry on manufacturing operations in those towns. Five members of the Court, including Appleton, were of the view that such a statute would be unconstitutional. The other three members were of the view that the statute would be unconstitutional if the gifts or loans were to aid purely private enterprises, in no way connected with public uses or public exigencies. Shortly after those opinions were issued, the Legislature enacted just such a statute. The Court, however, had the last word. As discussed above, the Court unanimously found that statute unconstitutional in *Allen*.

[504] 111 Me. 486, 90 A. 318 (1914).

statute authorizing municipalities to use money raised by taxation to establish and operate fuel yards to provide residents with fuel "at cost." The Court upheld the constitutionality of the statute, concluding that the legislation in question was constitutionally justified as a matter of public necessity.[505] In that regard, the Court noted the high cost of fuel caused by "monopolistic combinations" and the resulting difficulty people had in obtaining an adequate supply of fuel to get through the winter.[506] At the same time, however, the Court reaffirmed the point that if a tax is imposed in order to subsidize or otherwise benefit private interests, any indirect public benefits, regardless of amount, that may result from such a subsidy would not save the tax from being unconstitutional. As the Court put it:

> [T]axes cannot be imposed to aid a private enterprise, and a municipality cannot assist individuals or corporations to establish or carry on such business, either directly or indirectly.... If the direct object is private, the indirect benefits that may result to the public, even in a large measure, are unavailing to remedy the vital defect.[507]

---

[505] Not long after the Maine Court handed down its decision in *Laughlin*, several taxable inhabitants of the city of Portland launched another suit in an attempt to prevent the establishment of the Portland municipal fuel yard. This time, the plaintiffs took a different tack, contending that taxation of their property to establish the fuel yard amounted to a deprivation of their property without due process in violation of the Fourteenth Amendment to the U.S. Constitution. The Maine Court rejected that argument, summarily. *Jones v. City of Portland*, 113 Me. 123, 93 A. 41 (1915). On appeal by the plaintiffs, the U.S. Supreme Court soundly rejected that claim as well. *Jones v. City of Portland*, 245 U.S. 217 (1917).

[506] It is interesting to note that more than a hundred years ago the Maine Legislature was willing to use the purchasing power of government in the interest of citizens who could least afford the high cost of fuel.

[507] *Laughlin*, 111 Me. at 491, 90 A. at 320. The influence of the *Laughlin* case was not confined to Maine. For example, referring to *Laughlin*, the Arizona Court in 1926 upheld the constitutionality of a municipal ice plant in Tombstone, Arizona, stating that "if heat is necessary to the health, comfort and convenience of the inhabitants of Maine, ice is no less so to the inhabitants of Arizona." *City of Tombstone v. Macia*, 30 Ariz. 218, 226, 245 P. 677, 680 (1926).

That principle, which the Appleton Court of the 1870s believed was constitutionally required in order to protect property from "robbery," "spoliation," and "confiscation" by the "will of an irresponsible majority,"[508] thus survived into the twentieth century as a judicially enforceable rule limiting the power of taxation. As events would unfold, however, that principle did not survive into the twenty-first century.

In 1983, in *Common Cause v. Maine,*[509] the Maine Court adopted a new rule for determining the constitutionality of a tax or spending measure. It seems worthwhile to consider that new rule briefly here, in our consideration of the early years of Maine law, because the contrast between that new rule and the jurisprudence of the Appleton Court highlights the importance the Appleton Court placed on judicial protection of property rights in those early years.

Under the Court's new rule, the constitutionality of a tax or spending measure is decided by examining whether "the plan [at issue] threatens a detriment to the public which outweighs the benefit that could have been anticipated [by the proposed plan]."[510] In place of its long-standing rule that incidental public benefits are insufficient to justify what is essentially a governmental subsidy to a private enterprise, the Court in *Common Cause* explained that in weighing the costs and benefits of a spending measure, "indirect economic benefits" such as the creation of jobs, may be considered. "[W]e now hold," the Court stated, "that indirect economic benefits

---

[508] *See Allen v. Inhabitants of Jay,* 60 Me. 124, 142 (1872).

[509] 455 A.2d 1 (Me. 1983). In that case, the Court rejected a challenge to the legality of a subsidy from the State of Maine to Bath Iron Works ("BIW") for the development of a dry dock facility at the Maine State Pier in Portland. The Court described that subsidy as follows: "Plaintiffs are correct in their basic premise that the agreement has the effect of creating a subsidy to BIW out of public funds. The state is obliged to contribute as much as $20.1 million dollars of the first $24.6 million to be spent by BIW in rehabilitating the dry dock, without any right in the state to recover that amount, or the interest on it, from BIW by way of reserved rent or other payment." *Id.* at 20.

[510] *Id.* at 25 (quoting Note, "Legal Limitations on Public Inducements to Industrial Location," 59 *Columbia Law Review* 618, 647 (1959)).

may be taken into consideration in deciding whether public spending by the state is justified."[511] With that single sentence, the Maine Court erased a limitation on legislative power that was a central feature of Appleton's opinions in *Allen* and *Brewer Brick*—opinions that Appleton, in all likelihood, believed would rank among his most significant and longest-lasting legacies to the people of the State of Maine.

The Appleton Court would probably be particularly dismayed to find that, in erasing that limitation on legislative power, the *Common Cause* Court never mentioned the "unalienable property rights" provision of Maine's Constitution, even though that provision, which secures the property rights of Maine citizens, was a major part of the constitutional footing of the wall the Appleton Court had erected in *Allen* and *Brewer Brick*. The *Common Cause* Court, however, did explain that "*Allen's* implicit requirement that taxation meet the public-use requirement of eminent domain has been implicitly overruled by later cases and opinions in which the Court has recognized that the Legislature's taxing and taking powers are different and that the requirement of public purpose in taxation may be applied more liberally than the requirement of public use in eminent domain."[512]

Under the Maine Court's new rule, which entails a weighing of direct and indirect benefits and detriments, it is difficult to conceive of any statute providing a subsidy for a private business that could not be justified by reason of its claimed "indirect economic benefits." This is especially so because in *Common Cause* the Court made it clear that in applying that rule, the judiciary should give considerable deference to the Legislature's judgment and should invalidate governmental expenditures to private enterprises only when the Legislature's decision has "no rational basis."[513] As a practical matter, therefore, the Court's new rule for determining the constitutionality

---

[511] *Id.*

[512] *Id.* at 22.

[513] *Id.* at 25.

of a governmental spending plan is hardly an enforceable standard at all. The Appleton Court would be appalled. Indeed, it is difficult to see how the Appleton Court could consider the Court's decision in *Common Cause* to be anything other than an abdication of judicial responsibility.

The Appleton Court, however, might also find it interesting (and maybe even amusing) that, in one of those curious ironies of legal history, the Maine Court of the 1870s and the Maine Court of the 1980s both appealed to the importance of economic development in justifying their contrasting views concerning the legitimacy of governmental subsidies to private enterprises. In 1872, explaining its objection to such subsidies, the Court in *Allen* stated that "[n]o surer or more effectual method could be devised to deter from accumulation—to diminish capital, to render property insecure, and thus to paralyze industry."[514] One hundred and eleven years later, explaining its decision to allow indirect economic benefits to be taken into account, the Court in *Common Cause* noted that "unemployment is now one of the prime concerns of government"[515] and additionally pointed out that "[t]he chief indirect benefit predicted for the Portland project will consist of the jobs provided by the project itself and the economic 'ripple effect' of introducing new business into the state."[516]

One further point concerning *Common Cause* might be mentioned here. Just as the Maine Court in 1983, in *Common Cause*, reconsidered its earlier jurisprudence from the era of the Appleton Court, it is possible that, at some future date, the Court might reconsider the rules it established in *Common Cause* if, for example, those rules prove to be incapable of restraining imprudent governmental expenditures. If the Court were to do so, that would not be the first time the Court, on reconsideration, has expressed concern about the extent to which it had allowed the State to advance the

---

[514] *Allen*, 60 Me. at 142.

[515] *Common Cause*, 455 A.2d at 24-25.

[516] *Id.* at 23.

interests of private enterprise at the expense of individual property rights. Decisions of our Court in the nineteenth century include two prominent illustrations of judicial reconsideration along those lines.

The first such instance was *Jordan v. Woodward* (1855),[517] where the Court expressed serious reservations about the constitutionality of Maine's "Mill Act."[518] That statute allowed owners of water-mills to flood the property of upstream landowners in order to raise a head of water for the working of mills, subject to the payment of compensation for damages caused by the overflowing. In effect, the statute allowed the mill owner to "take" the private property of another, without consent, on payment of compensation. The Court explained that this statute grew out of a time in "the early history of this country, [when] the erection of mills was deemed matter of great public convenience and necessity, and as such deserving the special protection of the legislative power [of eminent domain]," but that with the more recent investment of private capital for private gain in all kinds of mills and enterprises, it had become difficult to distinguish the public importance of water-mills from the public importance of other private businesses, for example, the "shop of the smith, the store of the grocer, the house of the inn-holder, and a great variety of business enterprises in which our citizens employ their labor and capital." As the Court observed, "In fact there is no branch of lawful business which may not contribute to the public good, and for which there may not, to a certain extent, exist a public necessity." Yet, as the Court also noted, "to authorize the appropriation of private property for all these various purposes, would be destructive to private rights, and unsettle the tenure by which property is holden." Under these circumstances, the Court stated:

---

[517] 40 Me. 317 (1855).

[518] Me. R.S. ch. 126 (1841). Maine's Mill Act was originally enacted by the Maine Legislature in 1821. As our Court has explained, that statute derived from the early statutory law of the Province of Massachusetts Bay. *See Dorey v. Estate of Spicer*, 1998 ME 202, ¶¶ 9-12, 715 A.2d 182, 184-85 (discussing history of Maine's Mill Act).

> The mill Act, as it has existed in this State, pushes the power
> of eminent domain to the very verge of constitutional
> inhibition. If it were a new question, it might well be doubted
> whether it would not be deemed to be in conflict with [the
> eminent domain] provision of the constitution....[519]

But despite the Court's doubts concerning the constitutionality
of the Mill Act, the Court felt it was too late in the day to reconsider
the question. Turning a blind eye to the question of the statute's
constitutional infirmity, the Court concluded:

> We do not intend to question the authority of the existing mill
> Act of this State. From its great antiquity, and the long
> acquiescence of our citizens in its provisions, it must be
> deemed to be the settled law of the State.[520]

The second nineteenth-century illustration of our Court's having second thoughts about the extent to which its jurisprudence
favored the interests of private enterprise at the expense of the property rights of Maine citizens is *Dyar v. Farmington Village Corp.*
(1878),[521] where we see our Court urging the Legislature to exercise
caution in authorizing municipalities to use tax dollars to subsidize
private enterprise:

> We do not mean to question the authority of the legislature to
> confer upon towns and cities the right to use the coercive
> power of taxation to raise money to build railroads. In this
> state the question is *res judicata*, and further discussion of it
> would not be profitable. But it may not be out of place to say
> that the constitutionality, as well as the expediency, of such an
> exercise of the taxing power, has always met with a vigorous

---

[519] *Jordan*, 40 Me. at 323.

[520] *Id.* at 324. It bears noting that the Court's theory of "antiquity," as there
stated, could "justify" the most egregious constitutional violation of long
standing.

[521] 70 Me. 515 (1878) (holding that one part of a town cannot be burdened with a
tax, as distinguished from an assessment for local improvements, from which the
remainder is exempt).

opposition. The reasoning by which its constitutionality is maintained is not satisfactory to some of the best judicial minds of the country. In several of the states it has been rejected altogether. Unfriendly competition, wasteful expenditures of money, and an amount of municipal indebtedness that must end in repudiation or the most oppressive taxation have been the result. And, as was well remarked by Mr. Justice Barrows, in his reply to the legislature, 58 Me. 612, "the fact that one step of doubtful propriety has been taken is never a good reason for taking another in the same direction; but rather, on the contrary, it should induce us to pause and revert to fixed principles."[522]

As we conclude our discussion of the extent of the power of government to tax the property of its citizens in the early years of

---

[522] *Id.* at 528. The Court here was quoting from Justice William G. Barrows' opinion in the Court's 1871 advisory-opinion proceeding concerning the question of the constitutionality of governmental subsidies to private manufacturing businesses, discussed above. *See Opinion of the Justices*, 58 Me. 590, 607-14 (1871). In accord with the Court's majority view, Barrows was of the opinion that such subsidies were unconstitutional. Most significantly, in distinguishing between such subsidies, on the one hand, and governmental support of paupers, on the other, Barrows suggested that the right of paupers to "necessaries of life" was grounded in Maine's Constitution. As Barrows explained:

"Among the rights declared natural and inherent in all human beings by our constitution, is the right to life, and that necessarily includes and carries with it a right to the means of sustaining life. It is not merely common humanity, but common justice, that demands that no one shall be suffered to languish for lack of food, clothing, and other necessaries of life. To provide the means of preventing it is strictly within the line of public duty.

"Thus far we may safely proceed toward an agrarian distribution of the fruits of the earth and the products of human industry; and in doing so, we are only establishing justice and insuring tranquillity. But this is no precedent for going further, and furnishing to any beggar, however wealthy, influential, or clamorous (and these are they whose applications are likely to be successful), out of the public treasury the means of trying some pet scheme for adding to his own gains at the public risk."

Opinion of the Justices, 58 Me. at 611.

Maine law, it seems fair to say that what was once a pillar of our constitutional law—the principle that the State may not take the property of one person and give it to another—has in recent years been so eroded by the Maine Court's 1983 *Common Cause* decision and by the Supreme Court's 2005 *Kelo* decision, that it now bears little resemblance to its former self. Our legal grounding has shifted significantly here, and the resulting tremors continue to be felt.

Restricting the Use of Private Property in the Public Interest — The "Police Power"

In addition to clarifying the limits of governmental power to take and to tax private property, the Maine Court in its early years also clarified the scope of the related power of government to regulate and restrict the use of private property in the public interest. Generally speaking, the Court sustained the exercise of that regulatory power, viewing that power as an aspect of the inherent power of government to enact legislation to secure the safety and general welfare of the people. During the nineteenth century, as is still the case today, that broad, inherent power of government was widely known in the law as the "police power."[523]

---

[523] Courts have occasionally referred to the police power as the protective power of government, the most notable illustration perhaps being the U.S. Supreme Court's landmark decision in *Home Bldg. & Loan Ass'n v. Blaisdell*, 290 U.S. 398, 440 (1934) ("Whatever doubt there may have been that the protective power of the State, its police power, may be exercised....") (majority (5-4) opinion of Chief Justice Charles Evans Hughes, upholding constitutionality of Minnesota statute that afforded mortgage debtors temporary relief under the emergency conditions then existing). Hughes' reference to the state's "protective power" as a synonym for its "police power" at several points throughout that opinion not only more accurately described the power of the state legislature to grant the temporary relief involved in that case, but also made the Court's ultimate ruling more readily understandable, and probably more persuasive, than it would otherwise have been. Except where police and law enforcement are directly involved, the term, "protective power," would today seem more accurately to capture the original meaning of the term, "police power," as that term was initially used when it became part of the judicial vocabulary many years ago.

The principle that the government possesses the power to regulate and restrict the use of private property in the public interest got off to a strong start in Maine with our Court's decision in *Wadleigh v. Gilman* (1835).[524] In that case, the plaintiff sued the street commissioner and city marshal of the city of Bangor for damages for having "taken down" a wooden building he owned in that city. The defendants said they were justified in having done so because a city ordinance prohibited the erection of wooden buildings in that part of the city where the plaintiff's building was located. As the defendants pointed out, the plaintiff had moved his building from one lot to another within that restricted area after the ordinance had been enacted. The plaintiff, on the other hand, claimed that the ordinance was unconstitutional and that in any event he had not erected a building in violation of the ordinance, but had merely moved his building from one location to another. The plaintiff also claimed that the defendants had no right to destroy his building because the only penalty provided by the ordinance was a fine not to exceed fifty dollars. In a forceful opinion authored by Chief Justice Nathan Weston, the Maine Court rejected the plaintiff's claims and dismissed his lawsuit.

In ruling in favor of the municipal officials, the Court broadly interpreted the ordinance as applying to wooden buildings placed on lots where none had existed before, "whether newly built, or removed there from some other quarter." In response to the plaintiff's contention that the city was limited to imposing a monetary fine, the Court replied:

> Is this all [the municipal officials] can do? After exacting the penalty, must they submit to the continuance of a mass of combustible matter, erected in defiance of their ordinance, in the heart of the city? We think not.[525]

---

[524] 12 Me. 403 (1835).

[525] *Id.* at 404.

Turning to the question of the constitutionality of the ordinance, Weston explained that the ordinance, which was designed to lessen the danger of fire, was a legitimate exercise of the city's authority to enact "police regulations" for the protection of the public and that, in prohibiting the erection of wooden buildings, the ordinance did not appropriate the plaintiff's property, but merely regulated its enjoyment:

> Police regulations may forbid such a use, and such modifi-cations, of private property, as would prove injurious to the citizens generally. This is one of the benefits which men derive from associating in communities. It may sometimes occasion an inconvenience to an individual; but he has the compensation, in participating in the general advantage. Laws of this character are unquestionably within the scope of the legislative power, without impairing any constitutional provision. It does not appropriate private property to public uses; but merely regulates its enjoyment. [526]

Sixteen years later, Lemuel Shaw, Chief Justice of the Massachusetts Court, developed the same principles further in *Commonwealth v. Alger* (1851).[527] Shaw's explanation of the "police power" of government in that Massachusetts case has been so influential with courts throughout the country, including Maine, that our discussion of that topic in Maine's early years would seem incomplete without at least some mention of that case here. Shaw grounded the police power of government in what he termed, "the nature of well ordered civil society," and by doing so, made the validity of that power seem self-evident. He also clarified the distinction between the regulation of property pursuant to the police power and the taking of property pursuant to the exercise of the power of eminent domain. In two paragraphs that became the classic

---

[526] *Id.* at 405.

[527] 61 Mass. (7 Cush.) 53 (1851) (upholding constitutionality of a Massachusetts statute that prohibited the erection of wharves and other structures beyond a designated line in the harbor of Boston).

explanation of the police power, Shaw explained that doctrine as follows:

> We think it is a settled principle, growing out of the nature of well ordered civil society, that every holder of property, however absolute and unqualified may be his title, holds it under the implied liability that his use of it may be so regulated, that it shall not be injurious to the equal enjoyment of others having an equal right to the enjoyment of their property, nor injurious to the rights of the community. All property in this commonwealth, as well that in the interior as that bordering on tide waters, is derived directly or indirectly from the government, and held subject to those general regulations, which are necessary to the common good and general welfare. Rights of property, like all other social and conventional rights, are subject to such reasonable limitations in their enjoyment, as shall prevent them from being injurious, and to such reasonable restraints and regulations established by law, as the legislature, under the governing and controlling power vested in them by the constitution, may think necessary and expedient.[528]

> This is very different from the right of eminent domain, the right of a government to take and appropriate private property to public use, whenever the public exigency requires it; which can be done only on condition of providing a reasonable compensation therefor. The power we allude to is rather the police power, the power vested in the legislature by the constitution, to make, ordain and establish all manner of wholesome and reasonable laws, statutes and ordinances, either with penalties or without, not repugnant to the constitution, as they shall judge to be for the good and welfare of the commonwealth, and of the subjects of the same.[529]

Over the years following its decision in *Wadleigh v. Gilman* (1835), the early Maine Court frequently had occasion to discuss the

---

[528] *Id.* at 84-85.

[529] *Id.* at 85.

meaning, extent, and importance of the police power. One such case was *Boston & Maine Railroad Co. v. County Commissioners* (1887).[530] There, the railroad company challenged the constitutionality of a statute that made it the responsibility of railroad companies to construct and maintain that part of a county road that crossed railway tracks. The railroad company contended that, as the law applied to it, that requirement amounted to an unconstitutional impairment of its charter from the state, which contained the stipulation that it was not subject to amendment, alteration, or repeal. The Court rejected that impairment-of-contract argument and sustained the validity of the statute on the basis of the police power of the government, noting that the purpose of the statute was "evidently to promote the safety of travelers both upon the railroad and the county way." The Court described the police power as follows:

> This power of the legislature to impose uncompensated duties and even burdens, upon individuals and corporations for the general safety, is fundamental. It is the "police power." Its proper exercise is the highest duty of government. The state may in some cases forego the right to taxation, but it can never relieve itself of the duty of providing for the safety of its citizens. This duty, and consequent power, override all statute or contract exemptions. The state cannot free any person or corporation from subjection to this power. All personal as well as property rights must be held subject to the police power of the state.[531]

With the seemingly endless number of state and federal regulations that exist today, we are apt to look back upon the first hundred years of Maine's statehood as a regulation-free time in which the citizenry went about their business as they pleased, doing what they wanted to do, with hardly any governmental interference at all. But that would be a misreading of history. As the decisions of the Maine

---

[530] 79 Me. 386, 10 A. 113 (1887).

[531] *Id.* at 393, 10 A. at 114.

Court indicate, a considerable amount of governmental regulation existed for the protection of the public during those early years.[532]

When the culture and economy of Maine were largely agricultural in nature, there was no great need for extensive governmental regulation. But as Maine became more industrialized and as society became more complex, more governmental regulation became necessary for the protection of the public. In the *Boston & Maine Railroad* case discussed above, the Court listed numerous examples of governmental regulations permitted under the police power of government. These included regulations dealing with matters such as liquor, lotteries, building codes, sidewalk safety, consumer protection, and disease prevention. The Court also pointed out that legislation enacted under the police power of government was even more extensive with regard to railroads, steamships, hotels and other institutions and places of public accommodation. Significantly, and presciently, the Court noted that with the "progress of society," the exercise of the police power "must become wider, more varied and frequent."[533]

The fundamental importance of the police power of government was a recurring theme of our Court during the early years of Maine law, as the following descriptions of that power illustrate:

> Take away the police power of the State and you at once put in jeopardy both life and property. It is the one inherent power of all government. It antedates and supersedes constitutions. It is founded upon the maxim that self-preservation is the first law of nature. The police power is inherent in every form of government.[534]

---

[532] For a comprehensive study of regulatory law in the nineteenth century and an insightful analysis of the development of the doctrine of the police power, see William J. Novak, *The People's Welfare: Law and Regulation in Nineteenth-Century America* (Chapel Hill: The University of North Carolina Press, 1996).

[533] *Boston & Maine R.R. Co.*, 79 Me. at 393, 10 A. at 114.

[534] *Inhabitants of Skowhegan v. Heselton*, 117 Me. 17, 23-24, 102 A. 772, 775 (1917) (upholding validity of ordinance requiring that plans for repairing wooden buildings damaged by fire be approved by two boards of officials). The Court's statement that the police power "supersedes constitutions" calls for some

> The police power of the State is co-extensive with self-protection, and is not inaptly termed "the law of overruling necessity." It is that inherent and plenary power in the State which enables it to prohibit all things hurtful to the comfort, safety and welfare of society.[535]

> The police power is inherent in all sovereignty and is exercised for the protection of the people, the preservation of the peace and order of society, and the health and safety of its members.[536]

Consistent with these expressions of the importance of the police power, the Court carefully preserved the power of the government to regulate and restrict the use of private property in the public interest. From an early date, as we have seen in the case of *Wadleigh v.Gilman* (1835), the Court established the point that the regulation of private property did not amount to the appropriation or "taking" of property for which compensation had to be paid. In *Opinion of the*

---

clarification inasmuch as the Constitution of Maine is the supreme law of the State (except as limited by the federal Constitution). *See LaFleur ex rel. Anderson v. Frost*, 146 Me. 270, 280, 80 A.2d 407, 412 (1951). In describing the police power as a power that "supersedes constitutions," the Court probably had in mind judicial decisions such as its 1887 decision in the *Boston & Maine Railroad* case discussed above. Strictly speaking, however, the constitutionality of the statute involved in that case was upheld, not because the Court permitted the Legislature to "supersede" the Constitution, but because, under the common law's conception of the "well-ordered civil society," the corporation's charter, like other property rights, was "held subject to the police power of the State," with the consequence that, since the corporation's charter was already, inherently subject to that limitation, the State's exercise of its police power did not "impair" the charter in violation of the Constitution.

[535] *State v. Starkey*, 112 Me. 8, 12, 90 A. 431, 433 (1914) (upholding validity of ordinance adopted by the town of Houlton, requiring official inspection of meat sold in that town).

[536] *Opinion of the Justices*, 118 Me. 503, 516, 106 A. 865 (1919) (discussing Legislature's authority to construct water storage reservoirs and impose franchise taxes).

Justices (1907),[537] the Court reaffirmed that point in an advisory opinion issued in response to an inquiry from the Maine Senate.

The question at issue in that proceeding concerned the constitutionality of a proposed statute that limited the cutting of trees on wild and uncultivated lands in order to prevent the erosion of land and to preserve the quality of the natural water supply. The statute provided no corresponding compensation for the owners of such lands. In considering the question presented, the Court first explained that, in contrast with courts in some of the other states, the courts in Maine and Massachusetts had always defined the "taking" of property narrowly, as not including restrictions on the use of property, in order to allow the government sufficient latitude in regulating the use of private property in the public interest. In support of that view, the Court quoted from Massachusetts Chief Justice Shaw's explanation of the police power in the *Alger* case, discussed above, where Shaw reasoned that all property is held subject to "those general regulations which are necessary for the common good and general welfare." The Court was satisfied that the proposed statute was within the scope of the Legislature's police power because "if the owners of large tracts can waste them at will without State restriction, the State and its people may be helplessly impoverished and one great purpose of government defeated."[538] The Court was also satisfied that the statute's restrictions on the cutting of trees did not rise to the level of the taking of land by eminent domain. As the Court stated:

> [W]e do not think the proposed legislation would operate to "take" private property within the inhibition of the Constitution. While it might restrict the owner of wild and unculti-vated lands in his use of them, might delay his taking some of the product, might defer his anticipated profits, and even thereby might cause him some loss of profit, it would nevertheless leave him his lands, their product and increase, untouched, and without diminution of title, estate or quantity.

---

[537] 103 Me. 506, 69 A. 627 (1907).

[538] *Id.* at 511, 69 A. at 629.

He would still have large measure of control and large
opportunity to realize values. He might suffer delay but not
deprivation. While the use might be restricted, it would not be
appropriated or "taken."[539]

In looking back at the early Maine cases involving the
government and private property, we have seen that where the
taking and taxing of property were concerned, our Court established
and enforced definite limits beyond which government could not go.
The Court considered those limits necessary in order to safeguard the
constitutionally protected right of private property from encroach-
ment and usurpation by the governing powers. On the other hand,
where the regulation of the use of property in the public interest was
concerned, the Court allowed the government considerable leeway.

From one perspective, it might seem that in allowing the
government relatively broad leeway to regulate the use of private
property, the Court was compromising the right of private property,
which it so carefully protected where the taking and taxing of
property were concerned. But that perspective overlooks the point
that in upholding the government's legislative power to restrict or
prohibit uses of private property that might be harmful to the
property of others or to the community as a whole, the Court was
safeguarding the property rights of all. What one person might see as
an infringement of his or her right of private property, other
members of the community might see as a much appreciated
protection of their same basic right.

---

[539] *Id.* at 511-12, 69 A. at 629. The Maine Court has recognized that where
regulation goes "too far," it may result in a taking of private property. *See Seven
Islands Land Co. v. Me. Land Use Regulation Comm'n*, 450 A.2d 475 (Me. 1982)
(quoting *Pennsylvania Coal Co. v. Mahon*, 260 U.S. 393 (1922)). In *Seven Islands*,
however, the Court concluded that certain restrictions on cutting trees did not
amount to a taking of the plaintiff's property. *See also State v. Johnson*, 265 A.2d
711 (Me. 1970) (holding that the prohibition against the filling of the appellant's
land, upon the facts peculiar to that case, was an unreasonable exercise of the
police power).

The Court's support of the police power of government, including the government's power to regulate and restrict the use of private property in the public interest, was of a piece with its endorsement of two legal maxims we encountered in earlier chapters, namely, *salus populi suprema lex* (the safety of the people is the supreme law) and *sic utere tuo ut alienum non laedas* (use your own so as not to injure another's property). Those maxims, together with the doctrine of the police power, were the framework of a jurisprudence, at the center of which was the vision of the "well-ordered civil society," in which government was seen as a reliable ally of the people, securing the welfare of the community and protecting the people from harm. Although history has taught us to regard the grand scope of that vision with a measure of skepticism, it nevertheless remains true, as our Court observed many years ago: "Take away the police power of the State and you at once put in jeopardy both life and property."[540]

---

[540] *Inhabitants of Skowhegan*, 117 Me. at 23, 102 A. at 775 (1917).

CONCLUDING THOUGHTS

This seems a good place to bring our ramble through the early years of Maine law to a close. Were we to proceed further, this endeavor would be at risk of turning into something much more formal and comprehensive than it was ever intended to be.

Along the way, we have looked at the early development of a number of topics of Maine law. Considered separately, those topics may seem to have little to do with each other. From that perspective, the law, taken as a whole, resembles a quilt that has been patched together with no coherent pattern or design. Yet if we step back and look at this fabric from a broader perspective, some patterns emerge that help us to understand the developments we have seen. On closer examination, we will see that these patterns have been formed by certain threads that run through the various topics we have considered. Three such threads, each representing a different theme, stand out clearly, even though in practice they sometimes overlapped and crisscrossed each other. Those themes can be described as economic progress, social stability, and the struggle for equal rights under the law—more succinctly, progress, stability, and equality.

Economic Progress

The period 1820-1920 was a time of unprecedented industrial and commercial growth in Maine and throughout the rest of the country. The importance of enabling that growth and thereby advancing the economic well-being of all Maine citizens was not lost on the Maine Court. As we have seen, the Court frequently mentioned the importance of economic growth and the role of the Court in furthering that growth.

For example, as early as 1829 our Court declared, "It is our duty to regard and protect the interests of agriculture as well as trade."[541] In 1842, our Court credited the "liberality and far-sightedness" of England's mercantile regulations in playing an important role in advancing the "pride, wealth, strength, and fame" of that country.[542] In 1862, the Court emphasized the economic importance of water mills and the lumber industry, in explaining the importance of the Court's not allowing either of those enterprises to destroy the other: "These two great interests mutually sustain each other. Without the mill, the lumber which now floats on our streams from the distant forests would be comparatively valueless, and, without the unobstructed streams on which to float the product of the forest, the mill would be of little worth."[543] In the same case, our Court emphasized the economic importance of its doctrine concerning the public nature of Maine's floatable streams: "[T]he right of the public to the use of our *floatable* streams has ever been guarded with jealous care by our Courts. They are the great highways over which vast amounts of the property of our citizens are transported to market, and without which much of the wealth of the State would be locked up in inaccessible forests."[544]

In 1887, in developing the common law concerning the respective rights of the ice-harvesting industry and travelers over the ice on Maine's rivers, the Court described the ice-harvesting industry as an industry that "has assumed extraordinary importance on our rivers."[545] Similarly, in a case decided in 1896, our Court explained that if trains were required to materially reduce their speed at every country road-crossing, the "great benefit of railroads to the public, viz., quickness and economy of transportation, would be greatly lessened if not destroyed."[546] Summing up its view that economic

---

[541] *Lassell v. Reed*, 6 Me. 222, 224 (1829).

[542] *Owen v. Boyle*, 22 Me. 47, 66 (1842).

[543] *Veazie v. Dwinel*, 50 Me. 479, 487 (1862).

[544] *Id.* at 487.

[545] *Woodman v. Pitman*, 79 Me. 456, 461, 10 A. 321, 324 (1887).

[546] *Giberson v. Bangor & Aroostook R.R. Co.*, 89 Me. 337, 343, 36 A. 400, 401 (1896).

progress unquestionably serves the public interest, our Court in 1905 said:

> It is beyond question that any instrumentality which tends to promote the manufacturing industries of a state, to furnish labor for its mechanics, to create the need of markets for its products, and to develop and utilize its natural advantages, is of great public benefit.[547]

With the Court being so strongly of the view that economic progress was of "great public benefit," it is not surprising that, in shaping the common law during Maine's first hundred years, our Court gave considerable weight to commercial and industrial interests. Indeed, in the Court's eyes, those interests were virtually indistinguishable from the "public interest." As we have seen, in almost every area of the common law in which the factor of economic progress was a consideration, the Court developed rules of law that facilitated economic progress.

Regrettably, however, as we have also seen, the Court considered economic progress so important that, in shaping the rules of the common law, it sometimes allowed its support for commercial and industrial interests to almost entirely override legitimate interests of other parties, most notably, employees who suffered injury or death in the workplace, victims of railroad crossing accidents, and widows and children in wrongful death cases. As we conclude our ramble through the early years of Maine law, the question still persists: Why did our Court allow that to happen? Didn't our Court see that this was unfair?

In our earlier discussion of these questions, we suggested that the Court probably believed that in one way or another its jurisprudence that facilitated economic development ultimately redounded to the benefit of everyone concerned and that its rules that favored business interests were justified on that account. We have also suggested that the Court's vision of a unified, non-

---

[547] *Brown v. Gerald*, 100 Me. 351, 361, 61 A. 785, 789 (1905).

polarized community probably played a part in the Court's coming to that conclusion. All of that may well be true, but something still seems to be missing here in terms of understanding the mind of the Court in the last half of the nineteenth century.

In explaining the outlook of the builders of America's industrial empire in the Gilded Age, the eminent historian Richard Hofstadter found it useful first to describe the environment in which they flourished:

> In the years from Appomattox to the end of the nineteenth century the American people settled half their continental domain, laid down a vast railroad system, and grew mighty in the world on their great resources in coal, metals, oil, and land. There is no other period in the nation's history when politics seems so completely dwarfed by economic changes, none in which the life of the country rests so completely in the hands of the industrial entrepreneur.[548]

As Hofstadter goes on to explain, in these circumstances, the business barons believed that they were effectuating a "benign transformation of tremendous magnitude." So overwhelming was the might of that vision that it effectively obscured the malignancies that were a part of it. As Hofstadter puts it,

> Because the abiding significance of their deeds would be so great and so good, they did not need to fret about their day-by-day knaveries.... To imagine that such men did not sleep the sleep of the just would be romantic sentimentalism. In the Gilded Age even the angels sang for them.[549]

Consequently, for the most part, those empire-builders "felt secure in their exploitation and justified in their dominion":

---

[548] Richard Hofstadter, *The American Political Tradition and the Men Who Made It* (New York: Vintage Books, 1957) (1948), 164.

[549] *Id.* at 165.

Assured by intellectuals of the progressive and civilizing value of their work, encouraged by their status as exemplars of the order of opportunity, and exhilarated by the thought that their energies were making the country rich, industrial millionaires felt secure in their exploitation and justified in their dominion.[550]

Functioning in much the same setting, and during the same time frame, the members of the Maine Court, like the industrial millionaires described by Hofstadter, probably believed that they too were playing a central role in effectuating a benign and historically significant transformation of the economy. And like those millionaires, those jurists were probably so sure of the "progressive and civilizing value" of that transformation that they came to regard any harmful consequences of their jurisprudence that favored economic progress to be not injustices, but simply "collateral damage," unavoidable consequences of a great work that was being accomplished. This is hardly a comforting view of the mind of our Court during the Gilded Age, but it seems likely that this is how our Court considered the circumstances at that time.

Social Stability

The second major theme that characterizes our Court's jurisprudence during the early years of Maine law is the importance the Court ascribed to maintaining the stability of society, beginning with the family and extending to the community as a whole. At the same time that the Court was advancing the interests of economic development, to the extent it was within its power to do so, it was applying the brakes to forces of change that were affecting the social sphere. Strongly supportive of economic progress, our Court seems to have been just as strongly wary of social developments that could upset the stability of the established order of the community.

---

[550] *Id.* at 169.

The Court's concern for maintaining a safe, stable, and orderly community is shown by its early decisions concerning a wide array of issues we have covered here, for example: the status of paupers (paupers of dissolute habits must be removed from society to "preserve the community from contamination");[551] the unity of the family (the purpose of the rule that "marriage makes the husband and wife one person, and that person is the husband," is to establish "an indissoluble union of interest between the parties" in order to "insure the unity and preservation of the family");[552] the rationale behind Maine's morality laws (the Lord's Day statute is designed "to enable man to derive the benefit designed to be bestowed upon him by Providence, in the consecration of the Lord's day to the duty of doing good");[553] the importance of maintaining law and order ("The substitution of law for brute force, in the maintenance of the rights of property, is one of the greatest triumphs of civilized society and good government.");[554] the constitutionality of Bible reading in public schools (to allow exceptions to school rules on the basis of an individual's religious belief "at once surrenders the power of the State to a government not emanating from the people");[555] the conflict between free speech and blasphemy ("stability of government in no small measure, depends upon the reverence and respect which a nation maintains toward its prevalent religion");[556] the use of corporal punishment in schools ("To become good citizens, children must be taught self-restraint, obedience, and other civic virtues.");[557] the prevention of public nuisances ("The moral sense, the correct principles, the temperate, regular and industrious habits, which are the basis of a happy and prosperous community, are frequently

---

[551] *Adeline G. Nott's case*, 11 Me. 208, 211 (1834).

[552] *State v. Burlingham*, 15 Me. 104, 106 (1838); *Haggett v. Hurley*, 91 Me. 542, 550, 40 A. 561, 563 (1898).

[553] *Towle v. Larrabee*, 26 Me. 464, 469 (1847).

[554] *State v. Yeaton*, 53 Me. 125, 128 (1865).

[555] *Donahoe v. Richards*, 38 Me. 379, 407 (1854).

[556] *State v. Mockus*, 120 Me. 84, 93, 113 A. 39, 42 (1921).

[557] *Patterson v. Nutter*, 78 Me. 509, 511, 7 A. 273, 274 (1886).

impaired or destroyed [by resort to bowling alleys].");[558] the foundational concept of the well-ordered civil society ("We think it a settled principle, growing out of the nature of well ordered civil society, that every holder of property, however absolute and unqualified may be his title, holds it under the implied liability that his use of it may be so regulated that it shall not be injurious to the equal enjoyment of others having an equal right to the enjoyment of their property, nor injurious to the rights of the community.");[559] and the need for obedience to the law ("Free political institutions are possible only where the great body of the people are moral, intelligent, and habituated to self-control, and to obedience to lawful authority.").[560]

The Court's reliance on the maxims, *salus populi suprema lex* (the safety of the people is the supreme law) and *sic utere tuo ut alienum non laedas* (use your own so as not to injure another's property), as rules for resolving disputes and controversies, further illustrates the Court's consistent concern for maintaining the safety and stability of the community.

Although the Court placed a high value on maintaining the stability of the social order, so many changes were occurring in society during the period 1820-1920, at such a rapid pace, that the Court's vision of the social order as static and traditionally structured was becoming increasingly unrealistic with each passing year. Consequently, those opinions of the Court that were predicated on that vision—for example, the Court's early (1834 and 1856) pauper workhouse decisions;[561] the 1874 advisory opinion of a majority of the Court to the effect that women could not be justices of the peace;[562] and the Court's 1921 opinion in Maine's blasphemy case[563]—

---

[558] *State v. Haines*, 30 Me. 65, 76 (1849).

[559] *Opinion of the Justices*, 103 Me. 506, 510, 69 A. 627, 628-29 (1907) (quoting *Commonwealth v. Alger*, 61 Mass. (7 Cush.) 53, 84-85 (1851)).

[560] *Patterson*, 78 Me. at 511, 7 A. at 274.

[561] *Adeline G. Nott's case*, 11 Me. 208 (1834); *Portland v. Bangor*, 42 Me. 403 (1856).

[562] *Opinion of the Justices*, 62 Me. 596 (1874).

[563] *State v. Mockus*, 120 Me. 84, 113 A. 39 (1921).

soon found their place, along with that outdated vision, in the dust-heap of history.

The Struggle for Equal Rights Under the Law

The third important theme that runs throughout the early years of Maine law represents the ongoing struggle for equal rights under the law. The framers of Maine's Constitution considered the principle of equal rights under the law to be of such supreme importance that they gave it the place of highest honor (Article I, Section 1) in Maine's Constitution:

> All people are born equally free and independent, and have certain natural, inherent and unalienable rights, among which are those of enjoying and defending life and liberty, acquiring, possessing and protecting property, and of pursuing and obtaining safety and happiness.

As we have seen, from the outset the Maine Court was often called upon to give these words meaning in deciding various cases and controversies. We first encountered the theme of equal protection under the law in Maine's landmark "separation of powers" case, *Lewis v. Webb* (1825), where, describing that theme as "the great principle of constitutional equality," our Court explained that it could never be within the power of the Legislature to enact a law exempting an individual from compliance with the general laws of the State.[564] The principle of equality under the law again arose in 1834 in *Adeline G. Nott's case,*[565] which concerned the commitment of a pauper to Portland's workhouse without a pre-commitment hearing of any kind. In considering that case, we saw that the Maine Court at that time rejected Nott's contention that her commitment violated her constitutional right to defend her liberty. Yet the principle of equality of rights under the law was to prove so strong that some forty-two

---

[564] 3 Me. 326, 336 (1825).

[565] 11 Me. 208 (1834).

years later, in *Portland v. Bangor* (1876),[566] the Maine Court reversed course completely and sustained a similar plea grounded in the Fourteenth Amendment to the U.S. Constitution.

The principle of equal rights under the law was also a cornerstone of the Maine Court's early jurisprudence prohibiting the government from granting economic subsidies to privately-owned businesses. "How can our property be protected," Chief Justice Appleton asked in *Allen v. Inhabitants of Jay* (1872), "if the legislature can enable a majority to transfer by gift or loan, to certain favored and selected individuals through the medium of direct taxation, such portions of one's estate as they may deem expedient."[567]

The principle of equal protection of the law was also at the heart of the Court's decision in *Leavitt v. Dow* (1908),[568] Maine's first "civil-rights assault case," where the Court set aside the jury's verdict based on the Court's concern that the verdict was contaminated by prejudice against the plaintiff.

The enduring vitality of the principle of equal rights under the law is perhaps nowhere better illustrated than by the historical development of the law concerning the civil rights of African Americans and women. Of special note here are the forceful opinions authored by Justices John Appleton and Woodbury Davis in 1857[569] in response to the U.S. Supreme Court's decision in the *Dred Scott* case and the powerful dissenting opinion written by Justice Jonathan G. Dickerson in 1874 in support of the right of women to be judges in Maine.[570] As we have seen, these Maine jurists were all ahead of their time. The principle of equal rights under the law on which they relied was so compelling that in time the views they expressed would become the law of the land.

---

[566] 65 Me. 120 (1876).

[567] 60 Me. 124, 133 (1872).

[568] 105 Me. 50, 72 A. 735 (1908).

[569] *Opinion of the Justices*, 44 Me. 505, 521, 576 (1857).

[570] *Opinion of the Justices*, 62 Me. 596, 600 (1874).

With the ratification of the Fourteenth Amendment in 1868, the equal right of African Americans to be citizens of the United States, articulated eleven years before by Justices Appleton and Davis, was at last constitutionally secured, and the states were prohibited from denying any person the "equal protection of the laws."[571] Many years would pass, however, before the U.S. Supreme Court, in *Brown v. Board of Education* (1954),[572] revived the Fourteenth Amendment's promise of equality by effectively overruling the "separate but equal" doctrine it had approved in *Plessy v. Ferguson* (1896).[573]

Similarly, with the ratification in 1920 of the Nineteenth Amendment, guaranteeing women the right to vote, and the U.S. Supreme Court's belated recognition, in the 1970s, that statutory classifications based on gender warrant heightened scrutiny by the courts under the Equal Protection Clause,[574] the equal rights of women, articulated by Justice Dickerson as long ago as 1874,[575] were finally established as a matter of constitutional law.

The power of the principle of equal rights under the law is also seen in the way in which the law concerning Bible reading in the public schools developed over the years following Bridget Donahoe's suit against members of the Ellsworth School Committee in 1854.[576] Although the Maine Court rejected Bridget's objections to the School Committee's "Protestant-Only Bible Policy" in that case, the validity of her constitutional argument—that the School Committee's policy

---

[571] The principle of equal rights under the law was also dramatically realized on the national level by the two other Civil War Amendments, the Thirteenth Amendment (ratified in 1865), which abolished slavery, and the Fifteenth Amendment (ratified in 1870), which secured the right of (male) citizens of the United States to vote, regardless of "race, color, or previous condition of servitude."

[572] 347 U.S. 483 (1954).

[573] 163 U.S. 537 (1896).

[574] *See, e. g., Reed v. Reed*, 404 U.S. 71 (1971); *Craig v. Boren*, 429 U.S. 190, 197 (1976) (explaining that classifications by gender must serve important governmental objectives and be substantially related to the achievement of those objectives).

[575] *Opinion of the Justices*, 62 Me. at 600.

[576] *Donahoe v. Richards*, 38 Me. 379 (1854).

constituted an unconstitutional preference in favor of one religious denomination, namely Protestantism—did not die with the Court's decision in that case. Like a smoldering ember that keeps burning long after a fire has gone out, that argument lost none of its vitality over the years. More than a hundred years later, in 1963, it was finally accepted by the U.S. Supreme Court when, in deciding that the practice of daily Bible reading in the public schools is unconstitutional, the Court clarified that under the Constitution, "[i]n the relationship between man and religion, the State is firmly committed to a position of neutrality."[577]

The historical fact that the principle of equal rights under the law ultimately triumphed in every context—race, gender, and religion—in which it was germane speaks volumes for the lasting power of that principle. That principle may not have always been accepted immediately by the courts, and it was never realized without a struggle, but such was its strength that, however long it took to be accepted, it would not be denied.

A Broader View

From a broader perspective, looking back over the entire expanse of the ground we have covered, we can see that the three themes that run through the work of the early Maine Court—economic progress, social stability, and the struggle for equal rights under the law—are parts of a larger picture that includes the nature of the times in which that work was done. The chief distinguishing feature of those times was dramatic change that was rapidly and irreversibly transforming society on every front. The Civil War and the abolition of slavery were, of course, the most significant events in that transformation. Other momentous developments that also took place during Maine's first hundred years of statehood included the evolution of the legal status and rights of women, the industrial revolution, the advent of rail transportation, the development of electrical power, the invention of the telephone and the automobile,

---

[577] *School Dist. of Abington Township, Pa. v. Schempp*, 374 U.S. 203, 226 (1963).

and the diversification of culture that resulted from waves of immigration.

From the outset, the early Maine Court faced the challenging task of adapting principles and precedents of the common law tradition to novel circumstances that were occurring with great rapidity and that could not have been even remotely imagined previously. In virtually every subject we have considered here, we have seen the tension that existed between old rules inherited from the past and radically new ideas and social conditions. As we have noted, to mention but a few examples, the previously accepted authority of government to commit paupers to workhouses ran up against a fresh spirit of liberty that was abroad in the land in the years following the Civil War; ancient common law doctrines that denied married women property rights and separate identities of their own were confronted by newly emerging principles of equality; common law rules of assumption of risk and contributory negligence found themselves strained to the breaking point in a new and increasingly dangerous world of high-speed locomotives and factory conditions that bore little resemblance to the days of the horse and buggy and the workbench at which master and apprentice plied their trade, working side by side.

From time to time, the Court in its decisions would remark on the ability of the common law to adapt to new conditions. But it is in the reflections of judges and lawyers, offered on the occasion of memorial ceremonies for deceased jurists, that we find the clearest insights into the challenge the early Maine Court faced in applying traditional common law principles in a "brave new world"—a world that must have seemed to the Court as being completely made over with each passing year. Those personal reflections often provide a more intimate understanding of the mind of the Court than could be gleaned from the Court's formal opinions.

One such ceremony took place before the Maine Court in Portland on Saturday, August 5, 1900, to honor the memory of Justice Charles W. Walton, who served as a member of that Court for thirty-five years and who died on January 24, 1900, in his eighty-first year.[578] The passing of that highly esteemed jurist at the close of the century, after a period of such lengthy service, provided a fitting opportunity to take a thoughtful, retrospective view of his influence and of the judicial process, generally, over a span of many years. Addressing the Court on that occasion, Justice Joseph W. Symonds, who had served as a member of the Court from 1878 to 1884, explained how the Court labored to shape "the guiding principles of conduct in human society" by adapting rules based on the experience of the past to modern conditions, including "all the relations of a complicated society throbbing with busy life." Relating the work of the Court to the rapidly changing times in which that work was done, Symonds stated:

> I hope the time will come when our countrymen will have a truer appreciation and therefore a higher estimate, than now, of the value of the labors of the men who devote their lives to shaping the guiding principles of conduct in human society, to doing this from the vast deposit, like the wealth of quarries and mines, in the learning, thought and experience of the past; and at the same time to applying such rules of action with more and more accurate knowledge and juster dis-crimination, in the clearer light of modern times, to the problems of advancing civilization, increasing intercourse, wider commerce, larger and more varied business interests, subtler rights of property, multiplied and diversified indus-tries, and to all the relations of a complicated society throb-bing with busy life, pursuing its aims restlessly as with fever in a myriad fields.[579]

Consistent with these observations, the development of Maine law during Maine's first hundred years of statehood can perhaps best be described, in summary, as a creative, ongoing, and intensely human process in which, out of the crunch of the collision between

---

[578] Memorial proceedings, 94 Me. 588 (1901).

[579] *Id.* at 592-93.

old rules inherited from the past and a society undergoing rapid and radical transformation, our Court, together with our Legislature, each exercising its respective constitutional powers, shaped the legal principles and rules that constituted the law of the State of Maine for those times. In shaping that body of law, the early Maine Court played several central roles—as enabler of economic progress, as guardian of the existing social order, and as architect of the scope of the principle of equality of rights under the law.

If in that process it seems that our Court was in some respects behind the times, it is interesting to note that the Court itself did not share that view. At another memorial ceremony for Justice Walton, which was conducted by the Androscoggin Bar on February 27, 1900, Justice Albert R. Savage[580] summed up the work of the Court over Walton's long tenure of service with the remark, "I think it is safe to say that in no state has the court kept up with the times better than in this."[581]

In the final analysis, however, even if it could fairly be said that in some ways the early Maine Court had not kept up with the times, we should hardly find that surprising. The rapid pace of change that occurred during Maine's first hundred years would have taxed the ability of anyone to keep current. But more to the point, we should not lose sight of the fact that, in comparison with legislative bodies, courts by their very nature tend to be conservative institutions, grounded as they are in tradition, custom, and judicial precedent. As such, then as now, it would be unrealistic to expect courts to be the dynamo that drives change at the cutting edge of each and every new development in the ongoing evolution of society. Yet that being said, as we have seen in looking back over the broad landscape of early Maine law, some of the most inspiring judicial opinions from that era are those that invoked the irrepressible power of simple justice in the face of lingering inequalities of rights, reminding us down through the years that justice remains the goal to which all law should aspire.

---

[580] Savage served on the Court as an Associate Justice from 1897 to 1913 and as Chief Justice from 1913 until his death in 1917.

[581] Memorial proceedings, 94 Me. 603, 616 (1901).

TABLE OF CASES

U.S. Supreme Court Cases

Other State Cases

INDEX